DIVINE REVOLUTION

Salvation & Liberation
in Catholic Thought

DEAN BRACKLEY

ORBIS BOOKS

Maryknoll, New York 10545

Library of Congress Cataloging in Publication Data

Brackley, Dean.
    Divine revolution : salvation & liberation in Catholic thought /
Dean Brackley.
        p.   cm.
    Includes bibliographical references and index.
    ISBN 1-57075-050-5 (alk. paper)
    1. Sociology, Christian (Catholic)—History of doctrines—20th
century. 2. Salvation—History of doctrines—20th century.
3. Liberation theology—History. 4. Catholic Church—Doctrines—
History—20th century. I. Title.
BX1753.B66   1996
230'.2—dc20   95-49739
                                                      CIP

Ad maiorem Dei gloriam,
Liberatoris pauperum

CONTENTS

FOREWORD

Jon Sobrino, S.J.

The basic theme of Dean Brackley's book is the relationship between Christian faith and salvation; more specifically, the changes that have taken place in Catholic theology in its understanding of salvation over the last fifty years. An epochal convulsion has occurred, the author declares—the passage from the notion of a unilateral spiritual, individual, and transcendent salvation to another, more integral understanding. That transition includes corporeal, social, community, and concrete historical salvation. This radical change is presented as "good news," since it entails the principle that nothing of the traditional doctrine on salvation is lost but much is gained as salvation is seen to be integral liberation from all that enslaves the human being.

This book analyzes the new understanding of salvation in the Catholic magisterium and in three theological models taken from important theologians of the second half of this century—Jacques Maritain, Karl Rahner, and Gustavo Gutiérrez. Brackley also adds important insights from feminist theology and the theology of Ignacio Ellacuría. Finally, he turns to Jesus of Nazareth and relates all this to him—thus showing a relationship between the origins of Christianity and our own day. We are caught by surprise in returning to Jesus, as our central argument, after twenty centuries of faith and theology.

The book's structure is clear, its argumentation convincing, and its analysis rigorous. Its content is supported by a very broad bibliography. The book can be read with profit in academe, but it ought not to be read only academically. Brackley himself recalls how important it has been for him in developing it to have lived and worked in the Bronx and in Jayaque, a little village of El Salvador that has under-

---

Translated by Robert R. Barr.

gone all of the horrors of repression and war and the disenchantment of today. And yet, the author calls our attention to something basic: in these places he has seen the growth of love and hope as nowhere else.

Thus, this a book of serious, critical theology. But its intent is not only the advancement of theological science. It is likewise to offer a response to the questions that have arisen for the author during these years in which he has lived in the world of the poor, the world of victims. What does it mean to be a human being, and what does Christian faith have to do with that? Therefore, and from this standpoint, the author rightly declares in his Introduction that "theology, and in particular Catholic theology, can and should interpret 'salvation' as liberation from all that de-humanizes us and as the fullness of life in communion with God and others."

This is a brief summary of the book that I am delighted to present. I personally share the author's theological point of view and can only add from my vantage amidst the reality of the victims of El Salvador certain reflections that may help the reader of the countries of the North to read this book with profit. To put it somewhat provocatively: *If the reader has no interest in the victims of the third world—and of the first—if the reader thinks that this reality is not a central reality for faith; if the reader does not to allow himself or herself to be affected by the real death of millions of human beings, then this book will not say much to that reader's faith and humanity. It is possible to read this book with the curiosity of those who scurry about after the latest novelties, or with the academic interest of those who study the history of ideas, but these approaches do not bring with them the preunderstanding and antecedent interest that are alone adequate for an authentic understanding of the book.* And this, in my opinion, is the major problem facing books like this one.

Having said this, I wish to offer three brief reflections concerning features in it that have attracted my attention and that may provide a kind of atmosphere for the reading of the book. The first is on an understanding of Christian salvation as a *quaestio disputata*. The second is on the meaning of a *return to Jesus of Nazareth*. And the third is on the title of the book, *Divine Revolution*.

•

Chapter one bears the title, "Salvation and Social Justice," and Brackley presents this, rightly, as a *quaestio disputata*. What I wish to do by way of clarification is to identify the "disputed" element in the question. The essential relationship between faith and salvation is not at issue, and, in official tradition, we are in possession of a (reductive) understanding of salvation in the line of redemption from sin and of transcendent salvation. The controverted element, then, is historical and social salvation.

But things are not so simple. First, we must recall that the traditional understanding of salvation corresponds to *one* New Testament, patristic, and conciliar tradition. That tradition is not the only one. What theology has developed in one direction—what has occurred in Christology, as well, without Jesus of Nazareth, or in an eschatology without the principle of hope, or in an ecclesiology without the people of God, and so on—does not mean that any other understanding of salvation should be subject to doubt until it is accepted. In other words, that it must hover in thin air as a mere *quaestio disputata*. This is not the case if we look at scripture as a whole. We need only recall that what we today refer to as social justice, although it must be well interpreted and complemented, is an expression of the salvific, central will of God that creation have life. Thus, the utopia of Isaiah 65:17-41 and Jesus' proclamation of the Reign of God to the poor regard salvation, indeed, they regard the most comprehensive formulation of salvation.

Now if we ask ourselves why something so central in the Old and New Testaments ceased to be such—why the "new" understanding of salvation is regarded as something disputed in the church and in theology—the answer has both a theological and a historical dimension. Theologically, the fundamental reason lies in the disappearance of the Reign of God proclaimed and initiated by Jesus from theological purview. Historically, the reason is that the dominant elements in society became uninterested in an understanding of salvation that would reveal, judge, and denounce society's profound sin. Society is interested rather in a conception of salvation upon which it can constitute itself as a respectable society, however permeated it be with sin.

Let us be very clear. The new understanding of salvation comports a dialectical dimension, a dimension of contradiction, and this in a very precise sense. The opposite of justice is not simply the absence of justice. The opposite of justice is active injustice. The latter actually struggles against the former, in a confrontation leading to another one, more basic for faith—the confrontation between God and the idols, between Jesus and the false mediators. And on this basis our current society must be unmasked and judged against the background of the ultimacy of the Kingdom.

In civil religion of the North, for example, or in the Central American "democracies" of today, God and the idols (neo-liberalism, an ideology of armament), faith can easily coexist with the injustice of ignoring the victims and active oppression. It is understandable that these social configurations should turn from a conception of salvation that reveals as sin what customarily passes as neutral, or even as grace. And something of the kind would have to be said of the church, since an acceptance of the "new" understanding of salvation plunges that church, of necessity, into conflicts. It entails a loss of privileges and worldly supports—something that the church, too, seeks to avoid! The present configuration of society and the church is easier to maintain if social justice and liberation from structures of sin are viewed merely as *quaestiones disputatae* and not as central to Christian faith.

The real, root locus of the controversy, then, seems to us to be our concrete, historical, ecclesial reality. The theological controversy is secondary. Although, obviously, it is important, that importance arises because the theology supports just or unjust views of society and the church. In this sense the controversy over social justice—*as a form of salvation*—is central, not secondary. And in this sense it is still unresolved.

Let us make two final observations on this theme. I suggest that an understanding of this question determines Christianity's identity and its very relevance. In vain do we speak of the church as a "sacrament of salvation" in a world of victims so broadly dehumanized and dehumanizing. In vain will the church claim to be an "expert in humanity," apart from the advancement of integral liberation and social justice.

I also suggest that it is dangerous to believe that the "disputed" element in the relationship between faith and salvation is only one pole of salvation, as if we had already adequately understood faith. This is not the case. Exegetes and historians of dogma never tire of reminding us that what has moved believers to this or that particular conceptualization of God and his Christ has always been the relevance of these views in regard to salvation. Thus, our *understanding* of salvation has an important influence on our understanding of God and the core understanding of faith.

I offer these reflections in order to put Christians on guard against any inclination to trivialize the theme of social justice as something upon which theologians might conduct a theoretical debate without personal engagement. Such a debate is impossible, since what is at stake is faith in God. It is not the same thing to believe in a *God* who only redeems from sin and only grants eternal life and to believe in a God who—in addition to these things—seeks the end of the oppression of victims at the hands of their executioners.

In one sense, of course, everything bearing on the mystery of God will be a *quaestio disputata*. We have to return to that mystery again and again because of the very nature of mystery. The case is the same

with "salvation," and this for the same reason, since salvation is the
human appropriation of ultimate mystery. This does not mean, however, that the basics of God and salvation must be everlastingly under
discussion. For it is indisputable that what God wishes is for creation
to live fully; that the glory of God is the human being fully alive; or
that in our cruel world this glory is the life of the poor. And if a
Christian theology seeks to place *this* under discussion, I fear that it
has not stood before the God of Jesus. What seems to me to be the
first important contribution of this book is its emphasis on what is
most profound in salvation—transcendent and historical—an emphasis on what is *not* under discussion.

•

My second reflection bears on the author's ultimate grounding of
his thesis in the return to Jesus of Nazareth. In itself, this is ironic,
since it implies that something centrally present in Jesus has disappeared in the course of the history of his movement. That process, to
be sure, began very early—in the New Testament itself. Once more
we have a *quaestio disputata*—a christological question with enor-
mous practical repercussions—whether and in what sense Jesus of
Nazareth is central for theology. Current theology rarely continues
to accept Bultmann's radical negative response to this question, but
neither do many theologies make Jesus of Nazareth central in any
consistent way.

But, for Dean Brackley, the centrality of Jesus of Nazareth is the
basic justification of his thesis. That centrality needs to be historicized and updated but the foundation is already present in Jesus.
Jesus of Nazareth is not only the factual beginning of Christian
tradition but also the primordial and essential origin of that tradition.
He is its *principium principians*—that which must be maintained
throughout the process of reflection, and that which will bestow upon
reflection its direction and supply it with its basic criterion for
historicization.

It is this return to Jesus that Brackley develops in chapter six, and
it is upon this return that I wish to comment because of its decisive,
irreplaceable importance for a determination of what salvation is.
When we take Jesus as our starting point, we rediscover the Reign of
God—the most important modern discovery for Christian theology.
And with Jesus as our starting point, one can discover an active
"anti-Reign," an omnipresent sinful force. John calls it the "sin of the
world," while the Synoptics describe it more concretely by actually
naming its historical agents, the purveyors of idols, and their victims.
The implication for an understanding of salvation consists in the fact

that this anti-Reign does not materialize on its own but in reaction to forces that seek to annihilate oppressive powers.

This is of capital importance today for understanding salvation and seeing the need to defeat a certain postmodern, naive, and at times self-interested irenicism, which is utilized to mask the true nature of the conflict so we can avoid it.

The return to Jesus also helps us understand the meaning of his death and resurrection for our salvation. The cross is no macabre "plan" laid by God, but a consequence of the quest for concrete historical salvation by Jesus. Nor is the resurrection an arbitrary action. Rather, it is God's reaction, doing justice to a victim, to the just and innocent one whom "you put to death" (Acts 3:15). It is hope for victims and—directly—for them alone.

Finally, and more specifically for the subject of the book, the return to Jesus specifies the privileged addressee of salvation. This will help us in a determination of salvation's content, given the transcendental relation between good news and addressee. As we well know, for Jesus the privileged addressees of salvation are the poor, the victims of this world. Salvation, then, consists in emancipation from all of their needs and slavery.

"Jesus of Nazareth" does not express the whole reality of the Christ as Lord and Son of God. But without Jesus, titles evaporate, and salvation is perilously abridged. We see it in the experience of recent decades—advances in the *theory* and *practice* of salvation are made when Jesus of Nazareth stands front and center. We need only consider such things as Medellín, liberation theology, solidarity movements, and the magisterium of the Latin American bishops who stand with liberation.

In the oldest Christian tradition, that of the Jesus-movement, we rediscover today something basic and indispensable for any statement of the essence of Christian salvation, as well as for any statement of the essence of Christian faith. This is another important contribution of Dean Brackley's book.

•

Finally, let us say something about the title of the book: *Divine Revolution*. "Revolution" means a radical departure from the past in a movement toward a future that it is hoped will be a better one. Etymologically, however, the word denotes a return to the past. We could seem to be dealing with an oxymoron. But actually we are not and we have perfect proof of this statement in what is happening to our understanding of Christian salvation. I have already spoken of the return to Jesus, but we need to go further. We need to go all the way back to God.

"Remember, Israel," is not a literary device for requiring formal fidelity to a tradition; it is a way of referring a people to the ultimate origin of its formation and its salvation. After all, what Israel must recall is the history of its deliverance. In what, then, does the divine revolution consist? Basically that liberation has no other logical explanation than to express the notion that "this is the way God is." The "way God is" consists in God's love for the victims, which emerges in the divine partiality for the poor—simply because they are poor. And on the basis of this partiality, one must profess the universality of that love. Many centuries later, Puebla will stand this partiality in a central place, and will cite the divine revolution: "Made in the image and likeness of God (Gen. 1:26-28) to be his children, this image is dimmed and even defiled. That is why God takes on their defense and loves them (Matt. 5:45; James 2:5)" (Puebla Final Document, no. 1142). It is in this same light that we should understand the fundamental demand that God's people do with others what God has done with them. Salvation in this key consists in being delivered in order to deliver. In New Testament terms, salvation means being loved by God in order to love others—and all of this in historicized fashion. And finally, it is from amidst the poor that hope and historically objective salvation, spring forth for those who enter into solidarity with the poor. In this consists the divine revolution. The repetition of this fact and its analysis is, in my view, the most important contribution of Dean Brackley's book.

Let us conclude with two brief reflections for theology. If what is revolutionary involves an element of a return to the past, it is because the process of thinking that has reached us today has lost a hold on important things. This occurs because in history, in the church, and in theology progress has not been rectilinear. The trajectory of progress spans both advance and loss. And from this we may draw the lesson that advances in theology—as progressive a theology as you wish to propose—cannot consist solely in extending the inertia of the Western theological process. My conviction is that to rethink critically the essential realities of faith, we must return to Jesus of Nazareth, to the Exodus and the prophets, whatever havoc this may wreak on things very dear to theologies traditional or progressive.

My second reflection is that "God's revolution" is accepted by us only with difficulty, and it is in constant danger of manipulation by the faint of heart. Let us therefore conclude by saying clearly what seems to me essential to the revolution in question—namely, *extra pauperes nulla salus* ("apart from the poor there is no salvation"). There is salvation, indeed, and in this hope lies the essence of

Christian faith. But that salvation has its locus in the poor of this world. And that same real locus becomes a locus for theology when theology seeks to reflect upon Christian salvation in its historical concreteness.

This is the theological revolution, a reflection assisted by Dean Brackley's excellent book and its underlying experience of the victims in the Bronx and Jayaque.

INTRODUCTION

The historicity of Christian salvation is still one of the most serious issues for the understanding and practice of faith. It is a problem in the North Atlantic countries, in the oppressed countries; and finally, in the magisterium and discipline of the institutional Church.

—Ignacio Ellacuría[1]

Sooner or later childhood faith enters into crisis. Reality, especially suffering and evil, weighs down on our fledgling faith until it cracks. When they penetrate our defenses, the horror of war, discrimination and poverty can shake the fault lines of our developing personalities and our worldviews.

This book grew from such a crisis. Years ago, once outside the shelter of middle-class childhood, I found my tender faith no longer adequate to a world as violent as this one. From where I stand today, it seems as though a bigger God was shoving aside a smaller one. Awash in confusion back then, I found questions emerging that were far more important than my old answers. Earlier, I had been asking, What must we do to be Christians in a world like this? Now, in my agnostic state, a second question arose from a deeper place inside and eclipsed the first: What must we do to be human in a world like this? A journey was beginning, fueled, I am sure, as much by subterranean complexes and self-doubt as by concern for the victims.

In time, the new question sparked another which continues to burn to this day: What does the salvation promised by the gospel have to say to society's victims? I wondered whether the churches, and my own Catholic Church in particular, announced a hope that really addressed the suffering of the poor.

This book represents a status report on a pilgrimage still underway. It suggests that the search has not been in vain and dares affirm that, despite one's own failings and the defects of the church, one can be a Christian and a responsible human being at the same time. It argues that the Christian message, and the Catholic formulation of it, when truly faithful to itself and its Christ, does proclaim a hope which responds to the pain and the deepest longings of the victims of history. But I'm getting ahead of myself.

In 1970, while working with youth on Manhattan's Lower East Side, I sought advice from Dorothy Day of the Catholic Worker. "Stay close to the poor," she said, "to the men on the Bowery who built the railroads and the women who sleep in doorways." Do that, she said, and much of my confusion would pass. Dorothy was right. Her advice suggested that we nonpoor people, a distinct minority in history, after all, live on the surface of things in a kind of chronic low-grade distraction from the great drama of life. And what was that drama?

Soon after, still on the Lower East Side, I met Carlotta Sarver, an aging eccentric barricaded in the most rundown apartment I'd ever seen. Carlotta survived from day to day, defending herself and her cats against drug addicts. One day Carlotta volunteered her secret of the meaning of life. "It's all about survival," she said. Carlotta was right, too. Around me, neighborhood youth were dying in drug-related shootouts and accidents. Men on the Bowery nearby were dying of exposure and drink. In fact, most people throughout history have spent their lives trying to keep themselves and their households alive. All that was new to me. The world, I was coming to learn, was a harsh and cruel place where most people could not take life for granted. Being human meant defending life, working for life. (As I look back, I have to wonder, in passing, whether those neoconservatives who claim to have been mugged by reality have tasted much of Carlotta's.)

In 1974 and 1975, two visits to Latin America confirmed Carlotta's thesis and helped me appreciate the international dimensions of rich and poor, powerful and dependent. The world showed itself still more profoundly disordered, unfair and violent. Our social institutions, especially the powerful modern state, seemed organized as much to threaten life as to protect it. We really did need revolution or, as Pope Paul VI had said in *Populorum progressio* (no. 32), bold and deep transformations.

The 70s were heady times. Revolution was in the air but, in the United States, only in the air. Still, one could do worse than question the social order to its roots and dream of fundamental change. These exercises moved some to serve the poor, and that would save many of them from premature hardening of the categories in later years.

By contrast, for me the 80s were sobering years, spent in New York's South Bronx as priest, educator and community organizer. The Bronx introduced my co-workers and me to what we now call postmodernism. Idealism took a beating; history seemed to lose its plot line. Where were we headed? My Bronx neighbors seemed less surprised than people like me when radical change refused to happen. They helped us look deeper.

Two Bronx lessons stand out. First, the root of most Bronx problems lay in the lack of community. New York had taken community away from African Americans who had migrated from the South and Latinos from still farther south. Carlotta had only seen part of the picture. Life was about staying alive, but it also meant living together. Life was hardly human without community. Being human meant liberation from the chains that blocked community and from the forces that tore it apart.

But the more difficult it grew to change political and economic conditions in favor of a humane society as a whole, the clearer we could see the need to build up local communities. We had to care for each other and form community where we found ourselves, even as "the system" rumbled along. Should revolution happen at all, it would have to come from "below." It would have to include new social relations—between women and men, Puerto Ricans and Whites, young and old. In fact, in order to arrest the destruction and build community, we had to *be* good people. Fortunately, there were plenty such people in the Bronx those days.

This brings me to the second lesson. Stereotypes aside, not all was wrong on those mean streets. I remember a morning when depression overtook me on the way to Rivera's store for a carton of milk, depression at the sight of run-down buildings and run-down people. But then the words of Paul came to the rescue: Yes, sin abounds, but grace abounds more. It was true. My neighbors Margarita and Grover struggled on, caring for family and fighting for justice with good humor. In fact, hardship seemed to bring out the best in them.

Thanks to people like them, the Bronx helped me appreciate that, besides the dying going on all around us, a "rising" is going on as well. Things are much worse than we usually dare admit. This I had understood. But things are also more wonderful than we usually suppose. In fact, it seems that we have to first let the evil crash through our defenses and blow our little worlds apart in order to appreciate that, along with the evil, love and humanity are also growing and spreading. In that case, being human means sharing people's dying, walking with them, and in that way sharing a rising that we often perceive only half-consciously.

In the Bronx, this rising took shape as joy, random acts of generosity, political windfalls and other surprises that seemed to well up from nowhere and for no apparent reason. In the face of this, I began to think of God carrying on a revolution of love deeper than any revolution human beings have devised.

Still, radical change was not happening in the Bronx in the 80s. It was happening in Central America, however, and many of us inner-city church workers allowed events there, and later in South Africa, to distract us from our daily rounds. Violent social crises in these places drew back the curtain on the daily drama of crucifixion and resurrection. It teased out the worst and the best in those societies and in their churches: the Somozas and the D'Aubuissons, on the one hand, the Archbishop Romeros and the Nelson Mandelas on the other.

The massacre at the Jesuit university in 1989 brought me to work in El Salvador to experience this drama firsthand. On the first anniversary of those killings, for example, Teresa Pérez stood up after the homily in her hamlet near Jayaque. She recalled that many people had left the parish after the murder of the Jesuit pastor, Ignacio Martín-Baró. "But I say," Teresa continued, "if death comes to us while we're working for the church here, well, let's welcome it!" Teresa was just one example of extraordinary faith under fire. Not every poor Salvadoran is a hero, but many who bore the brunt of the war are still disposed to share their last tortilla and their smile with a stranger, and even to forgive. Many seem capable of following in the steps of hundreds of catechists who gave their lives for others, for the poor and for the truth during the war. In them and people like them, a rising, a true revolution, seems to be going on, even if we can't see clearly where it's headed.

By the time the smoke had cleared in the 90s, it became clear that armed revolution had brought fundamental change neither to El Salvador nor to Nicaragua, or at least that the human cost exceeded the benefits attained. There were no more Winter Palaces in the world, and the Berlin wall had fallen. The violent determination of the privileged had made "taking power" not only reversible (as in Nicaragua), but prohibitively costly. In fact, the political forces of the left no longer seemed to know what they would do with power if they had it.

Central America, and many places like it, had begun to look to me a bit like the South Bronx. Now, in Central America, urban neighbor-hoods, families and psyches were crumbling, South-Bronx style. Both despair over the prospects of change any time soon and confusion about the path forward had a familiar Bronx feel to me.

I doubt it is a permanent situation, but to make sense of it, I find myself returning to old South Bronx insights and some principles of Catholic Worker anarchism. While people need to resist and change macro-institutions, the more urgent and realizable goal is the build-ing of local organizations and local communities. It will be a slow and permanent revolution from "below" requiring new social relations and new persons like Teresa Pérez of Jayaque—people capable of love under pressure.

This seems to be what we have to do, and be, in order to be human in this world, not only in El Salvador but most places I know. We need to be new persons capable of new social relations—between women and men, young and old, homo- and heterosexuals, administrators and workers, among races and peoples. We need to build local community even as we resist and transform death-dealing institutions.

The journey has brought me this far in the search for what it takes to be human in this world. Plenty of Christians, non-Christians and other searchers have walked similar paths over the last 20 years or so. But the telling of the journey has left a second question hanging in the air: What does faith have to do with all that? What does the "salvation" announced by the church have to say to the plight of the poor and the rest of us on this fragile planet?

The Bible had nourished and thrilled me from my years of deepest confusion and agnosticism. Still, the meaning of salvation in the face of suffering and injustice remained unclear to me. On the one hand, Jesus had said that "the poor will inherit the earth"; but on the other, hadn't he declared that his kingdom was "not of this world"? The church hardly spoke with greater clarity. On the one hand, the Latin American bishops at Puebla and Medellín had described God's saving work as "integral liberation"—a liberation at every level of human existence, including sociopolitical liberation. The Second Vatican Council, on the other hand, had sharply distinguished earthly progress from the reign of God.

This situation seemed to warrant sustained study, and the present book presents the fruits of that reflection to date. It owes a great deal to many friends, especially in the Bronx. It also benefited greatly from the guidance of professors David Tracy, James Gustafson and David Bartlett, who helped me complete a first version at the University of Chicago in 1980. Judy Vaughan and Jack Barron also provided crucial support at that time. I am grateful to Jesuits of the New York Province and the staff of the Woodstock Theological Center at Georgetown University in Washington, D.C., who provided the time and resources to work on a second phase of this project in 1988-89. I was able to extend that phase thanks to the theology department of Fordham University, which permitted me to assume a reduced workload in the fall of 1989. Thanks are also in order to the personnel of both the philosophy department and the Archbishop Romero Center at the Central American University in San Salvador for their support in completing a third and final phase of work during these years in El Salvador.

I also wish to express my gratitude for the kind help of the late Joseph Fitzpatrick. Finally, I am deeply grateful to John Breslin, Gene Palumbo, Martha Doggett, Charlie Beirne and Sagrario Núñez for their support and to Paula Genova and Richard Cassidy, without whose extraordinary kindness this book would perhaps never have appeared in print.

The pages that follow argue that theology, and in particular Catholic theology, can and should interpret salvation as liberation from all that dehumanizes us and as the fullness of life in communion with God and others.

In the 70s, controversy erupted over the social and political meaning of salvation and continued into the 80s. On Christmas 1988, as Cubans prepared to celebrate the thirtieth anniversary of their revolution, Cardinal Paulo Evaristo Arns of São Paulo, Brazil, wrote to Fidel Castro that "Christian faith sees in the gains of the revolution the signs of the reign of God reflected in our hearts and in the structures which transform political co-existence into an act of love." Conservative clerics and major newspapers took loud exception to Arns's statement (National Catholic News Service Report, Feb. 9, 1989). The cardinal, aware of the darker side of Cuba's revolution, surely had in mind the country's impressive advances in education, nutrition and health services. At stake theologically, however, as much as any ethical appraisal of the Cuban revolution, was Arns's close association of the reign of God—God's saving action in the world—with social liberation and development in Cuba.

The controversy over Arns's remarks reflected conflicting views about the social and political meaning of the kingdom of God. The way Arns characterized salvation clashed with the standard view and responded to the challenge which the contemporary world poses to the church's understanding of the hope it proclaims. That challenge, which had echoed in the questions that shook my faith some years ago, did not spontaneously generate in recent times. The fruit of a long gestation, its roots trail back at least several hundred years. Social injustice did not always challenge faith the same way it does today. In premodern societies, which largely took the social and natural orders for granted, social injustice engaged the church chiefly as a problem of personal morality. Classical theology, whether that of Augustine, Aquinas or Luther, understood salvation as forgiveness for personal sins, the life of grace in the soul and immortality. For this traditional theology, the kingdom of God on earth was simply the church itself. Christ did not come to bring social justice before we die; he came to bring happiness with God after we die.

Over the last few centuries, two developments have created a situation which challenges this traditional theology: First, generalized questioning of the social order helped reveal that poverty is not inevitable; more recently, modern communications and transportation have brought to vast numbers of people knowledge about suffering and injustice far beyond their immediate experience.

With the rise of modern society, the legitimation of the social order entered into crisis. When the feudal order crumbled before the growing power of capital and markets, serfs became proletarians. But if they were not fated to be serfs, perhaps they were not fated to be poor and powerless, either. And perhaps kings were not fated to be kings.

Besides political and economic forces, cultural factors helped liberate political imagination for widespread questioning of the social order. The Reformation and Renaissance humanism demolished the church's monopoly on truth. If Galileo's modern science could decipher the mysteries of nature, perhaps people could also unravel the inner workings of society—and make a new one.

In Europe, the French Revolution demonstrated once and for all—not just to elites, who may well have known already, but to everyone—that the social order is a human, not a divine construct and that our social future rests largely in our hands.

All these changes disclosed that sharp inequality is really injustice and that poverty is a human responsibility. This confronted the church with a new situation. Radical social change (for example, democracy rather than monarchy) seemed to many a moral imperative. How would the church respond? Would it advocate change or oppose it? And what about salvation? Did not salvation in the next world distract from changing this one?

Thanks to mass communications, these challenges have only grown more acute in this century of total war, Holocaust and genocide in Rwanda. Perhaps humanity has known misery on a greater scale in the past. But even if it has, before now only tiny elites could have known of massive suffering far beyond their own locale and as something to which they might be able to respond personally. Today news reports and travel opportunities burden most of us, even the poorest, with the knowledge of suffering inflicted by human beings and the institutions they create. To the extent that we can bear it, this knowledge has etched its mark on modern consciousness. It tugs at the rim of awareness and sets the context for the church's practice and preaching.

Some today believe the end of the Cold War marks the end of history, and they urge the church to move beyond social issues to more sublime activities. Unfortunately, our postmodern, post-Cold War world is hardly a post-poverty world—not by a long shot. Poverty thrives, and neoliberal capitalism shows no signs of addressing its root causes. The number of poor today and the gap between rich and poor continue to grow, generating conflicts and racial tension, creating waves of refugees and threatening the environment. Seventy percent of the poor worldwide are women.[2]

The industrialized nations hardly escape the crisis. Violence, mental and emotional anguish, and drug consumption among the affluent mirror the pain of the poor. The suffering of both rich and poor stems from a mutual separation that generates antagonism rather than political community. In the United States, for example, the richest 1 percent of households now owns more wealth than the bottom 90 percent (*New York Times*, April 21, 1992, p. 1).

If some are tired of talk about such things, the poor are far more tired of being poor. They, too, would like to move on to other things, but they cannot. If death-through-poverty in Chiapas, homelessness in New York and financing slaughter in Central America are secondary issues for the church—or non-issues—small wonder the gospel appeals little to people moved by the massive suffering and injustice of our world. To be human, to say nothing of Christian, the church as a community must respond, in its own ecclesial way, on behalf of justice in the world. Dispensing the church from this responsibility in the name of religion is the type of maneuver that most incensed Jesus of Nazareth. If these concerns are out of fashion, so much the worse for fashion.

Beyond the strictly moral issue, however, or rather at its base, is that other question: What does salvation mean for the victims of history? Even if the church should urge us all to work for justice, we must ask whether it preaches a salvation which undermines that call. That is the question this book addresses.

As the clamor of the poor and marginalized grows louder in coming years, the relation between that cry and the church's cry of salvation will continue to spark debate, perhaps the most important debate on the church's agenda for a long time to come. To proclaim a salvation that fails to address our inability to live together will risk distracting people from the most tangible and pressing human concerns and indirectly defend the status quo.

Yet, as frequently understood, salvation seems far removed from those pressing concerns. Is it so far over the rainbow that today's poor must forget their immediate needs to appreciate it? Is there anything to hope for *before* death that might answer to those needs? What does salvation have to do with the bread and dignity denied the poor? with our efforts to build a world of sister- and brotherhood? What, in short, is the social meaning of the reign of God here and now?

While theology has made important advances recently on this question, the matter is hardly settled. The churches, almost 2,000 years after Christ, still have not spelled out clearly the relationship between the salvation they announce and the just community people long for. Even official Catholic teaching reflects this ambiguity.

We examine this theological situation in the following chapter and lay out the strategy this book will follow in order to address it.

ABBREVIATIONS

AG — Second Vatican Council. *Ad gentes* (On the Missionary Activity of the Church).

CA — John Paul II. *Centesimus annus* (On the One Hundredth Anniversary of *Rerum novarum*).

EN — Paul VI. *Evangelii nuntiandi* (Evangelization in the Modern World).

GS — Second Vatican Council. *Gaudium et spes* (Pastoral Constitution on the Church in the Modern World).

IH — Jacques Maritain. *Integral Humanism.*

Instruction I — Sacred Congregation for the Doctrine of the Faith. *Instruction on Certain Aspects of the "Theology of Liberation."*

Instruction II — Sacred Congregation for the Doctrine of the Faith. *Instruction on Christian Freedom and Liberation.*

JW — Synod of Bishops, Second General Assembly. *Justice in the World.*

LG — Second Vatican Council. *Lumen gentium* (Dogmatic Constitution on the Church).

LP — Gustavo Gutiérrez. *Líneas pastorales de la Iglesia en América Latina.*

Med — Second General Conference of Latin American Bishops. *The Church in the Present-Day Transformation of Latin America* (The Medellín Documents).

PCG — Jacques Maritain. *The Person and the Common Good.*

PP — Paul VI. *Populorum progressio* (On the Development of Peoples).

PPH — Gustavo Gutiérrez. *The Power of the Poor in History.*

RM — John Paul II. *Redemptoris missio* (On the Permanent Validity of the Church's Missionary Mandate).

SD — IV Conferencia General del Episcopado Latinoamericano. *Nueva evangelización, promoción humana, cultura cristiana* (The Santo Domingo Document).

TDNT — Geoffrey W. Bromiley, ed. *Theological Dictionary of the New Testament.*

TI — Karl Rahner. *Theological Investigations.*

TL — Gustavo Gutiérrez. *A Theology of Liberation.*

1

SALVATION AND SOCIAL JUSTICE
AS A *QUAESTIO DISPUTATA*

Signs of the Times

The state of the world since the French and Industrial Revolutions has forced Christians to relate their faith to poverty, injustice, and politics. In recent decades, especially, social crises have stimulated fruitful theological reflection in this area. Since the Second Vatican Council, debate has raged in the Roman Catholic community over the relationship between the salvation the church proclaims and social liberation. Heated controversy surrounding Latin American liberation theology has demonstrated this dramatically. Now that the smoke has cleared over the battlefields of the seventies and eighties, we need to assess the state of the question as we advance toward the turn of the millennium.

Fundamental issues are at stake—political and economic, as well as ecclesial and theological—in these debates. Many remain unresolved and probably will not be resolved soon. In fact, it is probably fair to say that Catholic theology, perhaps even Christian theology generally, has not yet arrived at a satisfactory formulation of the relationship between salvation and the good of societies in history. The issue concerns nothing less than God's relationship to the world, a mystery which thought can never capture with precision. But beside this necessary imprecision, Catholic theology displays, even at the official level, remarkable ambiguity on the question.

The fundamental issue of the relationship between salvation and justice remains a *quaestio disputata*. More accurately, it has once again become one. For more than a century, traditional models have entered into deeper and deeper conflict with hard reality and, more recently, with alternative paradigms. We can illustrate the recent

1

conflicts and the ambiguity by briefly reviewing the most important official documents touching on the relationship between salvation (the kingdom of God) and social justice.

In this chapter, we first examine these documents. Then we locate the disputed question within the history of Christian thought on the subject. Finally, we explain how the rest of the book proceeds to address the problem.

Recent Catholic Documents

Beginning with Vatican II (1962-65), official Catholic documents display an instructive ambivalence about salvation and social justice. These documents represent only the bubbling surface of a caldron churning with pastoral and theological activity carried on in interaction with a world in the throes of change.

Gaudium et Spes

The Second Vatican Council's Pastoral Constitution on the Church in the Modern World, *Gaudium et spes* (GS), offers the most complete and authoritative presentation of Catholic teaching on the relationship of salvation to social justice. The Council rejected the dualism which regards the work of grace as wholly extrinsic to conscious life and divorced from created human values. Against those who supposed that human beings have a double destiny, natural and supernatural, GS (22, 24, 41, 92) insists on the single "integral vocation" (11, 35, 57, 63, 91) of each human being and humanity as a whole (1, 22, 24, 38, 43, 45, 64). All are called to communion with God. Yet GS makes careful distinctions: This destiny consists in more than the social justice we struggle to achieve (38). One distinguishes (without separating) "temporal," "secular," "earthly," "natural," activities and values, on the one hand, and "acts of worship," "the concerns of faith," "religious values," and "those aspects of the human condition which transcend this world," on the other (36, 43, 53, 61, 76). We distinguish human history from salvation history (41).[1] Finally, we must carefully distinguish earthly progress and salvation:

> Earthly progress must be carefully distinguished from the growth of Christ's kingdom. Nevertheless, to the extent that the former can contribute to the better ordering of human society, it is of vital concern [*magnopere interest*] to the kingdom of God. (39)

GS suggests that a right-ordered society disposes persons to hear God's Word and thus "prepares" salvation's way (38, 57); but, according to GS, earthly progress is not salvation.

What does GS mean by *earthly progress?* Some interpret the passage to rule out any identification whatever of salvation and the temporal good, including love and social justice inspired by supernatural charity. However, the passage distinguishes earthly progress from "the better ordering of human society." In GS, earthly progress almost always refers to the modern explosion of knowledge and advances in technical mastery of nature (15, 23, 33, 37, 54, 57, 63, 64; cf. also 10, 18; cf., on the other hand, 35), almost never to growth in human community and the realization of the common good. The question remains, therefore, whether, to what extent, and in what sense progress in love and justice and "the right ordering of society" can be identified with the growth of God's reign.

Certainly, advances in knowledge and what the Greeks called *techne*—our relationship to nature—can occur without salvation. We can have a "green revolution" without distributing grain equitably. We can turn advances in medicine and space technology to destructive purposes. But can we advance in love and justice and human community—what the Greeks called *praxis,* interpersonal and social relations—apart from the work of grace? Can salvation occur without love and justice? If not, to what extent can we identify love, justice and growth in sister- and brotherhood with God's saving gift? They can dispose and prepare for it, result from it, and reflect it, but can they be a part of salvation? Do they manifest or embody it? Are they a sign or expression of it? Does salvation take place *in* them? If so, how? In what sense?

GS attempts no precise formulations on this matter but, in many places, it suggests a close identification between salvation and building the earthly city. It traces "bondage" ultimately to sin (41). Christ and the Spirit work in hearts which seek to transform the social order (26, 38). Human labor helps realize the divine plan, not only by continuing the work of the Creator, but also by becoming "associated with the redemptive work of Jesus Christ" (34, 57, 67). The earthly task "make[s] ready the material of the celestial realm" (38). The blessedness of the "new heaven and new earth . . . will answer and surpass" the longings of human hearts for peace (39). What is sown in weakness and corruption will not simply be annihilated but "clothed with incorruptibility." Creation will be unchained from its bondage and "charity and its fruits," "the good fruits of our nature and enterprise," will somehow endure, purified and transfigured (38, 39, 45).

Indeed, the " 'kingdom of truth and life, of holiness and grace, of justice, love and peace' . . . is already present in mystery" here on earth (39; cf. 11). "Here grows the body of a new humanity" which "even now" foreshadows the new age (38; cf. 3, 42, 92). This people, and the reign of God in history, cannot simply be identified with the church (40, 42, 43; cf. 11 and the Constitution on the Church [LG] 28), for humanity as a whole is to be an offering to God (38). As God once formed the Hebrews into a people, the divine plan now is that "the human race might become the Family of God," its solidarity growing "until that day on which it will be brought to perfection" (32). *Fraternitas universalis* and the transformation of the world are the object of God's saving plan and human effort alike (38) (Vorgrimler, *Pastoral Constitution,* pp. 194-201; Segundo, *Theology and the Church;* Rahner, "Theological Problems," pp. 264-65).

Clearly, the Council did more than simply rule out false dualisms and facile identifications of "earthly progress" with the reign of God, but it still left much unresolved about just how they are related. While some imprecision derives from the nature of the problem and its share in the incomprehensibility of divine mystery, some also stems from the Council's unwillingness to consecrate one position, proscribing other views which do not appear irreconcilable with revelation.

Populorum Progressio

In his 1967 encyclical *Populorum progressio,* Paul VI advanced the discussion by introducing the concept of "integral development" for each person and all persons (14, etc.). The pope drew on Jacques Maritain's notion of "integral humanism," which seeks human fulfillment at every level of human reality, including the level disclosed by faith, that is, the level of sin and God's call to salvation. Stressing the importance of *being* more over merely *having* more (6, 19; cf. GS 35), the pope summarized the idea of integral development in the following well-known passage: "The fullness of authentic development . . . is for each and all the transition from less human conditions to those which are more human." Less-human conditions include the lack of material necessities, moral deficiencies caused by selfishness, and oppressive social structures. More human conditions include:

the passage from misery towards the possession of necessities, victory over social scourges, the growth of knowledge, the acquisition of culture. Additional conditions that are more human: increased esteem for the dignity of others, the turning toward the spirit of poverty, cooperation for the common good, the will and desire for peace. Conditions that are still more human: the acknowledgement by human beings of supreme values, and of God their source and their finality. Conditions that, finally and above all, are more human: faith, a gift of God accepted by the good will of human beings, and unity in the charity of Christ, Who calls us all to share as sons and daughters in the life of the living God, the Father of all Human Beings. (20-21)[2]

Pope Paul does not say how faith, charity, and divine adoption are related to the other values he mentions (manifestation?, partial embodiment?, etc.). They somehow embrace each other, however, for the labors of the Christian "share in the creation of the supernatural world" (28) and "union with the sacrifice of our Saviour contributes to the building up of the Body of Christ in its plenitude" (79; cf. 44, 76).[3] PP advances the discussion, but, like GS, it leaves room to develop the question.

Medellín

At their historic 1968 meeting in Medellín, Colombia, the Catholic bishops of Latin America addressed their own pastoral concerns in the light of Vatican II. They drew heavily on GS and PP to interpret the church's mission amid the misery and sociopolitical turmoil of their continent (Med., "Introduction," 7; "Pastoral Concern for the Elites," 13; "Catechesis," 6; "Lay Movements," 10; "Priests," 18). The Latin American bishops speak with greater power and precision than GS about the relationship between salvation in Christ and earthly human fulfillment: "In Salvation History, the divine work is an action of integral liberation and human development at every level." In this important statement, left largely undeveloped, the bishops explicitly enunciate what GS and PP left unspoken: God's saving work embraces the human values of integral human fulfillment.[4]

The thesis that God's saving work *is* integral development would soon occasion great controversy, for it implies that the reign of God includes or somehow embraces values of the created order, including, of course, social values. The Christian message offers people "the possibilities of full liberation, the riches of *integral salvation* in Christ our Lord."[5] This suggests that God's saving work integrates and deepens human fulfillment at its various levels. Rejecting "simplistic confusions or identifications," and aware that the definitive consummation must await Christ's return, the bishops nonetheless underline

the profound unity which exists between God's plan of salvation realized in Christ, and the aspirations of man; between the

history of salvation and human history . . . between the supernatural gifts and charisms and human values.[6]

Controversy over Marxist analysis and other aspects of liberation
theology has raged for more than twenty years now, with political and
institutional interests clashing in the debates. The most important
theoretical issue, however, has been whether or not salvation is, in
fact, integral human fulfillment—liberation and development, personal and social, at every level of human existence. (One could also
make a good case that methodological issues are even more important, especially those concerned with the relation between theory and
practice.) Needless to say, not everyone agrees with all the intuitions
of Medellín, as the example of Cardinal Arns's Christmas letter, cited
in the Introduction, clearly shows.

Justice in the World

Medellín reflected ferment in crisis-filled Latin America, but turmoil in the Latin American church was already spilling over on the
wider church. In 1971, Catholic bishops from around the world
gathered in synod in Rome. They produced a document, *Justice in the
World*, which declared that

> Action on behalf of justice and participation in the transforma-
> tion of the world [are] . . . a constitutive dimension of the
> preaching of the Gospel, or, in other words, of the Church's
> mission for the redemption of the human race and its liberation
> from every oppressive situation. (6)

The synod does not elaborate, but this statement implies a closer link
between human liberation and salvation (which the church announces) than previous Vatican documents had explicitly articulated.

Declaration of the Synod on Evangelization

Medellín had buried "integral salvation" in a few texts without
clearly spelling out its implications. But Medellín and the reality it
reflected were felt at the next Roman synod (1974), where third-world
bishops sparked lively discussion about salvation and liberation. The
synod's brief statement sparkled with the language of "integral salvation or complete liberation of human beings and of peoples," "the
total salvation of human beings or rather their complete liberation,"
"the true and complete liberation of all humans, groups and peoples,"
and so on. Adopting more of Medellín's language, the synod spoke of

the need "to eliminate the social consequences of sin which are translated into unjust social and political structures" (Synod, 308). For perhaps the first time, a universal synod spoke of a salvation which embraced, or included, created human values.

Evangelii Nuntiandi

The following year Paul VI issued his important apostolic exhortation *On Evangelization in the Modern World* in response to the synod's recommendations. "As the kernel and center of His Good News," wrote the pope,

> Christ proclaims salvation, this great gift of God which is liberation from everything that oppresses human beings but which is above all liberation from sin and the Evil One, in the joy of knowing God and being known by Him, of seeing Him, and of being given over to Him. (EN 9; cf. 18, 31)

True, Pope Paul stressed the primacy of the person and interior change (18, 20); he also insisted on the transcendent call to union with God, ultimately in the hereafter; and he rejected, finally, any reduction of salvation to merely economic or political liberation[7] (8, 27, 28, 32-36). But EN spoke the language of Medellín, declaring that God's salvation "is liberation from everything that oppresses human beings." For "the supernatural life . . . is not the negation but the purification and elevation of the natural life" (47; cf. 18-20). Paul VI left the implications of his brief statement undeveloped; however, EN took a major step forward by legitimating a pregnant and original concept of Medellín.

Puebla

In the face of growing social crises, pastoral practice in the Third World continued to nourish fresh thinking and controversy. This was true above all in Latin America, where Medellín had legitimated commitment to social transformation. Battle lines formed in the church around political options and pastoral practice, around the use of Marxist thought (class struggle) and the question of violence. In a charged atmosphere heightened by the visit of a forceful new pope, the Latin American Bishops' Conference convened for another historic meeting in Puebla, Mexico (January-February, 1979). The meeting produced a repetitious, nuanced document. Despite extraordinary efforts to undo some of Medellín's accomplishments, however, pastoral practice and thought had developed too far. Medellín had broad support. The Puebla document added much, including conservative theology, to what Medellín had said, but it restated the latter's main theses among its thousand-plus paragraphs (*see* Eagleson, esp. articles by Penny Lernoux and Moises Sandoval).

At first blush Puebla seems to avoid explicitly identifying salvation with the "integral liberation" mentioned throughout the document (*see* 141, 475, etc.).[8] But although the unusual expression "integral salvation" has dropped from sight (*see* 343, however), Puebla quotes EN 9: Salvation "is liberation from everything that oppresses the human being" (Puebla 354; cf. 482). The document elaborates: "Christian liberation" has two inseparable elements:

> The first is liberation from all the bondage of personal and social sin, from everything that tears apart the human individual and society and whose source is egotism, the mystery of iniquity. The second element is liberation for progressive growth in being through communion with God and other human beings; this reaches its culmination in the perfect communion of heaven....
>
> This liberation is gradually being realized in history, in our personal history and that of our peoples. It takes in all the different dimensions of life: the social, the political, the economic, the cultural, and all their interrelationships. (482-83, trans. emended)[9]

The obvious interpretation is that this "Christian liberation" is another word for salvation.

In another rich passage, Puebla declares that in their exercise of freedom, human beings encounter God; and when they accept God, this simultaneously affects their capacity for communion and participation with the world, especially with other persons. Thus salvation entails liberating ethical action on behalf of the neighbor, especially the poor (321-29).

The bishops further note that "even though the Kingdom of God comes to pass through historical realizations, it is not identified with these realizations nor exhausted in them" (193). But they declare in striking fashion that "lay people . . . are pledged to the construction of the Kingdom in its temporal dimension" (787). Finally, in the Eucharist, Christ changes humanity's history into a saving history (918).

Instruction on Christian Freedom and Liberation

As the theology of liberation spread both in and beyond Latin America, so, in the minds of some, did aberrations. The role of Christians, including priests and religious, in Nicaragua's ongoing revolution served as a focal point for tensions—as the papal visit to Managua in March, 1983, made clear. The Vatican summoned liberation theologians to Rome to explain their thought. Warnings were issued. Finally, in 1984, the Vatican's Sacred Congregation for the Doctrine of the Faith, headed by Cardinal Joseph Ratzinger, issued its highly critical and controversial *Instruction on Certain Aspects of the "Theology of Liberation"* to be followed a year and a half later by a longer, more constructive *Instruction on Christian Freedom and Liberation.*[10]

Building on the first Instruction, the second, which reflects the style of Pope John Paul II, treats our disputed question in greater depth. Although the Instruction adopts many expressions and categories of liberation theology (for example, in its prophetic criticism of economic and political oppression), it nonetheless parts with Medellín on the historical and social meaning of salvation. The Instruction acknowledges close and indissoluble links between salvation and integral liberation; for the power of eternal life penetrates history through the actions of believers (Instruction II, 23, 62). This does not mean that salvation *includes* or embraces integral liberation, however. The document warns that not only would it be a grave error to *reduce* salvation to earthly liberation[11]; they ought not be identified in any way, for they "do not belong to the same order." God's kingdom (or reign)—which does mean complete liberation when history is consummated—corresponds to "eternal life," while "earthly progress" corresponds to "temporal life" (60).[12] Thus integral salvation (chap. 4, sect. 1; cf. 96) is not identical with integral liberation (63).

Salvation (or the salvific dimension of liberation) is freedom from sin and communion with God (3, 22, 47, 51, 99), according to the second Instruction.[13] Salvation corresponds to the "transcendent order" and the "city of God." Liberation in the "temporal order" or the "earthly city" is its ethical consequence.[14] Therefore, the "essential mission" of the church is "evangelization and salvation" through word and sacrament, even though it has another, secondary task, namely, "human promotion," which seeks the "temporal good" in the earthly city (62-64).

In its zeal to condemn the reduction of salvation to social and political liberation, this second Instruction implies a reduction of salvation, strictly speaking, to the interior and personal (and ecclesial). To this extent, it backpedals from Medellín and EN.[15]

Redemptoris Missio

The Instruction was hardly the final word. But if that is not surprising, John Paul's 1990 encyclical on international missions, *Redemptoris missio*, is indeed surprising. Its break with the second Instruction serves as well as anything else to throw into sharp relief the ambiguous position of the church on the social and historical nature of the reign of God.

In this little-noticed encyclical, the pope claims that a " 'gradual secularization of salvation' has taken place, so that people strive for the good of the human person, but a human person who is truncated, reduced to the merely horizontal dimension." We might suppose that the pope wants to limit the scope of salvation; but his intention is the opposite. "We know, however," he continues, "that Jesus came to bring *integral salvation,* one which embraces the whole person and all humankind, and opens up the wondrous prospect of divine filiation."[16] The concept of Medellín—integral salvation—appears to have risen from the magisterial grave. The pope goes on to confirm this perception.

> At the beginning of his ministry [Jesus] proclaimed that he was "anointed . . . to preach good news to the poor" (Lk 4,18). To all who are victims of rejection and contempt Jesus declares: "Blessed are you poor" (Lk 6,20). What is more, he enables such individuals to experience liberation even now, by being close to them, going to eat in their homes (cf. Lk 5,30; 15,2), treating them as equals and friends (cf. Lk 7,34), and making them feel loved by God, thus revealing his tender care for the needy and for sinners (cf. Lk 15,1-32).
>
> The liberation and salvation brought by the Kingdom of God come to the human persons in their physical and spiritual dimensions. Two gestures are characteristic of Jesus' mission: healing and forgiving. Jesus' many healings clearly show his great compassion in the face of human distress, but they also signify that in the Kingdom there will no longer be sickness or suffering, and that his mission, from the very beginning, is meant to free people from these evils. In Jesus' eyes, healings are also a sign of spiritual salvation, namely liberation from sin.

The text affirms an integral understanding of the salvation proclaimed by Jesus. We might wonder if the vision is not still a bit privatized, focused exclusively on the forgiveness and the healing of the individual. But John Paul continues:

The Kingdom aims at transforming human relationships; it grows gradually as people slowly learn to love, forgive and serve one another. Jesus sums up the whole Law, focusing it on the commandment of love. . . . The Kingdom's nature, therefore, is one of communion among all human beings—with one another and with God.

The Kingdom is the concern of everyone: individuals, society, and the world. Working for the Kingdom means acknowledging and promoting God's activity, which is present in human history and transforms it. Building the Kingdom means working for liberation from evil in all its forms. In a word, the Kingdom of God is the manifestation and the realization of God's plan of salvation in all its fullness. (RM 14-15)[17]

These paragraphs are unique among modern papal documents in the manner in which they unambiguously affirm the integral character of salvation-liberation. Critics have frequently assailed liberation theologians for writing similar texts which fail to make a sharp distinction between salvation and secular human development. In this respect, RM constitutes a breakthrough in official Catholic teaching.[18] It reflects the impact of the cry of the believing poor—channeled through the local hierarchies and theologians of third-world churches—on the universal magisterium.[19]

Does *Redemptoris missio* signal a definitive change in magisterial thinking? One swallow does not a summer make. Two important subsequent documents declined to follow its daring lead.

A year after RM appeared, *Centesimus annus* (1991), John Paul's encyclical on the 100th anniversary of *Rerum novarum,* limited itself to restating fundamental theses on this topic. It reminded us that "no political society . . . can ever be confused with the Kingdom of God" and that

temporal societies . . . as the adjective indicates, belong to the realm of time, with all that this implies of imperfection and impermanence. The Kingdom of God, being *in* the world without being *of* the world, throws light on the order of human society, while the power of grace penetrates that order and gives it life. (CA 25)

The following year, the Latin American bishops, assembled in Santo Domingo, produced, under close Vatican supervision, a document with practically no echo of that "integral salvation" which includes the social liberation of the poor. The Santo Domingo document restricts itself to quoting RM 15 to the effect that the Kingdom is "communion among all human beings—with one another and with God" and to affirming that Jesus died and rose "to free us from sin *and all its consequences*" (SD 27; emphasis added). The consequences of sin would presumably include oppressive social structures, but the inference is not made (*see also* Hennelly, *Santo Domingo;* Codina, pp. 259-71; Sobrino, "Los vientos," pp. 273-92).

Clearly, it is too early to say that *Redemptoris missio* signals a sea change, a development of doctrine on this central matter. The church as a whole is far from assimilating the idea of "integral salvation," to say nothing of its practical and pastoral implications.

This study of recent official texts shows that the social and histori- cal character of salvation constitutes a genuine *quaestio disputata* for Catholic theology. Few have stopped to appreciate and marvel at how it is possible that, after 2,000 years, the church could find itself at such a juncture with respect to an issue so central to the practice and understanding of the faith. We will leave the search for historical reasons as a task for others to pursue. For now, we simply note the gravity of this situation for the church: Social crisis looms and spreads, with the need for the church to do battle, not as a political party but as church, on the social front. But "if the trumpet gives an uncertain sound, who will get ready for battle?" (1 Cor 14,8). The task of this book is to diagnose the present situation in Catholic theology on this central question in greater depth and to suggest directions for the future.

As we enter the third millennium of Christianity, basic issues remain unanswered for Catholic theology. Do the autonomy of the temporal and the transcendence of salvation require a sharp distinc- tion between salvation and social liberation? Do the secular task of the laity and the clergy's task of explicitly pointing to that transcen- dence through Word and sacrament imply this? This book argues that they do not, but that salvation is integral human fulfillment, integral liberation, although we should speak of salvation in different senses. It further argues that the church has a single integral mission which includes various subtasks and roles.

The relationships between faith and society, God and Caesar, church and state, religion and politics, and the relationship of clergy (and religious) and laity to the social order are all tied up with this question. The way we formulate and act out these relationships depends in part on the particular times and places in which we live; there can be no clear formulas for all situations. It also depends on how one construes the relationships between the temporal and eter- nal, natural and supernatural (nature and grace), the material and the spiritual, the personal and the social (and political), human action and divine action (God's gift and the human response). But the heart of the matter, it seems to me, concerns the relationship between the good of societies and the reign of God—in other words, the social meaning of salvation in history. This is less a matter of ethics (the human task, the *Aufgabe,* as the Germans say) than of soteriology (the divine gift, the *Gabe*).

Therefore this book treats the relationship between the salvation the church proclaims and social justice. The question is one part of a more general problem: the relationship of salvation to human fulfill-ment or the human good, generally. We are concerned, however, with the relationship of salvation to the good of the community, that is, of particular communities and the whole human community.[20] Our concern is, especially, the relationship of salvation to the liberation of the victims of all forms of oppression. This question, above all, challenges the churches today, and wide disagreement exists about formulating the response.

It will help to sort out the issue by viewing it historically and situating it within a broader doctrinal context.

The Context of the Question

In this section, we first sketch the general meaning of salvation in Christian theology and note the characteristics of "Catholic" and "Protestant" thinking. Next we trace the question of salvation and social justice through the history of Christian theology. Finally, we summarize H. R. Niebuhr's typology of "Christ and Culture," which will help steer us through contemporary debates.

Salvation

The Bible and Christian theology always present salvation as the overcoming of a negative condition and the establishment of a positive one. Salvation is the forgiveness of sins, justification; it is the healing of a wound. It is liberation from slavery—to sin, to the powers of this world, to the passions, to the fear of death and to death itself, to Satan. It is the overcoming of darkness and ignorance. More positively, it is reconciliation with God and with others. It is the restoration of humanity to its "original state." It is freedom. Ultimately, it is the resurrection to eternal life and the vision of God in a new community (Topmoeller; Rahner, "Salvation," pp. 423-33, 435-38; Topel, pp. 100-1). At this general level, as Karl Rahner has observed, "on the whole the [Catholic] Church's official pronouncements simply repeat the doctrine of Scripture," and "the history of soteriology in dogma contributes little" ("Salvation," p. 428; cf. Haight, "Grace and Liberation"). Indeed, we could make a similar generalization for Christian theology as a whole.

Granted this basic unity, the history of Christianity nonetheless reflects two basic perspectives on salvation (*see* Harvey, p. 225; Haight, "Grace and Liberation," pp. 552-58).

Catholic and Eastern Orthodox theology characteristically views salvation as humans' participation in the divine life. This theology emphasizes Christ's Incarnation and (in the case of Catholic theology, at least) speaks the metaphysical language of nature and grace. It stresses church and sacraments as instruments of grace.

Protestantism, on the other hand, conceives of salvation as the restoration of a broken personal relationship between God and the sinner. Language is more existential than metaphysical. Protestantism emphasizes Christ's Atonement (Cross and Resurrection) and speaks of salvation in terms of the sin-grace conflict. Stress falls less on the sacraments than on the Word of God, which promises forgiveness and liberates from sin.

Fundamental Historical Figures

It will further help to frame our discussion if we briefly characterize the most influential positions that have been taken in Christian tradition concerning the relationship between the social good and the ultimate hope of Christians.

Augustine. Augustine decisively shaped the issue in the West. He radically distinguishes the earthly city and the created goods proper to it from the City of God and its proper good ("salvation"). For Augustine, salvation does not take place at all in the earthly city as such, that is, in social and political life. It takes place in the City of God—in the church and in the soul of the individual. Salvation consists of the forgiveness of sins and the promise of immortality. Although its effects overflow in ethical action leading to a form of earthly peace, the saved are few. Augustine believes that the Fall has so corrupted the world that we can expect little or no real progress in history.[21]

Irenaeus. The Greek tradition had earlier taken a different tack, especially with Irenaeus of Lyons who, in reaction to the gnostics, insisted on the goodness of creation. For Irenaeus, the Incarnation means that God saves all that is human and creaturely, spirit as well as flesh. Christ culminates creation and recapitulates all in himself. Therefore God will transform not only human flesh but all of nature, restoring creation to its pre-Fall condition and perfecting it in Christ.

Irenaeus believed that the saved would one day live in a very material and concrete new world (*see* Carpenter, Chapt. 2). But the West followed Augustine, not Irenaeus.

Luther. Profoundly influenced by Augustine, Martin Luther distinguished the good of the earthly kingdom from that of the kingdom of Christ even more sharply. The earthly kingdom concerns the outer person—all temporal and social affairs—the kingdom of Christ concerns only the inner person and the righteousness of the heart (*see* Lehman, pp. 75-129, 231-37).

Calvin. Like Augustine, John Calvin viewed history as God's instrument leading the elect to sanctification. But Calvin sees more possibility for change in history. First, since he relies less on categories of Greek philosophy, he does not permit fixed natures and orders of creation to constrain God's sovereign action in the world; second, God's grace transfigures the social order through the ethical action of regenerated Christians. This transformation of history is not itself salvation, however. Apart from regenerated individuals and the church, "salvation" or "God's kingdom" refers to a wholly transcendent, suprahistorical beatitude—as in Augustine and Luther (Calvin, *Institutes*, Book III, Chapt. iii, 9 [p. 601]; III, vi, 1 [p. 684]; III, ix [pp. 713-19; *see* Gilkey, pp. 175-87).

Sects and Millenarian Movements. Medieval sects and the radical wing of the Reformation generally consign the world to the devil. The holy community constitutes God's reign at present, but hope for the future is vibrant. The sects vary greatly, however, as to where (heaven, earth, new earth), when (now or later), and how (with human effort, including even violence, or by divine miracle) the final victory of God's reign will come about. Some understand the reign of God in immanent, historical and social—at times, materialist—terms.[22]

Thomas Aquinas. Sooner or later, contestants in any serious debate about Roman Catholic theology have to come to terms with St. Thomas. This is no easy matter in the present case. To know what someone thinks about the relationship between society and salvation, one need often only determine what the person says about the kingdom of God. St. Thomas Aquinas, however, says almost nothing about this central theme of Jesus' teaching,[23] and his thought is open to different interpretations on the issue we are considering. In any case, Thomas's theology closely links the growth of human community in history and the work of God's grace. First, Aquinas regards human nature as merely wounded, that is, less drastically corrupted by sin than Augustine and the Reformers suppose. For him grace brings human nature to perfection. In addition, following Aristotle, Aquinas stresses the communitarian character of human existence more than Augustine and Luther did. Despite this, however, Thomism has never found it easy to relate grace to the social order. In this it is not alone.

Since Augustine, mainstream Christian tradition as a whole has treated salvation from the perspective of the theology of grace. Whether from a personal and existential perspective in the sin-grace problematic of Augustine and Luther or from an ontological perspective in the scholastic tradition, this approach to salvation has shown great difficulty conceiving sin, God's call, and salvation in social categories other than those of the church itself. The existential-personal sin-grace problematic begins with the individual turned in upon itself (*incurvatus in se,* as Luther said), addressed by the saving Word and liberated by grace. The ontological nature-grace problematic begins with human nature, an essence or substantial form given prior to social interaction. In the one case, salvation refers to a new relationship between the individual and God; in the other, grace is a quality inherent in the soul. But in either case, it is first of all a matter of the individual before God. What about God's call to concrete communities and God's forming of community? This question invites us to probe more deeply the social character of the human condition.

The Kingdom Revisited. The last 200 years have witnessed a dramatic retrieval of the symbol of the reign of God as an expression of the hope inspired by political and industrial revolutions and the Enlightenment. Immanuel Kant inaugurated this revival by secularizing the reign of God in the form of an inner-worldly ethical commonwealth (Kant, book 3). Hegel and other idealists went on to develop the kingdom theme in different ways, as did liberal Protestant and Catholic theologians and the Social Gospel movement in the United States.

Critical Exegesis. During roughly the same 200 years, the Enlightenment and the spirit of modern science gave rise to the parallel development of critical New Testament study. This research quickly established the centrality of the kingdom of God in Jesus' proclamation and the origins of that symbol in Jewish apocalyptic, with its decidedly political expectations. The meaning and implications of these discoveries continue to fuel today's debates about the relationship of political and social change to Christian hope.

These most recent developments form the theoretical matrix for the theology of hope, contemporary political theology, and the various theologies of liberation. They constitute the wider theoretical context for the controversy that rages today over the reign of God and social liberation.

Christ and Culture

The history of Christian thought on our topic is even more complex than our brief sketch suggests. Can we order this material in a way that can help sort out the contemporary discussion? H. Richard Niebuhr distinguishes five broad approaches that have been taken historically to formulate the relationship between Christ and culture. His well-known typology can provide us with reference points for evaluating contemporary positions. Niebuhr first identifies two extreme positions that he calls "Christ against culture" and "Christ of culture." In the first view, espoused by Tertullian and Tolstoy, Christ and culture stand in fundamental opposition. In the second, represented by Abelard and Ritschl, Christ and culture are in fundamental agreement.

Between the two extremes, Niebuhr distinguishes three broad categories, all of which seek to maintain the differences between Christ and culture while expressing their interrelation in more complex ways than the two extreme views. Closer to the view of Christ against culture is the position represented by Paul and Luther, which recognizes a polarity and tension between the two legitimate authorities of Christ and culture. Niebuhr calls this dualist motif "Christ and culture in paradox." Closer to the Christ of culture is the position that affirms that Christ fulfills what is good in culture but also represents a good and a fulfillment that is qualitatively different from and transcendent of culture. This spirit of "synthesis," which Niebuhr characterizes as "Christ above culture," is dominant in Clement of Alexandria and Thomas Aquinas. Occupying something of a middle position, one finds the conversionist position, "Christ transforming culture." Latent in Augustine, hesitant in Calvin, thoroughly consistent in F. D. Maurice, this perspective holds that Christ is the Incarnate Word who regenerates culture.

Niebuhr's concern is more general than ours. His "Christ" refers to both the divine gift of salvation and the values associated with the ethical task of Christians; "culture" refers to the (positive or negative) values of society generally. Our stress falls more directly on the divine gift and more narrowly (and positively) on social justice. With these differences, nonetheless, Niebuhr provides a typology to which we can refer in this study. In the light of Niebuhr's types, we may speak of the good of salvation in relation to the social good according to five broad approaches. Salvation and social justice can be 1) utterly distinct, with justice unrealizable in history, 2) in basic harmony (or identical), with justice fully realizable in history, 3) in polar or paradoxical tension, 4) qualitatively distinct but fundamentally compatible, or 5) God's saving action transfigures society and its justice.

Niebuhr believes that the two extreme positions have difficulty incorporating elements that are indispensable to Christian faith. Yet even they provide important correctives for the imbalances to which the more centrist motifs are inclined (pp. 68, 102). Indeed, each of the perspectives represents only a more or less adequate attempt at the synthesis of a reality which is too rich and complex for any single position. There is no definitive solution to the problem. Each of the five positions serves as a reminder of the elements which the others are liable to devalue or ignore.

The Plan for This Book

The following chapters trace the recent historic shift in Roman Catholic thought from its traditional Christ-above-culture perspective toward a more Christ-transforming-culture outlook. But we will also have to question whether contemporary Catholic thinking about salvation and society neglects important elements of the Pauline-Lutheran perspective—Christ-and-culture-in-paradox—or of the other positions.

Tracing the Paradigm Shift: Three Key Thinkers

The next three chapters trace recent developments in Catholic thought on salvation and the hope of the poor through the work of three influential thinkers, rather than official documents. Why? Official documents cannot sort out all that is at stake in the complex issue we are addressing. They typically reflect compromise and bulge with the tensions of various camps, leaving room for a variety of legitimate interpretations. To get at underlying issues, we want to examine the work of thinkers who argue their position in a more detailed and systematic way. Theologians rely more on the force of their arguments than on ecclesiastical authority and must explain themselves in a more thorough way, a way which allows us more easily to evaluate the soundness of their position.

The following chapters therefore examine the syntheses of French philosopher Jacques Maritain (1882-1973) (Chapt. 2), German theologian Karl Rahner (1902-84) (Chapt. 3), and Peruvian theologian

Gustavo Gutiérrez (1928-) (Chapt. 4) . Investigating these thinkers will enable us to trace a historic "paradigm shift" in Catholic thought on salvation and social justice. (*See* Kuhn for a classic presentation of the meaning and dynamics of paradigm shifts.)

Why choose Maritain, Rahner, and Gutiérrez? They are key players in this century's dramatic development of Catholic thought on the question before us. Each achieved a decisive breakthrough in relating Christian faith to contemporary social and political life, and each developed a comprehensive and representative synthesis, a paradigm, on the problem.

Without question, Maritain represents the classic twentieth-century neoscholastic solution. Perhaps more than any other Catholic thinker, and in the face of great opposition, he has provided the theoretical framework for helping the Catholic Church find its place in the modern world after generations of political and cultural reaction. Although Maritain resisted both transcendental Thomism and pluralism in philosophy and theology, his thought is brilliant, subtle, and modern. We dare not identify him with the doctrinally rigid, politically conservative manual scholasticism with which he frequently sparred. Neither is Maritain a mere "pre-Vatican II" figure. It was he who provided the concept of integral humanism which inspired the language of "integral vocation" in *Gaudium et spes* and "integral development" in *Populorum progressio*. His views—including his understanding of what he calls the temporal and spiritual orders—continue to echo in official and nonofficial expressions of Catholic thought. Anyone who wishes to move beyond traditional formulas will do well to understand them. For this, no one better than Maritain can be found, because he applied them with a creativity that has given his synthesis lasting power.

Most acknowledge Karl Rahner as a, perhaps *the,* foremost Catholic theologian of this century, one who has articulated the question under discussion in a way that challenges the classic neoscholastic synthesis from the standpoint of first-world Europe. Rahner's theology diverges from Maritain's theological presuppositions in important ways. Tensions between the two graphically reflect tensions in church practice and theology today. Karl Rahner probably influenced the doctrinal formulations of Vatican II's *Gaudium et spes* more than any other theologian (*see* Vorgrimler, *Karl Rahner*, p. 99).

Most today regard Gustavo Gutiérrez as the father of Latin American liberation theology. He has addressed our chief concern more systematically than any other figure in that movement and in such a way that almost all its participants accept the main lines of his position. The relationship between the reign of God and the struggle for social justice is the central theme of his masterwork, *A Theology of Liberation*. But Gutiérrez treats the question from his own third-world context in a way that challenges the paradigms which Rahner and Maritain represent. Indeed, as recent controversies between the Vatican and liberation theology demonstrate, Gutiérrez's theology poses a challenge to the Christian church as a whole. He was deeply involved in the drafting of the Medellín and Puebla documents, both of which reflect his thought.

In short, these three thinkers represent crucial moments, stopping points in the recent historic paradigm shift in Catholic theology concerning salvation and the hope of the poor. We will evaluate each of their paradigms for consistency, coherence, and comprehensiveness, for their adequacy to experience, especially the experience of misery, and their fidelity to authoritative sources such as the Bible, tradition and philosophy (*see* Tracy, *Blessed Rage;* Gustafson, pp. 138-44).

The Future of the Tradition

Maritain, Rahner and Gutiérrez represent what Catholic theology has been and much of what it is today. What about its future? We will uncover weaknesses that need to be addressed and discuss the following points in connection with these in Chapter 5:

First, the Catholic tradition suffers the lack of a feminist corrective. So far, no feminist thinker has engaged the tradition of Catholic thought concerning salvation and social justice with the same thoroughness as Maritain, Rahner or Gutiérrez. The tradition—and this book—is impoverished by this lack. But feminist theology has effectively sighted the ghost of Platonic dualism that has haunted Catholic theology for centuries and that is central to our concerns. Not all are convinced that Karl Rahner's transcendental theology has succeeded in dispelling this ghost. Besides feminist theology, Basque philosopher Xavier Zubiri and his student, Ignacio Ellacuría, one of the Jesuits martyred in El Salvador in 1989, have made signal efforts to confront this issue. We shall briefly examine their contributions.

Second, the study of our three paradigms will confirm the need for a solid theory to interpret the social character of the human condition and its relationship to social institutions and politics. Laying the basis for a strong sense of sociality will help fill in some gaps in the search for a more complete understanding of the relationship between salvation and liberation.

Third, Chapter 5 also addresses the "Catholic" tendency, which we noted, to neglect certain typical "Protestant" emphases.

Finally, in Chapter 6 we will turn to Scripture for a fresh look at the question of salvation and social justice, focusing on the meaning of "kingdom (or reign) of God" in the early synoptic traditions about Jesus. Our hypothesis about Jesus' understanding of God's reign will in part confirm and in part challenge the Catholic tradition on salvation and liberation.[24]

Five Key Issues

We bring a single question to all the sources we examine—the question of Christian salvation and the hope of the poor—but this fans out into several subquestions which can help us compare positions and trace the developing debate.

The larger question includes 1) the relationship between *the divine gift (salvation) and the human response* or task, a subtopic which arises as a matter of course. But how one links salvation and social justice also depends on 2) how one interprets the relationship between what Catholic theology, especially, calls *nature and grace,* or grace and the human condition. However, if "grace perfects nature," then the way salvation and human justice are related also depends on how one understands the human condition itself. A great deal depends, for example, on how one interprets 3) the relationship of *spirit to matter* and 4) *the social character of the human condition.* Finally, the relationship between salvation and the social good depends 5) on one's *theory of the eschaton,* or end time.

A great deal rides on how one interprets the human condition. You might hold, for example, that grace transfigures the human spirit; but if you understand the human condition dualistically, with spirit radically transcending matter, then the work of grace might have little effect on the body or on human society.

Similarly, even if you hold that grace transfigures the human condition and that body and soul constitute an indivisible unity, you might still consider human persons as isolated individuals, so that God's saving action, while affecting the entire person, might have no direct effect on human society.

Finally, the relationship of salvation and social good also depends on eschatology. You might well suppose that grace transfigures the human condition, that body and spirit are one, and that human beings are essentially social, but that, on the other hand, every concrete human achievement will vanish without a trace when God's final victory is established through a totally transcendent intervention which will consummate history.

As we investigate how Maritain, Rahner, Gutiérrez, feminist theology, and the Bible spell out the relationship between salvation and the social good, it will help us to attend to how each treats these subissues.

Tracing the paradigm shift will demonstrate that the Catholic tradition has great potential to articulate a hope which responds to the suffering of the poor in history. Catholic grace-theology's historic neglect of social relations can be partially remedied by showing that God's saving action (grace) touches and saves the whole human being and that human beings are social beings in a stronger sense than the traditional Thomist paradigm has affirmed. Therefore, God's saving action means new persons in a new community.

However, this argument, based on the principal "grace perfects nature," is insufficient. Liberation theology took the decisive step when it intuitively framed the central question in terms of the sin-grace polarity *and spelled out the social character of sin*. Sin is social; therefore, so is salvation. This, we shall see, is central to biblical theology. The Bible reveals not simply how God (and grace) relates to human persons, but also how God relates to social relations and, in particular, to social injustice. The Reign of God which Jesus announced replaces unjust social relations with just social relations. This understanding of salvation rests on nothing less than the identity of God who takes the side of victims, not because of any merit of theirs, but because of who God is: the compassionate one, the Liberator of the poor.

This means that, to be really faithful to its roots and to the task of articulating the faith for today, Catholic theology must be liberation theology. In order to realize its liberating potential, it must take as its starting-point and center the biblical God who rejects oppressive social relations and offers a new way to live together in community. It can then specify that God is carrying on a revolutionary transformation in history in the face of selfishness and sin and that, for all its secularity, social justice is no mere secondary problem which the church addresses under the heading of moral theology, but a strictly religious affair which lies at the heart of the church's single mission to announce saving Good News to all, especially the victims of history.

2

THE TRADITIONAL PARADIGM
OF JACQUES MARITAIN

The relationship between Christianity and the social order occupied Jacques Maritain throughout his long and fruitful career. Indeed, he has articulated a classic Thomist synthesis of the problem for our century, one which already represents a paradigm shift with respect to the Catholic "integrists" who attempted earlier in this century to resurrect a European Christendom whose day had passed. While Maritain's limitations appear obvious to some today, we do well to examine his synthesis closely, for its rich complexity transcends a narrow, passé neoscholasticism and its chief theses crop up frequently in official and unofficial expressions of Catholic thought.[1] Maritain's positions will help readers less familiar with earlier debates to better understand today's and tomorrow's.

In this first section, we shall offer brief comments about how the problem which engages us touched Maritain's life. Then we will present his diagnosis of modern theological dualism and his own solution, "new Christendom."

Maritain and His Times

Maritain maintained a passion for social justice throughout his life. As a member of a staunch Republican family, he declared himself a socialist at the age of sixteen and vowed to serve the proletariat.[2] After his conversion to Catholicism in 1906, Maritain traveled in conservative antidemocratic circles but distanced himself from social affairs.[3] In 1926, papal condemnation of the monarchist movement *Action Française* jolted him into undertaking the serious study of social philosophy which he kept up for the rest of his life. In 1954 he wrote that he never revoked his youthful vow to "serve the proletariat and humanity" (*Notebooks,* pp. 7-8).

At the turn of the century, the prevailing scientism at the Sorbonne nearly drove the student Maritain to "despair of reason" and the contemplation of suicide ("Confession," p. 331). He later came to view French positivism—and his personal crisis—as part of a far deeper problem. The attempt to understand reality apart from metaphysics and revelation is just one symptom of the great tragedy of the modern West: the divorce of the human enterprise from God. Human beings seek to achieve an earthly good without reference to the ultimate good of salvation and without reference to the truth that they are fallen and redeemed. This problem would inform Maritain's labors until his death in 1973. They included spelling out the meaning, for Christians, of the task of building a humane social order.[4] Maritain's central thesis is that the social and political task must be subordinated to the supernatural order.

Thomism amazed Maritain by its range and power, and it delivered him from his despair. In time he applied its principles with extraordinary versatility to the questions posed by contemporary society. Few Catholic intellectuals in this century would demonstrate a broader interest or a keener sensitivity to those questions than Maritain. But Maritain always held to key epistemological and metaphysical principles of the seventeenth-century Thomist commentator John of St. Thomas, principles that placed him on one side of a serious split among Thomists which deepened between the world wars. These principles, together with questionable theological assumptions, colored his conception of the relationship between Christianity and the social order (*see* McCool, "Jacques Maritain"; Harvanek; cf. McCool, *Unity to Pluralism,* Chapt. 9).

The times alarmed Maritain. In the twenties, Europe's war wounds scarred over painfully, and in the thirties the Great Depression violently polarized France. The working class suffered bitterly and continued to slip away from a church whose members too often divorced faith from social responsibility. Generations of bourgeois individualism and the growing appeal of bolshevism, Nazism, and fascism among the fearful masses seemed to Maritain to threaten Western civilization.

From 1926 to 1936, Maritain produced four important books of Christian social philosophy. They culminated in *Humanisme intégral,* the synthesis which forms the basis of all his later work on political philosophy.[5] Maritain diagnoses the problem of the modern West most clearly in the first two chapters of IH. We summarize his diagnosis in the following section.

The Tragedy of the Modern West:
Anthropocentric Humanism

Maritain greatly values democracy, technical progress, and many other advances of the modern period. He believes, nonetheless, that a fatal flaw has characterized the modern West—the severing of humanity and its historical projects from God.

For Maritain, the Renaissance and Reformation gave rise to an *anthropocentric humanism* that finally issued in twentieth-century totalitarianism (IH 27, 34).[6] Pessimistic Protestantism separates human beings from God by debasing them.[7] Renaissance optimism achieves the same by glorifying them. Christian children of the Renaissance such as Descartes consider grace "a simple ornament capping nature" (IH 21); neither grace nor revelation are needed to understand the world or to bring about a fully human life. From there it is a short step to rationalism and deism, which practically dispense with God and grace. In the end, human beings take on the task of salvation and even the attributes of God. For Rousseau, Hegel or Comte, the human person is

> a *purely natural* being . . . detached from any connection with a supernatural order . . . and nevertheless in reality . . . one reabsorbs into this man of pure nature all the aspirations and all the appeals to a life properly divine . . . which for the Christian are dependent on the grace of God. (IH 24)

Marxist communism is simply the most consistent and sophisticated expression of this outlook.[8] In the twentieth century, bourgeois anthropocentric humanism has led to the materialism of Nietzsche and Lenin, and so ironically to the defeat of humanity.

New Christendom

In short, in Maritain's view, modern Western culture has tried to solve the problem of life without reference to God and the help of grace. The modern age "has been an age of dualism, of dissociation, of splitting in two" (IH 27). The situation calls for a "total recasting of our cultural and temporal structures" (IH 71). It calls for a *new* Christendom, that is, a pluralist *lay* (secular) society inspired by evangelical values.

Maritain considers Thomism uniquely capable of inspiring this transformation:

[The] one solution for the history of the world . . . is that the creature be truly respected *in* its connection with God and *because* receiving everything from Him; humanism, but theocentric humanism, rooted where man has his roots, integral humanism, humanism of the Incarnation. (IH 72)

This solution takes into account what *revelation* says, both about human frailty and about the power of God to vivify human action. It permits human beings to undertake great historical enterprises with great humility. By its nature, integral humanism requires "new human being[s]"[9] of genuine sanctity, equipped with the post-Enlightenment critical awareness needed to completely recast the social order (IH 76-77).[10]

New Christendom is Maritain's solution to the dualism of modern Western civilization. Its theological basis is his conception of the relationship between the temporal and spiritual orders of human existence. In the next two sections, we will explain the distinction and interrelation of the two orders. Although we will reserve most of our criticism and evaluation to the end of sections and subsections, an occasional critical observation in the exposition will give the reader a sense of direction through the exposition of Maritain's complex system.

The Distinction of the Temporal and Spiritual Orders

According to Maritain, the various modern worldviews all fail to appreciate the key distinction—and interrelation—of the temporal and spiritual orders. Neither order can be denied or collapsed into the other; neither can be separated from the other in the concrete. Following the classical scholastic formula, Maritain distinguishes them in order to unite them.

Two Orders

Maritain bases this distinction of spiritual and temporal orders, of the reign of God and the world, ultimately on the authority of Christ, who distinguished the things of God and Caesar and so declared that Christianity transcends specific states and cultures (IH 98). The distinction derives from the fact that "two distinct worlds, the world of nature and the world of (participated) Deity [i.e., grace] meet and interpenetrate one another" in human life (*Science and Wisdom,* p. 180; cf. p. 119).[11] Although the two orders transcend the state and the institutional church, their distinction pertains principally to visible social life. The orders are Christianity (hence, the church) and the world (civilization or society). (While "natural order" refers to the whole creation, "temporal order" denotes, especially, "culture and civilization.")

In scholastic philosophy, an order is specified by its end. Those elements ("forms") of human life which are directly "ordained" to (i.e., which have as their purpose) the realization of the end of human nature (the temporal good) constitute the temporal order. Those which are directly ordained to the supernatural end (the spiritual good) constitute the spiritual order (IH 133-34).[12] The temporal order is defined by the natural good, "the earthly and perishable good of our life here below."

> In themselves and by their own end, [culture and civilization] are engaged in time and in the vicissitudes of time. . . . The order of culture or civilization appears then as the order of the things of time, as the *temporal* order. (IH 98)

For Maritain, the following terms go together and characterize the temporal order: nature (rather than grace), the social and political, time, the perishable, and the material. (Much that is immaterial also belongs to the temporal order, however: the human spirit, natural law, the rule of justice and love, beauty, and so forth.[13])

Everything directly ordered to the ultimate end of human existence pertains to the spiritual order—a fitting designation, not only because God is spirit, but also because the human spirit (and thus the whole person) is intrinsically ordained to the beatitude of union with God.[14] Thus,

> The order of faith and the gifts of grace, being concerned with an eternal life which is a participation in the intimate life of God, constitutes by opposition [to the temporal order] an order to which the name *spiritual* most rightly belongs and which, as such, transcends the temporal sphere. (IH 98)[15]

Maritain holds that the spiritual order, in complete contrast to the temporal order, is the order of grace, the immaterial, eternity, and so of the unchanging and imperishable. Clearly, therefore, although the two orders are inseparable in existence, they are really distinct. They do not overlap. They do not interpenetrate. What is temporal cannot be eternal; the imperishable cannot perish.

> And if, for the Christian, this spiritual order must vivify and superelevate the temporal order, it is not as constituting part of

it. It is on the contrary as transcending it, as being of its own nature absolutely free and independent of it. In a word, the spiritual order enjoys as regards the temporal order the very freedom of God as regards the world. (IH 98)

Not only are the two *ends* distinct on the basis of the transcendence of God and of grace over nature, the orders themselves are equally and utterly distinct.

Spirit and Matter

For Maritain, the "spirit" of the spiritual order is clearly the divine Spirit, first of all. Just as clearly, this is the order to which the human spirit aspires and in which it participates by grace. According to Maritain's interpretation of Aristotelian Thomism, the human spirit is "intrinsically independent of matter in its nature and in its existence" ("The Immortality of the Soul," p. 58),[16] for it is ordained (and this defines spirit) to an activity, contemplation, that is totally transcendent with respect to matter and time: "The pure essence of the spiritual is to be found in wholly immanent activity, in contemplation, whose peculiar efficacy in touching the heart of God *disturbs no single atom on earth*" ("Religion and Culture," p. 225, emphasis added).[17] Even when enfleshed, the dynamism essential to spirit carries it away from matter, time and change.[18] In view of this, since human beings participate in the spiritual order in virtue of the human spirit, Maritain associates the work of the divine Spirit and grace more readily with the interior dimension of life than with the exterior—the body, society, politics. He therefore contrasts "the social and visible domain and the spiritual, moral, and invisible one," or again, "that which is of religion and that which is of the socio-temporal" (IH 213, 301; cf. *Freedom in the Modern World*, pp. 139, 147).

Maritain's starting point—an understanding of spirit as transcending matter, time and change—is questionable from a theological point of view (Nottingham, p. 82). Linking nature with time, matter and the social, and grace with the timeless and nonmaterial in creation will give a decisive coloring to the relation between the orders.

The Temporal Common Good

Maritain does not hold that human beings have two distinct *ultimate* destinies, one natural, the other supernatural, but only one absolute (supernatural) end, beatitude. So the temporal good is not an absolute end. Neither, however, is it a pure means. Maritain calls the good of the natural order the temporal common good. Irreducibly social, both material and moral, it corresponds to what we have called the social good, or social justice.[19] It is not just the collection of private goods (anarchistic individualism) nor the good of a whole that sacrifices the parts to itself (totalitarianism) but rather the common good of *persons*. It therefore includes respect for the rights of persons and families (which are prior to the larger community) (PCG 49-51; IH 133).

From this it follows for Maritain that it is intrinsic to the temporal good to be subordinated to the good of the *spiritual* order, for society must respect the person's orientation to communion with God. With respect to the supernatural end of human life, therefore, the temporal order *does* function as a means. But it is also a good in its own right, a *"bonum honestum,"* with the dignity of a subordinate, or "infravalent," end (PCG 53).[20]

For this reason, Maritain and the Thomist tradition can affirm the *relative autonomy* of the temporal order with respect to the spiritual order. Human nature retains its consistency with respect to grace, which does not destroy it but perfects it. So too reason with respect to faith. Civil and political institutions retain their relative autonomy over against the church. Secularization, the modern disenchantment of the world celebrated so enthusiastically by the Enlightenment, constitutes in many respects a "real historical gain" (IH 177; cf. 26, 176-77, 180). The awareness of the world's relative autonomy undermines the "integrist" understanding of the relationship between Christianity and the sociopolitical order. The church ought not employ the state to police its ranks. "Confessional" Catholic political parties, like the nineteenth-century German Centrum party, are inappropriate for modern times. Politics and social life generally have a logic all their own. The hierarchy should not try to control the political activity of the laity. It ought only proclaim the moral limits of political options and enforce these within its ranks. Maritain's "New Christendom" is thus a *secular,* Christianly inspired social order.[21] This fundamental thesis of the relative autonomy of the world, championed by Maritain, has become a permanent achievement of Catholic theology and was enshrined by Vatican II (cf. GS 36; Vatican II, Decree on the Apostolate of the Laity, 1, 7).

We shall return to this point in subsequent chapters. More important for our purposes, however, is the fact that for Maritain the temporal common good is a *purely natural good* whose experience or realization does not *include* the supernatural good even though, as we shall see, it requires the latter for its own integral realization. Even when civilization is "superelevated" by the practice of Christian virtues, "its own end . . . still remains . . . a certain common good of man on this earth, in his terrestrial life" ("Religion and Culture," p. 221).[22] In this sense, Maritain holds there is a double human destiny, even though only the supernatural end is ultimate and the natural end requires grace.

This has clear implications for the mix of religion and politics. For one thing, Christianity's primary function as "road to eternal life" is distinct from its secondary function "as leaven in the social and political life of nations and as bearer of the temporal hope of mankind" (*Christianity and Democracy*, p. 37; cf. p. 43. Compare Instruction II, no. 64). The Church's primary task, entrusted to the hierarchy, is "religious"; its secondary task, a secular ethical one, is entrusted to the laity.[23]

History and the Reign of God

As we turn to the good of the spiritual order, we find that Maritain calls it the "kingdom of God" when he wants to indicate its *social* character. Precisely because of its social connotations, for Maritain "kingdom of God" refers chiefly to final beatitude. The kingdom of God is a

> city at once *earthly* and *holy*. . . . The Jews looked for this kingdom in time. For the Christian it will be outside time; it is an eternal kingdom which will have as its place the land of the resurrected. (IH 101)

"Kingdom of God" refers first of all to the life of posthistorical resurrected humanity, the "city of the blessed." But it is also "earthly," and insofar as earthly, it is identical to the church itself.[24]

A correct understanding of the reign of God, according to Maritain, depends on a sound theological interpretation of the world. One must avoid three typical errors, according to which the world is regarded purely and simply as 1) the kingdom of Satan, 2) the kingdom of God, or 3) the kingdom of "man." Each error oversimplifies the correct characterization of the world as a kingdom at once of Satan, of God, and of "man."

The World as Kingdom of Satan. According to the first error, the world is on its way to perdition, pure and simple. Gnostic tendencies in the early church and Reformation theology bore elements of this dualistic thinking which, according to Maritain, denies in effect that God has saved the world and intrinsically justifies human beings. God has abandoned the world to the devil (IH 103).

This first type of Maritain's corresponds roughly to H. R. Niebuhr's two relatively countercultural types, especially "Christ against culture" but also "Christ and culture in paradox." These two types lie to the "left" of Maritain's own "Christ above culture" Thomist position. We next treat the third error before turning to the second.

The World as Kingdom of "Man." Maritain's third erroneous understanding of the world, peculiar to modern times, is also dualistic. In this secularist outlook, the world is "purely and simply the domain of man and of pure nature," with no transcendent reference (IH 107). It includes modern anthropocentric humanism and all efforts to build an earthly utopia without God. (This third error has no clear parallel in Niebuhr's typology. Christ is irrelevant to culture.)

The World as Kingdom of God. Unlike the two dualist errors above, the second error is monistic. The world becomes, at least in part, the reign of God.

> Not only is the world saved in hope, but one believes that it is necessary—to the extent that the work of redemption takes place in it—that in its temporal existence itself it appear as already really and fully saved—as the kingdom of God. (IH 104)

One hopes and strives to realize the reign of God as a good of civilization.

Under this error, Maritain appears to combine Niebuhr's two (at least partly) culture-affirming types, "Christ of culture" and "Christ transforming culture."

In the West, notes Maritain, this error has taken a typically political utopian form. This can take a religious direction (clerical theocratism, integrism, *cujus regio, ejus religio,* etc.) (IH105-6).[25] Maritain faced this error in the Catholic "integrists" who, earlier in this century, struggled to resurrect a modern form of the cross-and-crown alliance. And he, as much as anyone, helped the Catholic Church move beyond this model. But Maritain held that this error made its full weight felt only in sacred missions of secular salvation. Hegel invested the state with such a mission; Marx, the proletariat; and fascism, the race or nation (*see* IH 106-7, 150; cf. *Moral Philosophy,* p. 230). In such instances, one attempts 1) to bring about a definitive human fulfillment on earth 2) by human, and in the end coercive, means.[26] Marx gives definitive expression to this *hubris* when he claims that communism is the *"total redemption* of history" (*Moral Philosophy,* p. 230; *see* Bottomore and Rubel, p. 182; cf. IH 47n.10). Marxism promises "a secularized kingdom of God which, though terminating history, remains *in* history and *in* the time of this world" (IH 58-59; cf. *Religion et culture,* p. 110).

Coercion aside, for Maritain the human condition is such that not even with "spiritual means" and divine assistance can the reign of God be realized in history, for neither sin, misfortune, nor pain, the insatiable desire for beatitude nor the reality of death can be eliminated from history.

We may object that none of this precludes *partially* realizing the reign of God in history. Maritain's warrants only rule out establishing the reign of God *fully* or *definitively* in history. They rule out the "Christ *of* culture" solution—by Henry VIII or Lenin—but not the "Christ transforming culture" solution. Maritain, however, will have none of this. The second error concerning the world

> goes against the Gospel words: "My kingdom is not of this world." It goes against the fact that Christ did not come to change the kingdoms of the earth or to accomplish a temporal revolution: *non eripit mortalia, qui regna dat coelestia.* (IH 105; cf. 59)[27]

Non eripit regna mortalia ("He does not take away mortal kingdoms"). Precisely because it entails a sociopolitical good, the reign of God (except for the church militant) is outside time.[28]

> The Jews looked for this kingdom in time. For the Christian, it will be outside time. . . . Insofar, therefore, as this idea is rightly that of a kingdom, a political city . . . this idea of the kingdom of God is an eschatological idea, an idea which concerns the end of time. It does not refer to the time of this earth, but to what will come after this time. (IH 101-2)

Maritain believes that whereas salvation in the Old Testament was material and political, Christians expect a salvation which transcends time, the material, the perishable, the sociopolitical. Like grace itself, the reign of God wholly transcends history.

Critique

Our reflections suggest that Maritain has overlooked some important distinctions. We have three objections to the way he distinguishes the orders and, with them, salvation and the temporal good. First, for Maritain, salvation remains extrinsic to the temporal good of the social order. This problem surfaces when he fuses H. R. Niebuhr's types, "Christ of culture" and "Christ transforming culture," neglecting important differences between them. It is not the same thing to say that Christianity is not "of a race, nor of a nation, nor of a [particular] civilization, nor of a [particular] culture" and to say that Christianity is "not of man, nor of the world . . . nor of civilization, nor of culture," period (IH 97).[29] The first quote says that Christianity completely transcends each *particular* civilization, the second that it completely transcends the temporal good and civilization, *generally*. The former expression rules out the "Christ of culture" synthesis, the latter "Christ transforming culture," as well. Unlike other religions of antiquity, Christianity is universal with respect to cultures. *Non eripit mortalia* says far more, however.

The ground crumbles under Maritain's attempt to enlist John 18,36, frequently translated "My kingdom is not of this world," in support of his thesis. Exegetes have long abandoned his interpretation. In the first place, "kingdom" (Hebrew, *malkuth*) refers here to God's active governance of the world, God's "politics," and not to a place. In addition, "of" translates *ek* (cf. *enteuthen*, vs. 36c), which is not our possessive "of" but the directional "from." It designates origin and hence characteristic features.[30] The verse therefore means: "My kingly activity derives from God, not from this world." Or, "Pilate, my politics are radically different from yours." The verse does not say that God and the Messiah have no politics or that God's politics are no threat to Pilate and the empire. It says that the new regime replaces violence with truth (vs. 36b) and domination with service (cf. Matt 20,25-28 par., a synoptic equivalent to our passage). Jesus' (and God's) is the politics of the new age which is replacing the politics of this age. God's politics is not exercised in some other realm.

At the basis of these problems is an underlying form of "extrinsicism." Since the beginning of the Counter-Reformation and until recently, the dominant forms of Catholic theology construed the saving action of God (grace) as extrinsic to concrete experience. While Maritain fought to overcome this dualism and succeeded in part, he nonetheless remained captive to a form of extrinsicism with respect to the social order. He rightly affirmed that nature and grace are absolutely distinct, for God completely transcends creation. But he also held that salvation (which is the experience of grace in the concrete) utterly transcends the temporal good. The reign of God (salvation) is not of this world in the same way that grace is not of this world. The temporal common good and salvation "are two specific ends, clearly distinct; they differ as heaven differs from earth" (*Scholasticism and Politics*, p. 225).

Maritain does not hold for a "pure human nature" in the concrete, that is, a human nature to which grace and orientation to participate in the divine life are wholly extrinsic.[31] However, he accepts a double human destiny insofar as he construes the temporal good as a purely natural good (although it requires grace for its consistent realization) and insofar as he considers salvation to be purely supernatural in the sense that it does not include the temporal good in any way. In this sense, salvation and the temporal good are separate in the order of experience.

Maritain is well aware that grace and salvation (the experience of grace) are not the same. However, he attributes to salvation a transcendence similar to that of God and grace with respect to the temporal order and the temporal good. The absolute transcendence of God and grace is one thing; the absolute distinction between salvation (the experience of grace and its results) and the good of history is another thing altogether. One *might* distinguish God from creation and nature from grace absolutely and still understand the experience of God as the experience by historical beings of the radically transcendent which transfigures history, embracing in its very transcendence what is material and spiritual, perishable and temporal, personal and political.

Our chief criticism of Maritain, therefore, is that he links grace closely with the interior life and disassociates it from the "exterior" life—of the body, society and politics. This derives not only from his understanding of "nature and grace," but also from his conception of matter and spirit.

This leads to a second objection. Maritain supports the radical distinction of the temporal and spiritual *orders* by drawing their boundaries with Aristotelian lines. One is the temporal order, the order of the perishable and material. The other is eternal and spiritual, where "spiritual" refers ambiguously to both the divine and the human spirit. Since the essence of spirit is transcendence of matter and time, salvation has no temporal, material or sociopolitical dimensions. One negates the salvation characteristic of the Old Testament ("the Jews") in favor of something completely different—rather than transforming it by assuming it into a larger synthesis.

If, as Maritain says, the historical condition of humanity precludes the full or definitive solution to history within history as we know it—and it surely does—it does not *ipso facto* preclude partial solutions in history.

We must now complete Maritain's picture by describing how he *links* the two orders he has so sharply distinguished. This will reveal how Maritain understands the relationship between divine and human action, eschatology, and sociality—all of which will also help us compare his overall position with others'.

The Unity of the Two Orders

The last section showed how Maritain distinguishes the spiritual and material orders together with their two goods (salvation and the temporal common good). But his chief concern is to *unite* what he has distinguished, counteracting the dualism of the modern West. He wants to show how God's saving action must join human efforts to build a more just world.

According to Maritain, each of the three erroneous conceptions of the world improperly separates or fuses the two orders. Each of the three errors falls short of the Christian solution, which views the world and the temporal city as "a kingdom *at once* of man, of God, and of the devil." God created the world; Christ redeemed it; and for as long as history lasts, human beings must labor in it to wrest it from Satan's control. Therefore,

> the aim the Christian sets himself in his temporal activity is not to make *of this world itself* the kingdom of God, it is to make of this world . . . the place of a truly and fully human earthly life. (IH 108; cf. 108-11)

In other words, the Christian has the ethical task to seek to bring about in the world "a refraction of the Gospel exigencies" (IH 108, 110) and so to make of this world not the reign of God, but a truly human world, so far as possible. On the one hand, this can only happen with the help of grace. On the other, by building a truly human earthly city, humanity sets the environmental conditions for salvation and thus prepares for the reign of God itself.

This means that there are two perspectives from which Maritain considers the *interrelation* of the temporal and spiritual orders. First, the spiritual order affects the temporal; grace and revelation assist— "from above," so to speak—the ethical task of achieving the temporal good. Second, the temporal order affects the spiritual order "from below." That is, the human task prepares for the divine gift of salvation (both in history and in the posthistorical reign).

The Spiritual Order Affects the Temporal

The spiritual order affects the temporal order chiefly in two ways: first, the pursuit of the temporal good must be subordinated to the spiritual good; second, grace must superelevate action in the temporal order.[32] The first way is really an imperative: All moral philosophy and action must take account of revealed truth.[33] In particular, Maritain insists that since each person is ordained to the absolute, individual persons cannot be wholly subordinated to society as the part is subordinated to the whole. On the contrary: "With respect to the eternal destiny of the soul society exists for each person and is subordinated to it" (PCG 61; cf. p. 42 and *passim*).[34] One may not sacrifice the things which are not Caesar's to the pursuit of the temporal good.

In an age when all modern societies submerge the individual, Maritain's emphasis is wholly fitting. Notice, however, that it is the (individual) *person* who is ordained to the ultimate supernatural end, whereas the good of the temporal order is more clearly *social* (and material) in character (*see* IH 132-37; PCG 61). As a result, the subordination of the temporal to the spiritual good turns out to be, ultimately, a subordination of the common good to the (supernatural) personal good.

The spiritual order affects the temporal in a second way that illustrates the relationship between divine and human action. Following St. Thomas, Maritain says that achieving the temporal good itself requires that grace *superelevate* the temporal order by informing human action (*see* pp. 29-30, above; cf. PCG 51, 62, 64; *Science and Wisdom,* p. 215; IH 134, 293).

In Thomistic thought, the acquired (or natural) virtues direct action to produce the temporal good; but they can only do so adequately and consistently with the aid of God's grace, operating by means of infused (supernatural) virtues which direct action to the ultimate supernatural end.[35] Along with sanctifying grace and supernatural charity, God bestows the other infused virtues. Through their mediation, charity interrelates and stabilizes the acquired virtues, superelevating them to the supernatural end. Acquired and supernatural virtues thus form a "vital and synergic union" which promotes the temporal good in a consistent and integral way (*Science and Wisdom,* pp. 211-12).

In this way, "a human work [is] brought about on earth by the passing of something divine, namely, love, into human means and into human work itself" (IH 203). Few themes recur as frequently in Maritain's works as the need for the vivifying "sap" of supernatural charity in the pursuit of human well-being.[36] When the enlightened political elements (*cives praeclari*) which guide and animate a society possess the infused virtues, that society "is in reality and to this extent . . . under the regime of Christ" (IH 169).

According to Maritain, therefore, God's saving work affects the social order "from above" indirectly by means of the synergism of the moral virtues. A relative disjunction, proper to traditional Thomism, between soul and body and between interior and exterior morality leads to an extrinsicism with respect to the social order. Being "under the regime of Christ" sounds like social salvation, but it is not. Maritain's understanding of the synergic union of virtues prohibits identifying God's gift of salvation in any way with the concrete fruits of the human task. God's saving work does not take place in and through the temporal good. The integral realization of the temporal good is a *consequence* of the saving work of grace. *Personal* salvation manifests itself outward in temporal *social* effects.

The Temporal Order Affects the Spiritual: Eschatology

The relationship between the two orders is bilateral. The temporal order affects the spiritual "from below" in at least two ways.

First, secular activity can be meritorious. When the infused virtues "proportion our action to our eternal end," they render action, including secular action, meritorious of eternal life (*Science and Wisdom,* p. 213).[37] However, merit does not concern Maritain in this context, for in Thomistic thought, action has salvific import if and only if executed out of a (conscious or unconscious) supernatural motive.[38] The concrete results of such action (the temporal good) do not constitute or bring about the reign of God. They can, however, prepare for it.

This is the second way, one more germane to our interests, in which Maritain understands the temporal order to affect the spiritual "from below." The temporal good disposes, or prepares, individuals for personal salvation and prepares all of history for the advent of the posthistorical reign of God. First, the temporal good disposes individuals for grace.

> The end of political society is not to lead the human person . . . to sanctity. . . . Nevertheless, political society is essentially destined . . . to the development of those environmental conditions which will so raise men in general to a level of material, intellectual, and moral life . . . that each person will be positively aided in the progressive conquest of his full life as a person and of his spiritual freedom. (IH 134; cf. IH 137; PCG 59)

Suitable "environmental conditions" help dispose individuals, with the prior help of grace, to receive grace.

Furthermore, "Temporal history prepares enigmatically its final consummation in the kingdom of God" (IH 110).[39] This brings us to eschatology. For Maritain, the struggle to wrest control of the world from Satan will last as long as history itself. Wheat and tares will be sorted out only in the end. Therefore, the history of the world in part marches toward the reign of God, while in part it marches toward perdition (IH 108-9).[40] The church, on the other hand, marches solely toward the reign of God (IH 109).

> The kingdom of God constitutes the final term which the movement of history prepares and to which it leads, and toward which converge, on the one hand, the history of the Church and the spiritual world and, on the other, the history of the secular world and the political city. (IH 102)

That part of history which marches toward the reign of God is the progress of societies insofar as they realize "the good and freedom of the person" (PCG 77). This presupposes that action is superelevated and directed toward the ultimate supernatural end.

The temporal good thus "prepares in history for the kingdom of God, which, for each individual person and for the whole of humanity, is something meta-historical" (*Scholasticism and Politics,* p. 10).[41] In this preparation, Maritain assigns a significant role to social structures (social *habitus,* institutions)[42]: The world "prepares the coming of the kingdom of God" to the extent that its structures "have as their measure justice, the dignity of the human person, and fraternal love" (IH 111). And, indeed, although human actions are rarely measured by such standards, social structures, namely,

> institutions, laws and customs, economic and political organizations . . . insofar precisely as they are things and not men . . . can be measured by justice and fraternal love. . . . They can be more just than the men who employ them and apply them. (IH 111n.9)

Maritain thus places a high value on politics without conferring on it a sacred mission.

Maritain's understanding of how history prepares for the final consummation in the kingdom raises important questions. Will the temporal common good perdure to share somehow in the final reign of God? Will the *fruits* of our work for justice (and not just interior dispositions) endure in the city of the blessed? Can social *institutions*—loving social relations, just structures—share somehow in the final term of the universe? Or does understanding salvation as "meta-historical" preclude any such thing? On the one hand, "the world is sanctified insofar as it . . . is assumed into the universe of the Incarnation" (IH 109). On the other, what is of time will pass away, including the temporal common good.

The history of the secular world will come to its final term only by means of a substantial "mutation," which is designated as the conflagration of the world and which will engender it into the kingdom. (IH 102)

Maritain and the traditional understanding of merit imply that there is no continuity or "carry over" from history to the final reign of God except the personal holiness of individuals and the social holiness of the church. Nonetheless, although there will be "an essential discontinuity which separates the 'penultimate' from the ultimate" (IH 111n.10), Maritain must contend with the biblical teaching of the resurrection of the body. The material universe will be transfigured rather than annihilated. At the

resurrection of the bodies . . . the universe of matter, fully reconciled to the victory over death, will be itself transfigured in glory and integrated in order to serve it [the glory] in the beatitude of the spirits. (*Church of Christ,* p. 47; cf. pp. 33, 51; *Moral Philosophy,* p. 218; *Philosophy of History,* pp. 137-38)

For Maritain, the history of the world converges with the history of the church, to be transfigured at the end of time. Yet the reign of God apparently will not include the temporal good that prepared its way. Individual persons, personal virtue and the church endure in glory.

We have been examining how the temporal and spiritual orders affect each other in Maritain's thought. What is the relationship between justice in the temporal order and the salvation worked by God?

Earlier we concluded that for Maritain the social good is in part the *consequence* or *effect* of the saving action of God. Now we find that the temporal good also *prepares for* salvation—both in history and as the posthistorical reign of God. The temporal good follows salvation as an effect and precedes it as a preparation. Salvation does not take place in or through the struggle for justice. The two goods are radically distinct. Though itself a *bonum honestum,* the temporal good functions as pure means with respect to the supernatural end of persons, as we saw. We now see it is also pure means for the posthistorical reign of God. There is no continuity between the social good, as such, in history and the city of the blessed. Therefore, Maritain posits *two parallel histories,* the history of the world and that of the church, which converge in the final reign of God.

The Social Character of Salvation

Maritain's explanation of final beatitude confirms the discontinuity between the good of history and the reign of God and pointedly raises the question of the social character of salvation.

Beatific Vision and City of the Blessed

In Thomist thought, the ultimate end of human beings is the "beatific vision" in which the soul enjoys direct union with God (*see* PCG, Chapt. 2). It transcends every created good and is not mediated by any created good. Partly for this reason, Maritain refers to the "ultimate end" of human beings ("man") as the ultimate end of *individual* persons. Beatitude neither consists essentially in human social relations nor requires social mediation. The direct communion with God is sufficient for the individual.

> The beatific vision is . . . the supremely personal act by which the soul, transcending absolutely every sort of created common good, enters into the very bliss of God. . . .
> Were there but a single soul to enjoy God thus, it would still be blessed, even though it would not have to share this beatitude with any other creature. . . . The beatific vision . . . is the most perfect, the most secret and the most divine solitude with God. (PCG 21-22)

For Maritain, however, the solitary vision forms the basis for a human society. The beatific vision is "the most open, most generous and most inhabited solitude. Because of it, another society is formed—the society of the multitude of blessed souls." Maritain stresses the accidental character of this society, however: "According to St. Thomas, it is neither essential to nor necessarily required by perfect beatitude; this society accompanies it" (PCG 22-23).[43] Social relations among the blessed come about "consequentially" and "*outside of the vision*" (PCG 24; emphasis in original).[44]

Maritain's "Individualism"

According to Maritain, beatitude is essentially solitary because the beatific vision takes place through "a personal and solitary act of each one's intellect." What is most Godlike in the human person, the speculative intellect, "grasps the Divine Essence . . . in the most immediate act conceivable . . . without any created intermediary," God thereby serving as the intellect's "impressed species." Because of the immediacy of this union, the "beatific vision . . . transcend[s] absolutely every sort of created common good," including the city of the blessed (PCG 25, 21).[45]

This argument rests on the autonomy and superiority of the speculative intellect. With St. Thomas, Maritain argues that the operation of the speculative intellect is superior to that of all other faculties. It alone has truth and God as its immediate object, and its mode of operation—unlike that of all other human faculties—is independent of matter, self-sufficient, and immanent (PCG 24-26). All other human operations are *transitive*. They depend on created goods. Such operations—and such relations with other creatures—cannot be essential to beatitude, for Maritain, for transitive activity "is quite visible, is characteristic of the world of bodies. . . . It passes away in Time and with Time." Immanent activity (contemplation), which is proper to the speculative intellect, "is the characteristic activity of life and spirit. Here the agent has its own perfection in itself. . . . This action, as such, is above time" (*Scholasticism and Politics*, pp. 171-72; *see* Chapt. 7, *passim*).

Behind this argument is Maritain's understanding of spirit as "intrinsically independent of matter in its nature and in its existence" ("Immortality of the Soul," p. 58) and his belief that the human spirit's specifying activity is transcendence, not only through but *away from* matter. This also means moving through but away from human society, mediated as this is by material relations. The solitary contemplative life, as St. Thomas says, is superior to life in society (PCG 26-28).[46]

Maritain's argument draws us into one of the most tangled controversies of scholastic thought, past and present: How to safeguard the *immediacy* of the relationship of the individual to God without falling into gnosticism and idealism—especially since knowledge comes through the senses as the intellect turns to the phantasm of imagination. We cannot solve this problem here, although we will return to it in the following chapter. What we can say here is that Maritain's highly speculative argument fails to persuade, because his stress on the derivative nature of social salvation rests on a theologically unacceptable foundation: the understanding of human spirit's characteristic dynamism away from matter toward intransitive activity.

In general, Maritain's explanation of the ultimate primacy of the person over the community reflects this understanding of human transcendence. Although he affirms the superiority of the community over the individual in the order of temporal values, nonetheless each person's "direct orientation to God transcends every created common good," including the city of the blessed.[47]

Maritain is no liberal individualist like Locke or Mill. For him, human beings are social animals who, as *individuals* rooted in matter, must depend on society because of their needs and who, as spiritual *persons,* can dispose of themselves and communicate with others by love and knowledge (PCG, Chapt. 4, esp. pp. 47-49). For Maritain, however, this double potentiality for communication belongs to already constituted individuals who need no social interaction to *be* human in the first place: "Man is constituted a person, made for God and life eternal, before he is constituted a part of the city" (PCG 75-76).[48]

I will criticize this position more thoroughly in subsequent chapters. For now, I will offer only the following observation. If one does not need others to *be* a person at all, then one might not need others for beatitude. All one's needs could be supplied by God alone in the beatific vision. If, however, human beings require social interaction in order to be human in the first place, their fulfillment would also have to be inherently social. This is not a matter of the sufficiency of God for the person but of the kind of being for whom God is sufficient. If beatitude is not complete without the resurrection of the body, this is not a reflection on the inadequacy of God but on the fact that one is not a full human person without a body of some kind.

Summary and Conclusions

Maritain labored to repair the breach, opened in the modern West, between the human enterprise and God. His solution was to subordinate the things which are Caesar's to the things which are God's, carefully distinguishing the temporal and spiritual orders in order to show how they interrelate.

Like nature and grace, Maritain's two orders are utterly distinct. So are the "goods" which specify them: Salvation does not belong to the temporal social order. Except for the church, the social and political dimension of salvation remains posthistorical. We said this implies that the temporal good, because temporal and social, is a purely natural good. Maritain's position depends in part on understanding spirit as that which transcends matter and time into immanent contemplation. This enables him to link grace directly with the interior dimension of life and indirectly with the exterior—the body, society, politics. Maritain therefore habitually speaks of salvation and beatitude as an affair of the individual, an idea further reinforced by the idea that humans are constituted persons prior to social interaction.

Although Maritain considers the temporal common good to be a true earthly end, it is only a means with respect to salvation. On one hand, however, the temporal common good requires grace-inspired action and results from it. Personal salvation manifests itself "outward" in ethical social effects. On the other hand, the temporal good also prepares for salvation by providing its environmental conditions, as society and church follow parallel, converging paths toward the final victory of God's reign. However, although the two orders closely interrelate, society constitutes the realm of ethics (the task), not salvation (the gift) (cf. *Scholasticism and Politics*, p. 203; IH 42). In the end, salvation is extrinsic to the social order and the temporal good.

The church has a double function corresponding to the temporal and supernatural "ends" which specify each order. The hierarchy dedicates itself to *religious* action which directly pursues the supernatural goal; the laity to the secondary *secular* task of infusing the social order with ethical value.

We argued that the transcendence of God and grace with respect to history does not by itself exclude a temporal and social dimension of salvation and that Maritain's theological principles need not rule out a partial realization of the reign of God *in confuso* in the social order, particularly if one were to view the relationship between spirit and matter (or history) in a different fashion.

Like his efforts in so many areas, Maritain's synthesis of the relationship between the spiritual and temporal orders is rich, complex and brilliant. I have tried to show its limitations. (Space has precluded developing many of the positive points we have mentioned here.) The overall thesis and its presuppositions reflect the way salvation and the social good have long been understood, and continue to be understood, often unthematically, in Catholic thought.

We have traced flaws in Maritain's model to his understanding of human spirit and, ultimately, to his theology of grace. The philosopher Maritain never plumbed the grace question in great depth. Just three years before his death, however, he completed a study of the *church* which surfaced important issues concerning grace—as well as contradictions in his paradigm.

In the light of the Second Vatican Council, Maritain's *On the Church of Christ* wrestled with the problem of grace and salvation outside the church. This question had occasioned serious turmoil in Catholic theology during the entire first half of the twentieth century and up until the Council. As we shall see in the next chapter, its solution depends on reformulating the relationship between grace and the human condition (and, incidentally, on the understanding of human transcendence itself).

In *On the Church of Christ,* Maritain described the church as a common *person* whose soul is the Holy Spirit and grace. Its body—the visible social organization—manifests this soul *"in confuso,* not distinctly" (pp. 10-11, 17-19, 34, 103-4, 139, etc.; quote from p. 139). But, with the Council, Maritain affirmed that the Holy Spirit and grace (salvation) also manifest themselves outside the formal institution of the church. Therefore, he argued, the body of the church must also be found beyond the formal community of the church in the form of "the visibility . . . of the acts accomplished by the non-Christian under the influx of the grace which is in him" (ibid., p. 103; cf. p. 239).

In other words, the Holy Spirit and grace—salvation—manifest themselves in and through acts of love and justice of Spirit-filled persons in the world. This happens on a significant scale, since there are probably more such "saved" persons formally outside the church than inside! (ibid., pp. 94, 107).

This presence of the Holy Spirit and grace in the world suggests that we speak of the reign of God manifest *in confuso* in actions of love and justice. Unless one wished to separate these actions from social relations and institutions (in the broad sense of social *habitus*), we could also speak of these latter as manifestations of God's reign in history. Maritain declines to speak this way, however. Although he had earlier identified the kingdom with the church militant, in 1970 he chose to expand the meaning of "church" but not the language of "kingdom."[49]

This is one of many examples which illustrate that the problem we are considering in this book concerns the use of words. That hardly trivializes the issue. It means the problem concerns how we name reality, what we take reality and experience to be. If we use "salvation" to refer to all the work of selfless love in the world, our understanding of salvation and the world both change. That is fraught with practical consequences concerning how the church and groups within it (clergy, laity) should operate.

During the middle decades of the twentieth century, the question concerning salvation and the church sparked intense debate in Catholic circles over the theology of grace. By the time of the Second Vatican Council, most pointed to the work of Karl Rahner as a key breakthrough.

Pope John XXIII referred to the reform inaugurated by the Council as *aggiornamento,* or renewal. Rahner was, of course, a key shaper of Council documents, which often reflect a theology of grace akin to his. The next chapter examines his *aggiornamento* interpretation of the relationship between Christian salvation and the just community.

3

THE *AGGIORNAMENTO* PARADIGM
OF KARL RAHNER

Introduction

Ordinarily in Catholic theology the relationship between salvation and social justice depends, in the end, on the relationship between nature and grace. It depends, secondarily, on the relationship of spirit to matter and on the social character of human existence. Eschatology, too, is entangled in the relationship between divine redemptive action and human praxis.

The present chapter shows how Karl Rahner's understanding of grace and human transcendence (spirit) leads to a different interpretation than Maritain's of the relationship between salvation and the just community. Rahner's theology also affords a distinctive eschatology and a stronger conception of social existence than Maritain's. With Rahner, the traditional paradigm shifts.

Maritain had developed his synthesis of the two orders as a major controversy was brewing in Thomist circles in Europe over nature and grace. The smoke from this battle only began to clear in the 1950s, when Rahner's imaginative theses began to win widespread acceptance. Today, whether they accept it completely or not, most Catholic theologians consider Rahner's work a definitive advance in the understanding of grace and the most important contribution to the theology of grace for the *aggiornamento* period of Vatican II.[1]

The Grace Debate

Post Counter-Reformation Catholic theology long suffered from an "extrinsicism" that separated grace from conscious, concrete experi-

45

ence and ran the risk of interpreting grace as "alien, scarce, and ultimately, superfluous" to a human fulfillment achievable without divine aid (Duffy, p. 9). During the Thomist revival of the first half of the twentieth century, the dominant "Dominican" school, drawing heavily on commentators Cajetan (sixteenth century) and John of St. Thomas (seventeenth century), reflected this outlook. They argued that, if humans were destined to salvation by nature, then grace would be owed to them and would no longer be grace. Therefore, they reasoned, human beings' orientation to God (affirmed by St. Thomas) must itself be a supernatural grace wholly extrinsic to human nature. From this they deduced that, although humans are in fact destined to a supernatural end, God could have created them in a "state of pure nature," as relatively complete persons destined to a purely natural human fulfillment. For some, this implied that actual human beings have two destinies, one natural, the other supernatural.[2]

Extrinsicism, pure nature and the idea of a double destiny came under heavy fire during the 30s, 40s and 50s. Following the lead of Maurice Blondel (1861-1949) and the transcendental Thomism of Joseph Maréchal (1878-1944), proponents of the *nouvelle théologie* such as H. de Lubac, H. Bouillard, and H. Rondet countered that an orientation to share divine life is somehow intrinsic to the human condition. Their critique, while not wholly successful in establishing a new synthesis, left the standard view in tatters. Catholic theology would never be the same. From the 50s on, extrinsicism, hypothetical states ("pure nature"), static essences and natures were abandoned; thereafter, concrete-existential, personalist, dynamic, historical and explicitly Christological categories would characterize any attempt to explain God's relationship to humanity and to creation in general.

Maritain was deeply influenced by the Dominican school. He affirmed the possibility (not the actuality) of a "state of pure nature" ("Immanent Dialectic," p. 71, with note; "Religion and Culture," p. 221; *Philosophy of History,* p. 132) and a nuanced conception of a double human destiny, natural and supernatural. With the help of theologians such as Charles Journet, Maritain avoided the excesses of extrinsicism, insisting on the need for grace to elevate the achievement of the temporal (natural) good. The idea of a purely natural human fulfillment had a paradoxical affinity, after all, with the secular dualism Maritain relentlessly opposed.

Rahner, of course, rejected extrinsicism, but he broke with the *nouvelle théologie* insofar as it regarded an orientation to union with God as something intrinsic to what theologians call "nature." Steering a middle course, he arrived at his famous notion of the supernatural existential.[3]

Both Rahner, closer to the *nouvelle théologie,* and Maritain, within the Cajetan tradition, occupy the space between the extremes of warring camps. Though incompatible in important ways, their positions are both reflected in the theology of Vatican II (GS). Although before and during the Council, Catholicism turned a corner, the break with extrinsicism remains incomplete, as we can see today. "Unfortunately," as Stephen Duffy observes,

> a loss of nerve and a virulent restorationism have, in the last two decades of this century, marked something of a return to the old dualisms that interiorize and privatize religion, thus again willy-nilly conceding "the world" to secularism, as the school theology had done. . . . (pp. 9-10)

Much is at stake in the differences between Maritain and Rahner. They reflect the lingering ambiguity of Catholic thought concerning grace and the human condition and, in particular, concerning the social meaning of salvation in history.

The Order of Creation within the Order of Redemption

For Maritain, as we saw, the experience of the spiritual good does not take place in and through the realization of the temporal good. In this sense, it is extrinsic to it; it does not encompass or include the latter—although it is necessary for it, has been prepared by it, and will ultimately further it. For Rahner, however, there is never any genuine human fulfillment that does not include the experience of God's self-bestowal (grace). Rahner explains the relationship of the "orders" differently. Although nature and grace are themselves radically distinct, the *order of creation* and the *order of redemption* (or the natural order and the supernatural order) are not identical to these, and we ought not construe their relationship in the same way ("Order of Redemption," p. 48; cf. pp. 40-41).[4]

Maritain in no way confuses the pair nature-grace with temporal order-spiritual order. As we saw, however, he does say that the two orders are as radically distinct as grace and nature and, indeed, as creation and God. Rahner views matters differently:

> We speak of the order of redemption *within* the order of creation . . . divine grace, the fruit of redemption, actually penetrates the created order itself, healing and sanctifying it . . . it incorporates the world, in all its abiding naturality, into the *mysterium Christi.* ("Order of Redemption," pp. 38-39)

The two orders are materially co-extensive.[5] They are "not identical, but neither are they adequately distinguishable from each other" (ibid., p. 41), as they would be if they were characterized on the basis of matter-spirit or temporal-eternal distinctions. They interpenetrate in a way that Maritain's orders do not. Rahner's orders are less identifiable, less institutional and concrete. He finds it harder to locate the boundaries between them. In order to appreciate this, we must enter a little further into the labyrinth of the grace debates.

The Supernatural Existential

Rahner interprets human beings' orientation to God as follows: God's universal saving will creates all human beings with an infinite emptiness or longing—which only God can satisfy—precisely in order to communicate divine life to them. More than a merely natural openness to grace—a passive *potentia obedientialis* for grace proper to nature as such ("Order of Redemption," pp. 49-50)[6]—this longing is an "ontological alert," a positive ordination of human beings to share God's life as their only real final destiny.[7]

The ordination is an "existential" (or constitutive determination) of humanity as it exists in history. But, since humanity can in no way tend toward salvation without divine help, such an essential constituent must itself be a gratuitous bestowal pertaining to the supernatural order. In his famous explanation of this "supernatural existential," Rahner wrote,

> If God gives creation and man above all a supernatural end and this end is first "in intentione," then man (and the world) *is* by that very fact always and everywhere inwardly other in structure than he would be if he did not have this end; and hence other as well before he has reached this end partially (the grace which justifies) or wholly (the beatific vision). ("Concerning the Relationship," pp. 302-3)[8]

The constant self-offer of God, who has objectively saved the entire human race, decisively stamps the human condition, even when this offer of salvation is not subjectively accepted.[9]

The *transcendental* and *supernatural* character of this particular existential has far-reaching implications for our concerns. The offer of the divine self-gift is not a *part* of human existence so much as its all-encompassing "horizon," that is, its boundary and context. The dynamism of spiritual existence manifested in the self-transcendence of freedom, love, and knowledge has this horizon as its ever-present goal as well as its origin and the condition of its possibility. This context is called a horizon because it is never experienced directly but always remains at the limit of experience. It is the Holy Mystery called God (*Foundations,* Chaps. 1 and 2). As a permanent horizon of the human condition, the offer of salvation stamps every aspect of human existence, not from without but from within.

When accepted, therefore, *salvation embraces absolutely every dimension of human existence, interior and exterior, material and spiritual, personal, social and political.* This is the most important implication of Rahner's theology for our question of salvation and social justice. But what does it mean to say that salvation "embraces" all of life? The following sections show how Rahner's anthropology combines with his theology of grace (to which it corresponds as the other side of a coin) to explain how Christian salvation answers and surpasses the deepest longings of flesh-and-blood human beings who struggle together in history.

Spirit and Body

In Maritain's traditional paradigm, the order of grace is the spiritual order, the order where divine and human spirit meet. Divine Spirit and grace relate directly to human spirit and indirectly to matter and society.

This seems to suggest that matter stands, in Neoplatonic fashion, at a greater remove from God than human spirit ("Unity of Spirit and Matter," pp. 156-57). Or it suggests too close a similarity between divine Spirit's transcendence of creation and human spirit's transcendence of matter: In fact, the single word *spirit* applies to divine and human spirit only very analogously. These differ far more between themselves than do human spirit and matter. In any case, Maritain and Rahner differ on the relationship of human spirit to matter, and their differences lead to divergent understandings of how grace touches the material world.

Maritain understands spirit as a drive to transcend matter (and time and change) in its quest for contemplation of the immaterial.[10] As a Thomist, he holds that the human spirit "informs" the body. From a Rahnerian point of view, however, he exaggerates spirit's transcendence when he writes: "The pure essence of the spiritual is to be found in wholly immanent activity, in contemplation, whose peculiar efficacy in touching the heart of God disturbs no single atom on earth" ("Religion and Culture," p. 225). If this is true, grace might conceivably transfigure the soul without disturbing a single atom, that is, without affecting the body or social relations. The transformation of social relations would then pertain to the ethical human task but not to the divine gift. In Rahner's view, such a "psychotherapeutic" understanding of salvation would be essentially gnostic. Christianity is more materialistic (*Foundations,* p. 196).[11] "There cannot be any grace which does not imply a quite definite putting into action of nature," says Rahner.[12] "Nature" here includes the body ("atoms") and social relations. But before we consider how *divine* Spirit and grace affect the human condition, we need to explain how Rahner understands human spirit.

For Rahner, human spirit is not a substratum underlying its own operations of transcendence (knowledge, love, freedom). Spirit actualizes itself in these operations. Human being (spirit) is transcendence toward the world.[13] The human spirit must have a body in order to be spirit. The body is the spirit expressed in the emptiness of space and time (*materia prima*) ("Body in the Order of Salvation," pp. 71-89).[14] Spirit thus actualizes itself in bodily form, and the unity of body and spirit precedes their distinction.

> Spirit and matter are not ultimately words referring to particular regions of the total reality, regions which lie side by side, but refer to factors which wherever encountered, though essentially different, are everywhere correlative constitutive moments of the one reality. ("Unity of Spirit and Matter," p. 171)[15]

The most "spiritual," or interior part of a person and the most "material" or exterior part are both dimensions of a single incarnate spirit. "The loftiest spiritual thought, the most sublime moral decision, the most radical act of a responsible liberty is still a bodily perception or a bodily decision." I experience nothing as wholly interior or wholly exterior. Everything that I experience comes both from within and from without me ("Body in the Order of Salvation," p. 82; cf. "The Intermediate State," p. 121).

Furthermore, for Rahner, since matter "makes possible an immediate intercommunication with other spiritual existents" (*Foundations,* p. 183), spirit's relation to matter determines the social character of the human condition. Human spirit necessarily expresses itself into a *public* space and time in such a way that every aspect of human existence, including the most "interior," is socialized, that is, related to other persons, to a world, to history ("Body in the Order of Salvation," pp. 82, 86-89). We shall return to this presently.

Therefore, for Rahner, one could never presume to limit the saving action of grace to some interior sphere clearly demarcated from the external world.[16] The person actualizes him or herself in general only by going out into the other in order to return to self. In particular, a human being "goes up towards God only by going out into the world," for "only by stepping out into the world can man so enter into himself that he encounters being and God" (*Rahner Reader,* p. 56).[17] Maritain stresses that spirit strives toward the nontransitive, immanent activity proper to it. For Rahner, transcendence takes place and human beings realize their properly spiritual nature only in a body and via interaction with, indeed transformation of, the material and interpersonal world.

Even prescinding from the materiality of the sacraments and the social institution of the church, Rahner holds that when saving grace erupts in the world via the deeply personal act of faith of individuals, each such person is embodied and socialized in such a way that accepting grace is always the act of the whole person—material, spiritual, social—and that grace embraces all of existence.

Before considering Rahner's views on the social character of human existence and salvation further, we can draw some inferences from what we have just shown.

The Blessings of Salvation

Rahner agrees with the traditional view that grace is required for the integral achievement of the natural good.[18] However, whereas neoscholasticism generally considers the good of society to be itself a purely natural good, for Rahner, grace envelops all of creation, and creation's "real crying need for grace" implies that

> everything natural, if fully and freely experienced, accepted and realized as what it really is (i.e., necessarily supernatural in its ultimate goal) is actually always, at every stage, more than purely natural. ("Order of Redemption," p. 51)

In particular, any time we truly accept the human condition, we explicitly or implicitly accept the God-given dynamism of the human spirit toward God and accept God's self-bestowal itself. But analogously, grace is also offered in *every* good of creation.

Natural goods such as

> Joy, seriousness, responsibility, daring, commitment to an unforeseeable future, love, birth, the burden of work and thousands of other aspects of life . . . are willed by God *as* factors in a supernatural order.

Their orientation to share in the salvation God offers already stamps their character. We meet God in any created good, provided we accept its inherent longing to share salvation ("Significance of the Individual," pp. 104-105; cf. "Order of Redemption," pp. 51-52).

Rahner's thinking invites us to consider such more-than-natural goods as blessings of salvation *when God's offer is accepted in faith.* We may distinguish the blessings of salvation in three senses: first, as justification and the indwelling of the Holy Spirit in the church and the individual; second, moral acts (ultimately acts of love); and third, the fruits of such action. Salvation in the primary sense—justification and divine indwelling—manifests itself in simultaneous effects which are blessings of salvation in the other two senses.[19] Thus, in a secondary sense, salvation is effected and manifests itself through actions of selfless love. Building on the doctrine of the virtues infused by supernatural charity, Rahner regards human works produced under its influence as part of God's saving gift, not simply, as for Maritain, an ethical consequence of God's gift to the individual.[20]

We can also speak of salvation in a third sense, inasmuch as these actions produce good results in the world. Fruits of the Spirit and loving action, joy, peace, patient endurance, etc. (Gal 5,22), even as natural goods, are part of the blessings of salvation. Salvation in the primary sense (justification and divine indwelling) manifests itself through acts of love (secondary sense) to produce such blessings as community, justice, peace, food and drink shared (third sense).

The idea that salvation manifests itself tangibly and visibly in the world raises no difficulty for a biblical theology or for Rahner. But, like the presence of grace itself, the salvific character of such blessings is always ambiguous (and threatened) in history. Just as specific human actions can never be judged for certain to be motivated by supernatural charity, so, too, tangible human goods (including justice) that result from grace remain as ambiguous as the presence of grace itself.[21]

Human Beings Are Social Beings

In the mid-sixties, Rahner's student Johann Baptist Metz began to criticize what he called the privatizing tendency of modern existentialist theology, charging in particular that Rahner neglected the social significance of Christianity in the face of the suffering of history (Metz, *Theology of the World,* pp. 95-96, 107-15).[22] Taking Metz's critique seriously, and further influenced by papal social encyclicals, by Vatican II's turn to the world, and by liberation theology, Rahner subsequently devoted more attention to sociopolitical life. He claimed and demonstrated that his transcendental theology opens into political theology.[23]

In one sense, sensitivity to human sociality comes naturally to Rahner. As a Thomist, he holds that being is one. Though not to the same degree as Spinoza or in the same manner as Hegel, he is a theologian-philosopher "of internal relations" for whom everything that exists is related to everything else. The universe is an interdependent world of becoming, a unity in its origin, history, and destiny. From the beginning to the end of his career, Rahner repeats Aquinas's dictum *Non enim plura secundum se uniuntur* (all plurality is founded on a prior unity).

"Everything that is . . . rests on an ultimate solidarity" in God the creator and redeemer ("Unity of the Church," pp. 154-55; cf. "Theology of the Symbol"). This unity expresses itself in "the physical unity of the cosmos, the space-time unity; biological unity; intercommunication in the unity of a single history of truth and love, untruth and hate; the unity of rootedness in God, etc." ("One Mediator," p. 179).

Rahner's understanding of human sociality is far more than a simple extension of this principle of cosmological unity, however. Rahner emphasized that his method is both transcendental (that is, proceeding from the universal, nonempirical presuppositions of human existence) *and* historical. That is, human transcendence (and God's action) always occurs in and through concrete historical conditions, for human beings are spirit in the world. Transcendence takes place as the spirit turns toward the world, toward what Thomas calls the *phantasmata* presented by imagination. Late in life, Rahner explained that this "*conversio ad phantasmata* . . . precisely may not be translated as 'turning to the sensible image,' but rather 'turning toward history, toward the fulfillment of freedom, toward fellow men and women'" (Guenther, p. 350n.8). Intersubjectivity lies at the heart of each person's existence (transcendence).

Furthermore, in the early work *Hearers of the Word,* Rahner had explained that transcendence is more than an affair of pure intellect. While the Thomist tradition stresses the transcendence of intellect, in fact, love and freedom are interior moments of knowledge and in no way subordinate to it.[24] Moreover, since the world toward which one transcends is primarily other persons,

the basic and original actualization of human transcendence does not take place in theoretical reflection, but rather in the concrete and practical knowledge and freedom of "everyday life," and this is what is meant by interpersonal relationships. (*Foundations,* p. 456; cf. p. 133)[25]

For Rahner, human sociality is neither the subsequent overflow of human beings already constituted as such prior to interaction with others; nor is it one dimension among others. It constitutes the heart of human existence at the transcendental, a priori level. Human beings are social in a stronger sense than was the case for Maritain and the tradition as a whole.[26]

For Rahner, finally, the self transcends toward *God* only through the world. Contrary to Maritain, "Mediation [of the experience of God in time and eternity] and immediacy are not simply contradictory" (ibid., p. 83).[27] This means that salvation comes in and through the community. Like Rahner's doctrine of transcendence in general (through the world), this idea that transcendence to God necessarily passes through others has drawn the fire of critics who detect the influence of German idealism. Rahner is a realist, however. In the end, "mediated immediacy" to God seeks to affirm and explain that one only loves God by loving the neighbor. For Rahner, love of God and love of neighbor form a unity in the concrete ("Reflections," *passim*).[28] In *Foundations*, he wrote that together they constitute the unified basic human act which "has itself two dimensions: an *existential* dimension of *intimacy,* and an *historical* and *social* dimension" which includes political life and love. The two dimensions of human love "correspond to the two aspects of God's self-communication": self-communication in the Spirit which justifies sinners and in the Logos who unifies history (*Foundations,* pp. 456-57).

The following sections develop the implications of Rahner's theory of intersubjectivity and his theology of grace for a social understanding of *salvation*.

The Social Character of Salvation

From the late 60s on, Rahner continued to "socialize" and "politicize" his theology. What we have said so far already implies that salvation, in particular, must be a social and political reality.

God's promise of himself to man is addressed not only to each individual in the freedom of his own unique personhood. From its very origins this promise is at the same time aimed at mankind as a unity, a unity which is always historically and socially constituted. It is aimed at history, society, the people of God. . . . Grace and salvation are wrought in what we call a socially-based saving history and Church, and these are in themselves a historical and social embodiment in space and time. . . . As a reality which is constantly also achieving visible form at the social level, it is quite impossible in principle for salvation not to be concerned with the social realities within which it has to be realized and made manifest in history. . . .

The sphere in which salvation is achieved is identical with the sphere of human existence in general . . . which also always involves social structures. ("Function of the Church," p. 238; cf. "Christian Humanism," p. 189 and *Foundations*, pp. 40, 41, 193, 343, 345)

Rahner notes how the biblical concepts of people of God, salvation history, covenant, original sin, Body of Christ, prayer of intercession, and so on, presuppose the basic human intercommunication sketched above in the previous section. The possibility of understanding Jesus' death *for me* depends on my connection with him and all others. We experience this intercommunication as unlimited. It includes all persons and all areas of life—-biological, political, cultural, and so forth. Human beings live out this intercommunication before God in all these spheres in such a way that, on the one hand, God's self-communication opens them up to radical and secure intercommunication. On the other hand, in genuine interhuman communication (accepted as open to the infinite), human beings communicate with God. Both the vertical and horizontal communications are rooted ultimately in Christ, the Logos, in whom all things hold together and through whom the grace of God comes. Since Christ is the goal toward which all salvation converges, the Spirit enlists these intercommunications in the service of that convergence to unity. No one is saved alone. We all depend on each other for salvation; we are all responsible for each other. Wherever salvation occurs in a person's life, it mediates salvation for all others. A saving event is "necessarily always involved in intercommunication[s]" which link the event to salvation history as a whole. This is the basis of the church, the mediatorship of Christ, and the communion of saints.

Since God's self-gift is mediated concretely at all levels of history (essentially love of neighbor), the social character of salvation transcends interpersonal intimacy to include social, cultural, economic and political life ("One Mediator," p. 181; cf. "Why . . . Saints"; "Reconciliation"; *Foundations*, pp. 322-23, 389).

Unfortunately, Rahner fails to elaborate on this point or draw out its implications. *How* does salvation take place in social, cultural, economic and political life? We call attention to this point here, in the form of two brief critical observations, because of its ramifications for the rest of this book.

First, Rahner's entire enterprise springs from the tradition of reflection on nature and grace. This tradition rarely asks how grace (or God's saving action) is related to our *social relations*. As we saw in reflecting on Maritain, Catholic theology usually relates grace directly to persons and indirectly to society by means of moral action. For Rahner, grace meets us at the horizon of existence as a whole. The human subjectivity to which grace directly relates is social subjectivity; we can even say a political subjectivity. This is an advance. But since he lacks a social theory which would permit him to pursue the implications of grace for society, Rahner's understanding of salvation in society remains vague and general.

Secondly, Rahner's Catholic tradition is more analogical than dialectic (Tracy, *Analogical Imagination*). Grace perfects nature—that is, persons. One temptation of this tradition is to neglect the struggle (dialectic) of grace against sin, especially sin incarnated in social relations and institutions. In this century of unspeakable suffering, few things stand out more clearly, despite our denial, than death-dealing social sin. It is in this context that we must ask the question Catholic theology traditionally neglects to pose and Rahner fails to develop: What is the relationship of God's saving action (grace), not simply to subjects (even to social subjects), but to the social relations and institutions, especially to oppressive social relations and death-dealing institutions?

Salvation and History: The Reign of God

Rahner's writings reflect growing appreciation that the drama of human transcendence and divine self-bestowal is the *deepest drama of history* as a whole. From this perspective, the language of orders—of redemption and creation—sounds static and incomplete. Maritain held that the history of the church and that of the world converge along parallel paths. For Rahner, however, history is one; salvation history and profane history are materially co-extensive and interpenetrating. Eternity does not stand above history or follow it temporally. As with the flowering of human freedom into genuine love, eternity comes to birth in time, its essential precondition. The deepest meaning of history, the only meaning it can have as a whole, is its theological meaning ("History of the World"; "Life of the Dead"; cf. *Foundations*, pp. 142-52).[29]

Rahner increasingly directed his attention to the reign of God in history. The reign of God

is not simply something due to come later, which later will replace the world, its history and the outcome of its history. The kingdom of God itself is coming to be in the history of the world (not only in that of the Church) wherever obedience to God occurs in grace as the acceptance of God's self-communication.

The reign of God, moreover,

> does not take place solely in a secret inwardness of conscience, in meta-historical religious subjectivity, but in the concrete fulfillment of an earthly task, of active love for others, even of collective love for others . . . in the unity, activity, fraternity, etc. of the *world,* the kingdom of God is at hand. ("Church and World," pp. 239-40)[30]

Contrary to the traditional paradigm, the reign of God comes to be—only partially and ambiguously, but really—in and through the realization of the human good (which we can only really explain in view of its supreme realization in the life of Christ, which ended in apparent failure on the cross). In this case, however, we cannot simply identify God's reign with the church.[31]

Eschatology

Rahner's understanding of God's reign in history raises the question about the relation of human achievement, especially social justice, to the final consummation. A post-Kantian thinker, Rahner is keenly aware of the limitations of our possible knowledge of God's revelation of the future. All we can know about the future consummation amounts to an extrapolation from the present situation of those who enjoy the first fruits of salvation. God promises to complete the work already begun ("Hermeneutics"; cf. *Foundations,* Chapt. 9).

According to Rahner, the Pastoral Constitution of Vatican II (GS) reflects the present lack of clarity in Catholic theology concerning the relationship between historical progress and the final consummation of history. Far from useless speculation, however, the question concerns the ultimate meaning and validity of our work for a better world. Until recently, humanity largely accepted the social order as given with nature. What little human skill produced appeared "merely to be the fuel for the future conflagration of the world." Eschatological victory meant taking "the moral element in the immortal 'soul' . . . into the 'life beyond'." The question of the consummation of *history* occupied the periphery of thought. Today, however, we naturally ask: Is the world which humanity more and more fashions only the test site for exercising moral virtues? Will the world simply disappear when the reign of God comes? Or will "human history at the material and physical level" pass via death and trans-figuration into the *eschaton*? Does the "new earth" simply come from God? Or do human beings construct it, thereby completing God's creation? ("Theological Problems," pp. 266-67; cf. "Church and the Parousia").

Rahner answers, first, that for Christian faith the final consum-mation comes as a deed of God and not simply as the outcome of evolution and human accomplishments (it cannot be planned or conceptualized). Second, because humans are essentially corporeal, we cannot construe Christian eschatology rationalistically as the immortality of the soul. (The Logos, the first fruits of the consumma-tion, remains forever human and bodily.) Third, because humans are essentially historical and social, the eschatology of the individual necessarily fits within the collective eschatology of humanity and the whole world. Fourth, individuals and history as a whole will enter their consummation "radically 'transformed'" via death ("Theological Problems," pp. 268-70; *Foundations,* pp. 273, 444-45).

Since history is the locus of freedom, it "demands . . . to be brought to a definitive consummation" (and not merely to a disconnected "reward"). Furthermore, enduring moral goodness "*consist[s] in* that which takes place in history as concrete," not simply one's interior intention or meta-empirical virtue. (The scholastic doctrine of merit cannot be understood as merely interior virtue producing meta-em-pirical results.) Therefore, not merely individual persons, but history itself, including the *opus,* the *industriae nostrae fructus* (GS 39), is taken up and transformed, as if it were the resurrected "body of history," into the reign of God. The fruit of the whole of history—not simply its final stage—will die and enter, transfigured, into eschato-logical victory ("Theological Problems," pp. 269-70; "Christian Under-standing of Redemption," p. 241).[32]

Nonetheless, although history moves irreversibly toward the ab-solute future (or rather vice versa) and although scientific and social progress occur, there is no general ascent of history. Human beings will remain human. We can expect no utopia, no final solution, in history. (In this respect, Rahner was a postmodern thinker.) The world moves toward its final goal "through collapse, futility, the zero of death" ("Church and World," p. 246).[33] The transformative resur-rection itself presupposes the death of all concrete achievements. Yet while these are always provisional and transitory, "it is only through them, and not in by-passing them, that man can realize his assent in faith and hope to his absolute future" ("Function of the Church," p. 239).

Hope—in the sense of abandonment to the uncontrollable absolute future beyond any future planned or achieved—is the essence of human existence as free transcendence in history. The realization of humanity requires, therefore, a continual questioning, a "revolutionary" posture vis-à-vis any status quo and every utopian project ("On the Theology of Hope," pp. 256-58; *see* LG 35).[34]

But, for Rahner, insofar as they are an expression of love, human projects, our efforts for justice, are the form and medium necessary to open human beings to the absolute future which for this reason is already silently at work in the midst of the human project. "The Kingdom of God only comes to those who build the coming earthly kingdom." The absolute future "supports" history and its projects "as an inner constitutive element . . . even though it is independent of" them ("Theological Problems," pp. 265, 272; "Christian Humanism," p. 201; "Experiment with Man," pp. 220-221; "Marxist Utopia," p. 60).

Rahner stressed, especially toward the end of his life, that the true and enduring achievement in history is sharing the cross of Christ in suffering love of neighbor. Salvation occurs within history wherever the humble abandon themselves into the mystery of God by bearing Christ's cross in love of their neighbor. It therefore occurs more among the defeated of history than the conquerors.

> Ultimately, then, there exists between this inner-worldly utopia (taking "utopia" in this context in a very positive sense) and Christian eschatology the same relationship of unity and difference which, for example, a Christian sees in the light of the New Testament with regard to the unity and difference between love for God and love for neighbor.

The reign of God comes in and through the love of neighbor. Or, since love and freedom ultimately coincide, "every free act . . . serves to mediate the acceptance of the absolute future" (*Foundations*, p. 447; "Salvation," p. 425; cf. "Christian Understanding of Redemption," p. 239).[35]

This love must be political as well as personal. In another late essay, Rahner wrote that from the chaotic sea of history, not just individual lives, but larger complexes of social and political meaning and goodness emerge. (He mentions the emancipation of slaves in the U.S.) We must expect that these will in some way share in the final victory of God.

> One must also grant that these good, supraindividual segments of history achieve their finality in and with God in the same way as individual persons as such achieve theirs. . . . It is no more possible to dissolve the salvation history of . . . "peoples" into the history of individual persons belonging to these peoples than it

is to dissolve profane history into the chaotic confusion of individual histories. . . . In this eternal kingdom . . . we must recognize and allow for the individuality of specific supraindividual collective histories of peoples. ("Profane History," p. 14; cf. p. 10)

For Rahner, particular "peoples" and, we may suppose, their necessary social *habitus* (institutions and social relations, patterns of behavior formed, in this case, by supernatural love) must endure, transfigured.

Finally, God's victorious consummation of history is wholly transcendent *and* wholly immanent. Not only is transcendence toward the absolute future (God) precisely what is most immanent and proper to the person. The same is true for history as a whole. The internal principle of history's unfolding is the absolutely transcendent God whose self-bestowal is directed simultaneously to each person and to the community of all persons ("Immanent and Transcendent").[36] For this reason, although the final victory is a complete gift of God, "history itself constructs its own final and definitive state." Gift and task fuse, and "a history that is constructed by man himself as event and as the end product of his activities has a final and definitive significance" ("Theological Problems," pp. 270-71).

Gift and Task: Divine and Human Action

Rahner presents us with a God whom we cannot shake, who presses upon us from all sides, offering him/herself to us in and through the particulars of daily life. That is part of our human situation, an "existential." God's self-offer (objective salvation) is itself the offer of a new way of being-in-the-world that the gospels call the reign of God. God asks, Will you allow me to take over your life? and, simultaneously, Do you want to live, to be, in a new way?

The ethical task (love, justice) is therefore the other side of the coin of God's gift. To accept the free gift of forgiveness (subjective salvation) *is* to assume the task. The gift is precisely the possibility of living in new ways. As Rahner says, since God is the ground of human history and God's self-gift addresses human freedom,

There is never a salvific act of God on man which is not also and always a salvific act of man. . . . The history of salvation and revelation is always the already existing synthesis of God's historical activity and man's at the same time. (*Foundations,* p. 142)[37]

According to Rahner, we must not understand this in Pelagian fashion, for the saving human act which allows God to enter our lives is precisely faith, the life-posture which invests our most strenuous efforts with a receptive and grateful character. The struggle to transform the world must assume the form of allowing the Holy Mystery of God to take possession of us. This understanding of the fusion of divine and human action presupposes that God's self-communication to the world occurs by way of what Rahner calls a quasi-formal causality, producing a uniquely intimate relationship that allows God to remain God and human beings to be (and become more) human. The heroic love demanded by the Gospel is made possible by the self-communicating love of God, which sustains it.[38]

This fusion (which includes an absolute distinction) between divine gift and human act calls into question Maritain's sharp disjunction of the gift of grace from graced moral action—and from the temporal common good which the moral action produces. Maritain might have argued instead that merit means that the concrete works of the justified actualize their participation in divine life and effect a growth in grace (Rahner and Vorgrimler, s.v. "Merit"). In that case, however, the *concrete* work of the infused virtues and the social justice they produce (the common good) cannot be construed *merely* as the consequence of and preparation for God's saving gift. That action and the common good itself are part of God's saving gift, which manifests itself ambiguously but tangibly in the blessings of salvation effected by human action under the influence of grace.

Conclusion

Maritain, and most Catholic theology, objected to an intrahistorical conception of the reign of God (outside the church), first, on the basis of the distinction between the two orders and, second, because the reign of God is not a human work but a divine gift. Rahner's theology of grace answers the first objection by demonstrating the inadequacy of traditional interpretations of the two orders. Maritain's second objection has in mind those social engineers who, ignoring both weakness and sin and our supernatural destiny, must resort to coercion in their efforts to bring us perfect happiness. Rahner would never suppose that weakness, sin, or misery can be eliminated before the final consummation, but partial and ambiguous realizations of the reign of God can happen in this "vale of tears," thanks to the fusion (not synergistic cooperation) of divine and human action which his theory of grace implies.

Rahner's brilliant interpretation of human transcendence and God's self-communication in history allows him to elaborate a more satisfactory explanation of the social meaning of God's saving activity than the traditional view. In Rahner's new paradigm, the reign of God takes place in and through the concrete realization of any genuine human good along the march of history, provided we understand that human good in a sufficiently profound sense—provided, that is, that it entails faith, hope, and love, in other words, surrender to the Holy Mystery and the love of neighbor exemplified in Christ's life and cross. On the other hand, no experience of grace in history is isolated from the experience of the good within history. Because God grounds human transcendence and because finite spirit realizes itself via interaction with the world in all its material, interpersonal, and institutional complexity, salvation encompasses human reality as a whole—material and spiritual, personal, social, political, economic, and cultural—and includes acts of love and the justice and peace they produce, even when salvation in this sense is manifested partially, ambiguously, and in fragile form. In this case, our historical human projects, insofar as they are fruits of love, and even though they must pass through the door of death, acquire salvific validity and will somehow share in God's final triumph.

We can end with three comments. First, critics have argued that Rahner's transcendental theology depends on questionable Kantian, Hegelian, and Heideggerian presuppositions (Bradley).[39] As Leo O'Donovan points out, however, Rahner's theology and philosophy are ultimately based on his experience of human transcendence and of God, an experience which has appropriated—and changed— Hegelian and Heideggerian concepts in an effort to explain itself (O'Donovan, "Orthopraxis," p. 57). Many others appear to recognize their own experience in this historically conditioned experience on which Rahner reflects.

Others, however, will continue to question Rahner's Kantian categories. Although he insists that the transcendental structures of subjectivity operate *only* in and through categorial—that is, concrete—human experience, some argue that these categories sometimes appear as mere foil or occasion for the self-gift of a God who, like a Kantian noumenon, comes to us from beyond history. We shall return to this point in later chapters.

Second, for Rahner, human action informed by grace is salvific; it fuses with God's action in history. But this suggests that the receptivity and gratitude characteristic of faith should profoundly stamp all the action it informs. In our bourgeois and patriarchal societies, which place such a premium on transitive activity, production, technical control, and coercion, we have to ask: What does it mean to say that all loving, and so truly revolutionary, activity must be grounded in the receptivity of faith which accepts the reign of God as a wholly gratuitous gift? We shall return to this question, too, in the following chapters.

Third, as Metz and others justly remark, Rahner's starting point is always the existential situation of the individual subject. He articulates an outstanding theological account of the situation of the modern person. His is much less the theology of the suffering world of the twentieth century, however—a world of total war and genocide, third-world poverty and mass starvation, ecological crisis and racial, sexual and other forms of discrimination. Rahner thus fails to give a satisfactory account of the social sin at the root of this suffering or to tell us how God liberates us from that social sin (Neuhaus). We have to look to political and liberation theologies to fill this gap.

The problem has two dimensions: a neglect of the kind of suffering and social sin characteristic of our world and a lack of attention to social relations and institutions.

Moltmann has pointed out the temptation for optimistic Catholic theology to understate suffering and the power of sin (*The Crucified God*). *Aggiornamento* theology stresses that grace superabounds, a welcome corrective to a post-Tridentine Thomism which tended to consider grace all-too-rare and too closely confined to sacramental life. But first-world Catholic theology sometimes forgets that *sin* abounds, especially incarnated in dehumanizing social relations and unjust institutions.

Although he stressed the cross and the paschal mystery more and more with time, Rahner's always remains a metaphysical theology of the Incarnation, a theology of grace-and-nature in classic Catholic fashion. It takes the social and historical character of salvation more seriously than the concrete history of sin, especially social sin. It is not always clear, socially speaking, what grace saves us from.

The second dimension to the problem is related: Rahner's detailed account of human subjectivity is not matched by a theory of social relations and institutions. He tells us how grace relates to the person but not *how* God's saving action is related to social relations and institutions. As we noted earlier, traditional Catholic theology typically relates grace directly to the person and only indirectly to the social order through moral action. Since for him human subjectivity is *social* subjectivity, Rahner overcomes this limitation in part. God's self-offer constitutes the possibility of a new way of being-*together*-in-the-world, which presumably requires new social institutions. (In this sense, Rahner developed Heidegger's notion of *Mitsein* more successfully than either Heidegger himself or his other famous theologian-disciple, Rudolf Bultmann.) Rahner's fundamental principles open the path to political theology. However, he relates the saving action of God to the social and political order only in vague and general terms. A metaphysical theology such as Rahner's can presume, dangerously, to dispense with the kind of social theory needed to explain the concrete and contingent world of economic, cultural and political reality. Such a social theory could help specify social sin and flesh out *how* grace relates to the social order.

Rahner thus represents a positive paradigm shift in conceiving the relationship between salvation and human longings for justice and fellowship. With him, however, the paradigm did not shift far enough. He failed to pursue in a sustained way the relationship of saving grace to an unjust social order. We will address both social theory and social sin in greater detail in Chapter 5, naming social sin and social salvation in more specific but still general terms, keeping in mind that both assume different forms in different times and places.

But first, in the following chapter we examine how Peruvian theologian Gustavo Gutiérrez articulates the relationship between salvation and the achievement of social justice. Gutiérrez combines a Catholic nature-grace-Incarnation theology with "Protestant" emphasis on sin and liberation. His narrative theology reflects the experience not of the modern individual (Rahner) or the First World burdened with violence and materialism (Metz), but of the victims of the Third World and so the great majority throughout history. Gutiérrez reflects theologically on the history of sin-as-injustice and liberation from it. He has used social theory as the (necessary) means to articulate this history in social and political terms, but without the kind of explicit philosophical base that Rahner complained was lacking in world-directed theologies.

4

THE LIBERATION PARADIGM
OF GUSTAVO GUTIÉRREZ

The Context

For the past four centuries the Catholic Church, long rooted in the cultural soil of medieval Europe, has been slowly adjusting to the new soil of modernity. Recent developments in Catholic theology reflect the quickened pace of adjustment in our own century of rapid change. The last two chapters illustrate how this adjustment has brought a paradigm shift in understanding the social meaning of salvation.

Up to Vatican II, the "modern world" that challenged Catholic life and thought was above all the post-Enlightenment bourgeois world of the industrial nations of the North Atlantic. The theological and pastoral ferment which led up to Vatican II reflected tensions between the church and this modern world—even in culturally Catholic places such as Latin America and the Philippines where the modern ethos has been less dominant.

Until the 1960s, Latin American theology reflected the glow of Europe and its debates. In the middle part of this century, the Latin American church drew heavily on the experience of European Catholicism to discover new ways to respond to the changing social order in each nation.

Industrialization, revolution, and neocolonial penetration were altering the social landscape. The post-World War II economic boom accelerated the growth of middle classes, secularization and urbanization. It also raised expectations for economic development. The triumph of the Cuban revolution in 1959 stimulated revolutionary hopes and activity elsewhere in the region and provoked new schemes for growth and distribution such as Kennedy's Alliance for Progress (*see* Dussel; Gutiérrez, *Líneas pastorales;* Richard). Phenomena like these and modern communications media spread a growing nationalism among elites and new social awareness among impoverished urban and rural majorities. However, when development plans failed to address their growing misery, this new social awareness "required" military takeovers in most countries in the sixties and seventies. All of these trends created unprecedented challenges for the Latin American church, which had carried out its mission for so long in relatively static, largely agricultural, societies.

The changes in Latin America belonged to larger worldwide shifts. Mass communications and travel both stimulated the changes and further exposed Latin America to modernizing currents on other continents. In this context and around the time of the Second Vatican Council, the church in Latin America—its hierarchy, its theology and, in time, its base communities—began to come into its own and to achieve, quickly and dramatically, its majority within the universal church. Indeed, the demographics of Catholicism had shifted dramatically. Europe had ceased to hold the majority of Catholics.[1]

The dashed hopes of the postwar period helped politicize the populace and polarize political forces in Latin America. The church hierarchy's traditional support of the status quo came under increasing attack from Christians themselves, more of whom began to work among the poor and side with them in the struggle for a more just society. The historic bishops' conferences at Medellín (1968) and Puebla (1979) bore witness to the depth of the new challenges and to the turmoil and change of direction they had provoked.

The theology of liberation emerged from this ferment to articulate the meaning of Christian faith in these new circumstances. Among the most important expositors, and the key originator, of liberation theology was Gustavo Gutiérrez of Peru.

We have already mentioned Gutiérrez's contributions to the final documents of the Medellín Conference. Shortly thereafter he published the major work for which he has been hailed, and vilified, as the "father of liberation theology." The power and originality of *A Theology of Liberation* occasioned a storm of controversy which has continued since its appearance in 1971 and helped draw attention to the remarkable developments occurring in the Christian communities of a Latin America in social upheaval.[2]

Gutiérrez has articulated a distinct paradigm—one truly representative of liberation theology—which centers on the question of the meaning of salvation for the victims of injustice.[3] He has always described his theology as a "theology of salvation" (TL xxxiv; LP 29; PPH 63; Manzanera, p. 20).[4] "To speak about a theology of liberation is to seek an answer to the following question: What relation is there between salvation and the historical process of human liberation?" The central preoccupation of his masterwork is precisely that "classic question," as he says, "of the relation between faith and . . . social reality, between faith and political action, or in other words, between the Kingdom of God and the building up of the world." (TL 29).

Unlike the earlier paradigms we have examined, Gutiérrez's liberation theology reflects the faith and the reality of the Third World; and this affects his understanding of "salvation." As he says, progressive European theology has the nonbeliever for its interlocutor. It develops an understanding-of-the-faith for a world dominated by the bourgeois ethos. Liberation theology takes as its interlocutor the nonperson—the poor person, the exploited classes and oppressed races—and develops its thought within the context of massive poverty and oppression.[5]

This implies that the theologian has entered the world of the poor and assumed their cause and destiny (PPH 18-21, 50-51; We Drink, pp. 122-26; La verdad, pp. 19-21; "Option for the Poor," pp. 236-37). More than new contents, therefore, the theology of liberation represents above all a new way to do theology. From 1968 on, Gutiérrez based his theology on two key methodological principles (PPH 200-1): First, theology reflects from the perspective of the poor; second, theology is a "second step" (TL 9) which follows commitment to their liberation. Therefore, liberation theology "is critical reflection—in the light of the Word accepted in faith—on historical praxis" (TL 81).[6]

In recent writings, Gutiérrez also speaks more generally of reflection on the *experience* of God (*We Drink*), unjust suffering (*On Job*), and some of the existential concerns of progressive theology. In *El Dios de la vida* and subsequent writings, *contemplation* and practice constitute the "first step" on which theology reflects.[7] Thus, as Rahner's thought expanded from existential to social and political concerns, Gutiérrez's theology has developed in an opposite and complementary direction.

Gutiérrez's career divides conveniently into three parts. In the first, from 1960 to 1968, he strove to critique the pastoral practice of the Latin American church in the light of progressive (mostly European) theology. This was a "Vatican II" period, a period of formation. The second period began in 1968 ("Toward a Theology of Liberation," document 7) and extended to roughly 1979 and the publication of the *La fuerza histórica de los pobres*.[8] During this "Medellín" period, Gutiérrez presented and developed the basic insights of liberation theology. He focused on the practice of Christians engaged in the liberation process. We might call the third period a "Puebla" period. It dates from roughly 1979 to the present. In response to criticism both fair and unfair, Gutiérrez expanded the horizon of his concerns to include points previously neglected and liberation movements beyond Latin America (Black theology, feminism, Asian theology; cf. TL xix-xxiii); he qualified one-sided expressions and solidified original positions. This has been a period of deepening. The first period was ecclesiocentric, the second Christocentric (and world-centered); the third is a stage of synthesis combining both perspectives.

From Church to the Liberation Process

The first period of Gutiérrez's career culminated in a decisive turn to the world which led him to make original contributions concerning the relationship between salvation and social justice. Prior to TL, Gutiérrez formulated the "classic question" by focusing on the mission of the church and its contemporary challenges. Later, in TL, he focused directly on the process of social liberation in Latin America, allowing social reality to challenge the church to explain its mission— and the meaning of the salvation it proclaims. Tracing this shift in perspective will help us understand Gutiérrez and his relationship to the paradigms that Maritain and Rahner represent.

As a committed young student, Gutiérrez witnessed how the general social crisis of the 50s and 60s provoked a parallel crisis in the (Catholic) church's pastoral ministry. The pastoral crisis challenged common understandings of the relationship between church and world—and of salvation itself (LP 7, 29, 36).

Four Pastoral Approaches

To address the problem, in the mid-sixties Gutiérrez traced the development of pastoral practice in Latin America through three overlapping stages leading up to the crisis. He called the corresponding models of pastoral practice "Christendom," "New Christendom," and the "distinction of planes." He then proposed a fourth, prophetic, model.

Christendom. This first approach held sway from Augustine to the twentieth century! (LP 13-19, 29-33; TL 34-35). We saw how Maritain helped the church break with this "integrist" outlook in Europe. It still lives in Latin America and even predominated up to the time of Medellín. Based on elements of Augustine's theology, the Christendom model is markedly ecclesiocentric. The church is not only the sole vehicle of salvation but also an indispensable civilizing force in society. The sinful world requires *direct* intervention of the church in political affairs.

According to Gutiérrez, Christendom fails to appreciate the self-consistency of creation. It lacks clear distinctions between temporal and spiritual, sacred and profane, nature and supernature—and the role of clergy and laity. In recent decades, however, the obvious inappropriateness of this approach for the modern world has given rise to several new competing models.

New Christendom. Gutiérrez notes how Maritain's critique of Christendom inspired a new pastoral approach in progressive Latin American circles in the 1930s and how it continues to play an important role in Latin America today (LP 19-24, 35-41; TL 35-36; PPH 40, 188-89).[9]

As we have seen, this approach affirms the relative autonomy of the temporal order. For New Christendom, the world has its own ends and proper means which the church need not supply. According to Thomist doctrine, grace perfects a nature which has its own self-consistency. But as "wounded" nature requires grace, the world needs the church's *indirect* intervention to realize the temporal common good. Thus the church promotes secular institutions of Christian inspiration—Christian democratic parties, etc.—and the laity enjoys considerable, though not total, freedom from clerical guidance in secular affairs. Temporal and spiritual, nature and grace, and the tasks of clergy and laity are carefully distinguished. Here is a shift to the world, a recognition of secularization. However, the church remains the center of God's saving work.

The Distinction of Planes. Gutiérrez notes how New Christendom came under attack in the fifties from Latin Americans who judged its "reformist" efforts inadequate to the social crisis. They witnessed how the hierarchy appealed to the (merely) *relative* autonomy of politics to keep Christians away from leftist parties. Meanwhile, French theologians were arguing that the time for *any* Christendom had passed (LP 24-26, 43-54; TL 36-38; PPH 40-41, 198-99).[10] A mature laity, they reasoned, needs no political guidance from the clergy; the "adult" world has its own function in God's plan on a plane distinct from that of the church.

This "distinction of planes" position translates the distinction between nature and grace into a sharp disjunction between temporal and spiritual orders. It affirms the *complete* autonomy and secularity of the temporal order with respect to the church. In the temporal order, natural ("human," "temporal") values occupy neutral ground between grace and sin. Nevertheless, the world is said to have a definite function within God's saving plan. Indeed, that plan gives rise to both church and world, with their distinct functions (LP 46-49).[11]

Latin American Christians such as Gutiérrez (*La verdad,* p. 177), who were sympathetic to the left, at first welcomed this approach. Before long, however, it became apparent that its prohibition against church involvement in politics carried a high price. It meant the hierarchy and lay apostolic groups (Young Christian Workers, etc.) ought not take a public stand on important issues. From the late fifties onward, however, the deepening social crisis led to constant interventions by just such parties on behalf of the poor. This created serious tensions in the church (TL 39-41, 58-62). This crisis provoked Gutiérrez to spell out a new pastoral model which would later develop into the theology of liberation.

The Prophetic, or Liberation, Model. Agreeing substantially with the distinction of planes, Gutiérrez argued nonetheless that in the current crisis the Gospel required the church to assume a prophetic role. Specifically, the church should 1) break its traditional alliance with the established order, 2) denounce injustices and their systemic causes, 3) announce the Christian hope for a humane social life, 4) politicize as it evangelizes, and 5) allow for new kinds of involvement by clergy and religious in the struggle for social change. Finally, 6) lay apostolic groups *as such* should commit themselves to the revolutionary process (LP 26-27; TL 150-56, cf. 65-71).

Gutiérrez's prophetic pastoral model required a theology which simultaneously affirmed the autonomy and self-consistency of the world—permitting sufficient freedom to a laity committed to liberation—and an understanding of God's saving action which would commit the church as such to the struggle for a more just society. Gutiérrez wanted to integrate a secular and autonomous world into God's saving plan. In traditional terms, this required reformulating the relationship of grace to the world.[12]

Grace and History

As we saw in the previous chapter, the grace debates in Europe did just that. They demolished the dualism ("extrinsicism") which separates grace from human experience and limits salvation to a supernatural order. Gutiérrez hails the decisive contribution of Karl Rahner, for whom no aspect of human existence escapes God's grace, at least as an offer (TL 104). In the concrete, "it is not possible to indicate the boundaries between grace and nature" (LP 60).[13] There is no purely natural human fulfillment. Human beings have only one real destiny, communion with God (and, Gutiérrez always adds, with other human beings). Paul VI's *Populorum progressio* (21) reflects this vision, says Gutiérrez, when it speaks of the life of grace not as supernatural but as "more human, finally and above all." The text greatly influenced Gutiérrez's formulation of integral liberation (*see La verdad,* pp. 169-70; TL xxxviii-xxxix).

Gutiérrez draws two more decisive conclusions from the grace discussion. First, the new perspective retrieves an authentic Thomist perspective. But, as Henri DeLubac showed, a proper understanding of grace also retrieves important Augustinian insights. In his early critique of the two-planes model, Gutiérrez emphasized the centrality of the sin-grace opposition in Augustine's thought.[14] This has permanently stamped his theology. While he recognizes the relative autonomy of the world vis-à-vis the church in Thomist fashion, his is "a strongly religious perspective, in a certain fashion like that of the pastoral model of Christendom" which calls for the church to intervene in the social order (LP 60; *La verdad,* p. 176. *See* Manzanera, p. 34).

It is worth noting that TL's affirmation of an "entirely secular" world (suggesting the laity's complete independence from church guidance in secular affairs and the complete autonomy of social science) clashes with this "strongly religious perspective" (TL 41-43; cf. LP 62-65).[15] More recent writings retreat from the kind of radical secularity which isolates faith from reason (LP 58-59. *See* the section "Marx and the Enlightenment" below).

Secondly, the new theology of grace turns the church to the world. As we saw, the grace debates reflected a crisis over *salvation*—over who can be saved and how. Gutiérrez notes that both Christendom and New Christendom reflect the principle *extra ecclesiam nulla salus* and, with it, pastoral concern for bringing members into the church, where the sacraments nourish a life of grace leading to salvation beyond this world (LP 16-17, 29-41; TL 83-84; PPH 39). The distinction of planes model, on the other hand, affirms that persons outside the church can be saved. (This solution depends on the high Christology of Ephesians and Colossians: All human beings are saved in principle by Christ; all were created "for him" [Col. 1,16].) But in this model, too, the reign of God remains essentially post-historical (LP 43-45).

Gutiérrez argues that if Christ's grace is available to all, even nonbelievers, the criterion for salvation must be valid for believer and nonbeliever alike. This criterion, he says, is love: "The one who loves is the one who is saved, that is, the one who enters into communion with others is the one who enters into communion with God" (LP 54-57; cf. *La verdad,* p. 178; TL Chapt. 10, *passim*). This means that salvation occurs not simply in the church and in heaven but in the heart of history, in and through the practice of love. A sound theology of grace thus turns the church—and the theologian—toward the world.

> One looks then to this world, and now sees in the world beyond, not the "true life," but rather the transformation and full realization of the present life. The absolute value of salvation—far from devaluing this world—gives it its authentic meaning and its own consistency, because salvation is already, initially, in it. (TL 85)

When he turned to the world, the signs of the times which arrested Gutiérrez's attention were Latin America's intolerable misery and the aspirations of the poor for a truly human life. This led him to pose the question of salvation in terms of the liberation process:

> What is the relationship between salvation and the process of the liberation of man throughout history? Or more precisely, what is the meaning, in the light of the Word, of the struggle against an unjust society and the creation of a new human being? (TL 83, trans. emended)

This manner of posing the question led to an answer in the form of Gutiérrez's well-known distinction and interrelation of "three reciprocally interpenetrating levels of meaning of the term *liberation,* or in other words, three approaches to the process of liberation" (TL 24).

The Threefold Liberation Process

According to Gutiérrez, the liberation process is a differentiated unity with three distinct levels of meaning: "political liberation, human liberation throughout history, liberation from sin and admission to communion with God" (TL 103).

The first meaning level responds to the more apparent (hence more material) human needs and aspirations. It includes economic needs and the social conditions (politics) necessary to meet them (PPH 146). At this level, liberation means changing social structures. It is here a question of more quantitative aspects of liberation. The empirical social sciences—economics, political analysis, sociology—disclose this level. (For the kinds of knowledge which correspond to the three levels, *see* LP 9-10 and Manzanera, pp. 29, 117-21.)

The second meaning level of the liberation process responds to more profound needs and aspirations—for freedom and solidarity.

Liberation here and now is part of the wider process of the self-generation of humanity, through liberation, down through history. This level includes the more qualitative, less material, cultural, and interior aspects of liberation, as disclosed by philosophy and utopian imagination.

The third level of liberation is the deepest and least apparent, for the liberation process arises from the deepest needs and aspirations of human existence, the radical desire for communion with God and others. Oppression is revealed in its most radical character—as sin. Liberation is the radical gracious gift of salvation. The liberation of human beings throughout history, including the liberation of Latin America today, is part of God's all-encompassing plan that all may enjoy complete fulfillment as human beings. This is the dimension of meaning disclosed by theology whose object is the Word of God addressed to the person of faith.

We now take a closer look at each level.

Level One: Social Transformation

Until the 1960s, Gutiérrez notes, "development" seemed to express the process and goal which responded to the aspirations of the world's poor. However, closer examination soon revealed that development is a *political* problem. The solution for poor classes and nations is not to "catch up" with the rich. National underdevelopment and internal misery are a function of *oppression* and the fruit of social, political, and cultural *dependency* (TL 51-54; PPH 45-46, 78, 191-92). But in that case, the solution to poverty is better expressed as *liberation* than as development.

More specifically, says Gutiérrez, liberation means social transformation leading to socialism. The failures of "developmentalist" schemes, together with studies demonstrating Latin America's economic dependency, have shown that piecemeal reform of capitalism can never solve the problem of misery (TL 54-57).

Gutiérrez's interpretation of Latin America's economic and political reality takes place "at the level of scientific rationality" (TL 17), that is social science (including Marxist concepts; see below). This first level of liberation thus depends on particular social contexts and on social scientific interpretation. Both the course of events and studies following the publication of TL led Gutiérrez and other Latin American intellectuals to qualify their positions on the possibility (and costs) of economic development in Latin America under capitalism, as well as their belief that a revolutionary process would sweep the continent (PPH 45-46).[16] The theory of dependency, in particular, which Gutiérrez adopted (critically and tentatively) in TL, has since come under criticism from across the political spectrum (TL 51-54, pp. xxiv and 183n.31). Like most, Gutiérrez today regards it as unserviceable.[17] He has recently elaborated in nuanced language his understanding of the kind of society that is desirable in Latin America.[18]

The "essence" of the first level is institutional transformation, but structural change in different times and places must be guided by a utopian vision appropriate to that context. That utopian vision belongs to the second level of the liberation process.[19]

Level Two: Human Liberation in History

The Historical Becoming of Humanity. It is not enough simply to transform institutions. The liberation process must go deeper. Understanding development as liberation entails viewing structural change as part of the larger process of humanity's self-realization through the quest for freedom. The meaning of liberation in this more universal, philosophical sense varies less with historical conditions.[20]

According to Gutiérrez, the "best philosophical tradition" reveals that nothing less than human fulfillment is at stake in the liberation process. He observes how the most fruitful modern thinking has taken the form of "reflexive and thematic awareness of human experience and of humans' relationships with nature and among themselves" (TL 18, my trans.; cf. TL 7, 42).[21]

Gutiérrez recalls the signal contributions of Hegel and Marx to this line of thought. In his famous master-slave parable, Hegel shows that freedom requires self-consciousness, that self-consciousness requires recognition by another, and that all this entails a struggle. The historical process of humanity's becoming by means of conflict is the progressive "genesis of consciousness" and a gradual realization of human freedom. In this dialectical process, humanity forges itself; human beings gradually direct themselves toward a social existence free of servitude.

Marx recast Hegel's principles in more materialist form. Freedom, for Marx, requires an awareness of material conditions and their practical transformation within the conflictual encounter of social classes. But Gutiérrez also stresses the need for personal transformation, observing how Freud diagnosed the internal constraints to freedom, which are similarly overcome through self-awareness and struggle. (See TL xxxviii, xl; La verdad, pp. 188-93.)

The themes of freedom, awareness, self-generation, conflict, taking up the reins of history, and especially the historical becoming of humanity recur throughout Gutiérrez's writings.[22] He also shares with Hegel and Marx an interactive interpretation of human existence and becoming. "Human beings transform themselves by conquering their liberty throughout their existence and their history" (TL xiv) through work and transformative social praxis.

Moreover, to conceive of life as the conflictual struggle for freedom, says Gutiérrez, is to recognize that all life has a political color. Surely, not all life can be reduced to politics. But once we recognize that all humans struggle to realize themselves as free social subjects, we come to recognize that politics is more than a peripheral spare-time activity, more than the pursuit and exercise of state power by elites supposedly destined to rule. Politics—in the broad sense of the daily struggle for freedom—becomes everyone's day-to-day struggle for human self-realization (TL 30-31; *see* TL 188n.12; PPH 46-47; *La verdad*, pp. 184-86; *see also* Assmann, Chapt. 1).[23]

New Human Being, Qualitatively Different Society. At the second meaning level, therefore, the liberation process is "the continuous creation, never ending, of a new way to be human, a *permanent cultural revolution*" (TL 21). It is a question of a new human being in a qualitatively different society, a society of solidarity but also of freedom for all.

The liberation process must include the "unfolding of all dimensions of humanness" (TL 24). By interacting with nature and with others, says Gutiérrez, human beings do not simply develop their innate potentialities; they create new ways to be human. The new human being, a common idea in neo-Marxist circles, has obvious affinities with Christian thought. For Gutiérrez, it provides the crucial link between structural change and Christian salvation (TL xl, 24-25, 56-57, 81-82, 121, 202n.47; PPH 46, 192-93; *La verdad*, pp. 191-92).[24]

The second level of liberation is personal and interpersonal rather than structural, qualitative rather than quantitative, cultural rather than economic or political (in the narrow sense). Liberation means *new social relations*.

Utopia. This second dimension of liberation, argues Gutiérrez, enjoys a relative autonomy from theology similar to the first dimension, which is disclosed chiefly by social science. But he rejects any dogmatic approach to social liberation—whether in the form of theological fundamentalism or social-scientific positivism. Utopian imagination guards against both.

Following Paul Blanquart, Gutiérrez appropriates the line of reflection on utopia opened by Karl Mannheim earlier in this century (TL 135-40).[25] When grounded in reality and reason and verified by praxis, utopian imagination criticizes shortsighted political tactics;

by recalling the depth of the liberation process, it mediates the values of Christian faith to political action. In this way it helps orient practice toward a *qualitatively* different future.[26]

Level Three: Salvation

If "the driving force of history is the difficult conquest of freedom" (TL 19), if nothing less than human fulfillment is at stake in the liberation process, then, says Gutiérrez, that process challenges the church and the salvation it proclaims.

Salvation and Liberation. Moreover, if there is but one human destiny, must not the ultimate goal of the liberation process be what Christians call salvation? In that case, the goal of that process is more marvelous than we can imagine: the gift of complete communion with God and other human beings. But then the alienation to be overcome is also more radical than it appears. It is sin. Without liberation from sin—which only God's gratuitous love can effect—the genuine liberation at which the first two levels aim cannot be achieved (*La verdad*, p. 173). The single complex process of liberation "finds its deepest sense and its full realization in the saving work of Christ" (TL 25). Gutiérrez observes that conflict and liberation is precisely the language of the Bible. The work of Christ is a liberation *from* sin and *for* love, that is, for communion with God and with others. "Liberation from sin is one side of the coin; the other is communion with God and with others" (*La verdad*, p. 199). Christians share in the conflictual process of Christ's paschal mystery: "the passage from the old to the new person, from sin to grace, from slavery to freedom" (TL 23).

History Is One. Starting with liberation in history leads Gutiérrez to historicize the work of grace from the beginning. He stresses the unity of the liberation process and of history. "This is not a matter of three parallel or chronologically successive processes, however. There are three levels of meaning of a single, complex process" (TL 25). The three dimensions interpenetrate.

In particular, while he affirms the relative autonomy of the first two levels and their epistemological sources, Gutiérrez does not restrict the third level to the spiritual (nonmaterial), the interior, the personal (excluding the social), the imperishable, or the church. History is one.

There are not two histories, one profane and one sacred, "juxtaposed" or "closely linked." Rather there is only one process of human becoming in history, irreversibly assumed by Christ, the

Lord of history. His redemptive work embraces all the dimensions of existence and brings them to their fullness. The history
of salvation is the very heart of human history. . . . The historical
becoming of humanity must be definitively situated in the
salvific horizon. (TL 86, trans. emended)

Gutiérrez's argument boils down to this: The goal of the liberation
process is human fulfillment. A sound theology of grace recognizes
only one human destiny. Therefore, communion with God and others—salvation—is occurring in the liberation process. In traditional
terms, this is the main thesis of Gutiérrez's theology of grace.[27] The
first two levels of liberation correspond to "nature," the human
condition. Maritain calls this the common good of the temporal order,
noting that it is both material (compare level one) and moral (compare
level two). For Rahner and Gutiérrez, and unlike Maritain, salvation
occurs in and through its realization.

The following sections fill out Gutiérrez's paradigm by examining
his understanding of sociality, history and eschatology, and spirit and
matter. We will consider divine and human action toward the end of
this chapter.

Sociality

Early on, Gutiérrez wrote that "the whole of life is a relation with
the neighbor, since a human being is social, a being-with-others" (LP
63). In TL, he complained of theology's need to "break out of a narrow,
individualistic viewpoint," since in the Bible "human beings are called
to meet the Lord insofar as they constitute a community, a people"
(TL 45). The sole human vocation is a con-vocation; salvation is
communion with God *and with others* (ibid.; cf. PPH 31, LP 45).
Although translations frequently overlook it, Gutiérrez repeatedly
speaks of God *convoking* (*convocar*), not simply calling, human beings
into a church and to communion.

The threefold liberation process presupposes a relational understanding of human existence: Human beings are related to nature, to
other human beings, and to God. The first dimension of liberation
concerns human beings' need for, alienation from, and active (work)
and passive relation to things; the second concerns social relations;
the third, people's relation to God. This way of interpreting the
process is only implied in TL. It becomes explicit when Gutiérrez
identifies his own conception with that of the Puebla Document,
which adopts a similar framework without embracing the specifics of

his level-one social analysis or his level-two philosophy (cf. TL xxxvii; PPH 145-47). [28]

However, Gutiérrez does not develop the philosophical basis for his social anthropology. He is more explicit in arguing the theological basis for the unity of the liberation process and the concrete social character of salvation. The following two sections examine these arguments.

Creation, Political Liberation, and Salvation

Gutiérrez claims that progressive European theology fails to grasp the real unity of history insofar as it narrowly interprets history in terms of technical progress (see, for example, TL 219n.14).

Consider the following oft-cited passage from Vatican II:

> Earthly progress must be carefully distinguished from the growth of God's kingdom. Nevertheless, to the extent that the former can contribute to the better ordering of human society, it is of vital concern to the kingdom of God. (GS 39; cited in TL 98)

According to Gutiérrez, this vague paragraph reflects a lack of consensus at the Council, and in theology, concerning the relationship between the good of creation and God's saving work. He addresses this ambiguity by developing two complex lines of argument that intertwine, sometimes in confusing ways. The first connects creation, political liberation, and salvation in the Bible; the second develops a biblically based theology of history and eschatology. Together they converge to affirm that salvation is partially realized in ambiguous forms of human liberation which point to a definitive liberation in the future.

Creation and Liberation

Gutiérrez observes that theologians in industrialized countries have naturally devoted effort to interpreting scientific and technological progress. (For what follows here, see especially TL 100-2; PPH 43.) Unfortunately, he believes, they frequently separate human beings' relation to nature (what we earlier called *techne*) from economic, social, and political relations (*praxis*). (Rahner's earlier thought would fall under this general criticism.) At worst they interpret the drama of history in terms of the dominion of nature.[29] Although this permits them to interpret work and technical progress as the prolongation of God's act of creation, it obscures the connection between temporal progress and the "order of salvation," because the dominion of nature only indirectly concerns sin and redemption.

From the perspective of the poor of the Third World, says Gutiérrez, one must reflect on work and technology in terms of alienation, exploitation and the longing for liberation. Since history is a political drama of struggle for human fulfillment, that must be the context for interpreting temporal progress (*techne*). By failing to assume this perspective, theology in the developed world allows interpretations suited to relatively nonconflictual scientific progress to spill over into the political arena in the form of the ideologies of evolutionary development.

Liberation and Salvation

In this context Gutiérrez invites us to consider how the Old Testament presents creation as *part* of God's work of salvation (TL 86-87). [30] Salvation also means the formation of a new people through liberation, however, according to the paradigmatic exodus event (TL 86-89). This shows once again that we can bring work and technical progress (understanding both as extending God's *creating* activity) into relation to God's *saving* activity in a satisfactory way only if we first situate them in their sociopolitical context (TL 90; cf. TL 101; PPH 32). [31] But the exodus also illustrates the meaning of salvation as liberation from a sinful situation and for covenanted *communion* with God and others. These reflections suggest to Gutiérrez that salvation takes place in the self-creation of humanity through work and political liberation (TL 86-91; cf. TL 100; PPH 32; *La verdad,* pp. 166-69).

Latin American theology's recourse to the exodus, especially in developing the theme of salvation, is significant from the standpoint of the history of theology. Christian theology has not only traditionally failed to appreciate the centrality of exodus traditions to the Old Testament as a whole, it has also habitually bypassed the historical meaning of the narratives in the search for allegorical prefigurement of the New Testament. [32] The truth is, however, that this story—more than any other—told the people of Israel who they were, who Yahweh was—the liberator of slaves and the defender (the *go'el*) of the poor—and therefore what God's saving action was like. [33]

Gutiérrez's use of exodus is not problem free, however, as we shall see. But neither does he lean exclusively on the exodus to link social liberation and salvation, as some have charged. He also relies on a rich theology of social sin.

Sin

Progressive theology defines the issue of salvation and temporal progress in the "Catholic" language of nature and grace. The order of creation corresponds to nature, the order of redemption to grace; but the locus of sin is society. Politics, says Gutiérrez, more directly than technology and science, is the arena of freedom and social relations— and so of sin, the root cause of injustice. Pervasive injustice makes history a drama of enslavement and liberation. Gutiérrez therefore locates the entire nature-grace paradigm within a more Augustinian-"Protestant" sin-grace framework. "In our theological perspective," Gutiérrez wrote recently, "sin occupies a central place" (La verdad, p. 197).[34] The centrality of sin and conflict in history here contrasts with Catholic social thinking's relatively irenic outlook on society and with the two paradigms we have examined.

> We are far . . . from that naive optimism which denies the role of sin in the historical development of humanity. This was the criticism . . . [made of] all those theologies enthusiastic about human progress. (TL 102)

TL contributes richly to the theology of sin, especially in its social dimensions (TL 23-25, 102-3, 153; cf. PPH 62-63, 135-36; La verdad, pp. 194-99). Since salvation and human fulfillment is communion, sin is the absence or rupture of friendship with God and with others. It is the refusal of God's offer of love and so "an interior, personal fracture" (TL 103). A matter of the will, sin is nonetheless always concrete. There is no sin-in-itself apart from concrete instances of injustice and alienation—just as salvation, too, takes place under determinate historical conditions.

Sin is the fundamental alienation and ultimate root of a situation of injustice.[35] In this sense, sin can be said to be "in" oppressive structures. Sin produces situations of injustice and unjust structures and social systems. Salvation is liberation from sin and all the consequences of sin. At the first two levels, liberation addresses the consequences of sin, at the third level it addresses the root (La verdad, pp. 185-86).

In the context of this systematic argument concerning salvation and liberation, the introduction of the concept of social and institutional sin (already present in the exodus narrative) by Gutiérrez and liberation theology constitutes a decisive contribution to the Catholic tradition concerning salvation. Why? First, Gutiérrez speaks the language of liberation and sin (not simply grace and "nature"); secondly, he socializes and politicizes sin itself. From that point on, grace does not simply overcome personal sin and perfect human "nature" as the tradition has always affirmed. Now grace liberates from *social sin,* investing salvation itself with a political character. The concept of social and structural sin has, of course, been adopted and emphasized by John Paul II (*see* Letter on Reconciliation and Penance 16 and *Sollicitudo rei socialis* 36-37).

The Difference Christ Makes

Gutiérrez regards Jesus Christ as the hermeneutical key to Scripture as a whole (PPH 60-61; *La verdad,* pp. 13, 45).[36] But he believes that Christ takes up and deepens the understanding of salvation as seen in the exodus: The New Testament presents Jesus' saving work as a new creation crowning the first. It is the creation of a new people "which this time includes all humanity" (TL 90; cf. PPH 12-13, 15). Christ liberates from sin and for communion. In that case, salvation occurs in and through social and political liberation today. The Spirit of Christ is the driving force of history, the deepest source of the desire and the efforts of human beings to be free for communion in history.

> In Christ and through the Spirit, persons are becoming one in the very heart of history, as they confront and struggle against all that divides and opposes them. . . . Salvation—totally and freely given by God, the communion of human beings with God and among themselves—is the inner force and the fullness of this movement of human self-generation initiated by the work of creation. (TL 91; trans. emended)

Therefore,

> building the temporal city is not simply a stage of "humanization" or "pre-evangelization" as was held in theology until a few years ago. Rather it is to become part of a saving process which embraces the whole of humanity and all human history. (TL 91)

Many would object, however, that Christ completes these exodus themes by bringing a *wholly spiritual* salvation that is "not of this world." Like Maritain, they would argue that *Christian* salvation is a suprahistorical reality different from the carnal, historical salvation of the Old Testament: The prophets' descriptions of the messianic age refer to Christ in a metaphorical, spiritual sense.

The problem has two aspects. The first concerns the meaning of salvation in the two testaments. The second is the related question as to whether and how the reign of God (salvation) is a reality in present history. The first concerns matter and spirit; the second, eschatology.

Promise and Fulfillment

In Gutiérrez's view, the idea that earthly salvation in the Old Testament prefigured a (nonearthly) spiritual salvation in the New derives from an unbiblical dichotomy between matter and spirit and a failure to understand biblical eschatology.

The Promise Unfolding.[37] In TL, Gutiérrez draws on Gerhard von Rad, for whom the Bible is "the book of the Promise" of God's salvation. "Human history is . . . the slow, uncertain, and surprising fulfillment of the Promise" (TL 91-92; cf. 59-60).

For von Rad, the Promise of salvation unfolds down through history in specific promises and partial fulfillments which herald the complete fulfillment of the last days. The Sinai covenant, the kingdom of Israel, Jeremiah's new covenant, and Jesus' proclamation of the reign of God are all concrete fulfillments of past promises. Each specifies God's great Promise; at the same time, each points beyond itself to the ultimate fulfillment of the Promise. In this sense, the Promise is always *already* fulfilled and still *not yet* fulfilled. "It is a matter of partial fulfillments through liberating historical events, which are in turn new promises marking the road towards total fulfillment" (TL 96).

Subsequent promises and fulfillments do not invalidate earlier ones; they incorporate these so they continue to reveal the Promise. For example, God continued to promise "the land" and "rest" to Israel after the conquest. The prophesies of the messianic age, which the New Testament claims to fulfill, conform to this pattern. One must not invalidate their historical (literal) sense by an exclusive appeal to a "spiritualized" allegorical meaning.[38]

Spirit and Body. Gutiérrez believes that posing the alternative of a wholly spiritual (historically transcendent) and a wholly temporal salvation betrays a Western assumption that "spiritual" means non-material and nonhistorical (TL 95-97; cf. 207). "In the Bible the spiritual is not opposed to the corporal nor to the material, but rather to the carnal—understood as a selfish turning in upon oneself" (TL 223n.72, trans. emended; cf. PPH 203). Biblical anthropology prohibits reductively "spiritualizing" the fulfillment of the Promise. Christ takes up the prophesies of the Old Testament and brings them to completion. "In Christ 'all the promises made by God find their fulfillment' (2 Cor 1,20). All the promises" (TL 168; cf. PPH 4).

Indeed, we can add that, precisely because salvation in the New Testament is *radically* transcendent, because it is a sharing in the divine Spirit, it is all-embracing. Spirit (human and divine) penetrates and confers life (human and divine) on material and social human beings.

More recent works by Gutiérrez offer two important reinforcements to his argument that salvation in Christ embraces "the whole human being." One is a deeper reflection on Pauline anthropology; the other draws on the Chalcedonian Christological formula.

Life and Death. Gutiérrez interprets the Pauline triad of flesh, body, and spirit with striking richness and depth in *We Drink from Our Own Wells* (Chapt. 4). Catholic thought traditionally develops its anthropology metaphysically in relative independence from theology. But Gutiérrez shows that Paul roots his anthropology in a *soteriological* framework, the antagonism between sin and grace, from the very beginning. Here, as in all his recent writings, Gutiérrez stresses that the theology of liberation speaks about the God of life (*The God of Life, passim*). We can only understand flesh, body, and (human) spirit in Paul in reference to the dialectic between life and death. The flesh leads to death,[39] (divine) Spirit to life. Flesh and spirit, life and death, struggle within each person (Rom 7,15).[40]

For Paul, says Gutiérrez, the human person is wholly body and wholly spirit, depending on one's perspective. These are not component principles, as in Plato and popular understandings of Aristotle. If one walks according to the flesh, one's spirit is carnal. On the other hand, the power of the Spirit can transfigure the body (not the flesh) into a spiritual body. The divine Spirit transfigures the entire person (*see* 1 Thes 5,23; *We Drink*, pp. 102-4).[41]

The Chalcedon Principle. Related to these reflections is Gutiérrez's recent appeal to the ancient Christological formula of the Council of Chalcedon, which affirms the distinction without separation of Christ's divinity and his humanity. What Christ assumed—the human condition as a whole—he redeemed, incorporating it into the saving plan of God. The saving action of Christ is united to human liberation, which retains its own character and autonomy (TL xxxix; *La verdad*, pp. 25-26, 172-74).[42]

Christology, therefore, like biblical eschatology and anthropology, supports Gutiérrez's contention that salvation in Christ embraces the whole of human existence.

However, there is one last piece to add to the puzzle. The *complete* fulfillment of the Promise obviously did not come with Jesus. Gutiérrez is concerned to interpret our own time, theologically. What is the saving work of God today?

The Reign of God Today

Pauline anthropology and the Chalcedon principle already take us into the age of the church. With Jesus' death and resurrection and the sending of the Spirit, Gutiérrez writes, the Promise enters a definitive, final phase. Nonetheless, the kingdom will not be fully realized until the end of history as we know it. Now, as before, the Promise "illuminates and fructifies the historical process of humanity's becoming, carrying that process along through incipient realizations towards its fullness" (TL 92, trans. emended; cf. PPH 12).[43]

The biblical logic of promise and fulfillment is more than a tool for understanding the Bible. It is a tool for understanding history. Today, too, history remains "the slow, uncertain and surprising fulfillment of the Promise" in partial realizations that point beyond themselves (TL 92).

Von Rad shows that the prophets' oracles announce, first, that God will act to save in new and unexpected ways; second, that salvation is very near and will respond to the *present* historical situation; and, third, that the saving action points to a less determinate but more complete fulfillment of the Promise in the distant future (TL 123-26; cf. TL 11).[44]

Today, too, writes Gutiérrez, "there exists a dialectical relationship between the Promise and its partial fulfillments" (TL 92). God's reign is partially realized in and through liberating historical events that are themselves *ambiguous* and point forward to God's final, complete victory.[45]

> The growth of the kingdom is a process which occurs historically *in* liberation (insofar as liberation means a greater fulfillment of humanity) which is the condition for a new society, but the kingdom is not exhausted in it. While it is realized in liberating historical events, it denounces the limitations and ambiguities of historical liberation, announces its complete fulfillment and impels it effectively toward total communion. (TL 104, my trans.; cf. PPH 204)

No definitive establishment of God's reign can take place in history. Gutiérrez has repeatedly insisted that the coming of God's reign is not exhausted in and can never be identified, without qualification, with any historical arrangement.[46] "Whole books of imprecations of liberation theology would have been unnecessary" if their authors had attended to Gutiérrez's clear affirmation of this truth (Brown, *Gustavo Gutiérrez,* p. 129).

The traditional paradigm of Maritain rejected an intrahistorical reign of God on the grounds that it denies the "peregrinal" character of the human condition by affirming the possibility of the definitive solution to the "riddle of history" within history. Gutiérrez, too, rejects any such definitive solution in history but argues instead, like Rahner, that partial solutions occur and cannot be confined to individuals' consciousness or to the church. They embrace every dimension of life and take place when human beings struggle to achieve communion in society.

Summary

In short, for Gutiérrez, Christ's saving work embraces all human beings and the whole human being, material and moral, personal and political. History is one.

The conclusion to be drawn from all the above is clear: salvation embraces all persons and the whole person; the liberating action of Christ—made human in this history and not in a history marginal to real human life—is at the heart of the historical current of humanity; the struggle for a just society is in its own right very much a part of salvation history. (TL 97)

Assuming and transfiguring human reality as a whole, Christ and his Spirit are present and working in the liberation process, for it is in this process, understood in the broad sense as the struggle for freedom at every level of existence, that people are becoming more human and becoming one. In this process, "the pulse of history beats" (TL 104, *see* Spanish ed.; PPH 76). Liberation is

a single process; but it is a complex differentiated unity, which has within itself various levels of meaning which are not to be confused: economic, social, and political liberation; liberation which leads to the creation of a new human being in a new society of solidarity; and liberation from sin and entrance into communion with God and with all persons. (TL 137, trans. emended)

The three dimensions of the liberation process—institutional, cultural, and theological—are distinct but inseparable. They interpenetrate. "One is not present without the others, but they are distinct; they are all part of a single all-encompassing salvific process, but they are to be found at different levels" (TL 103). Real liberation cannot occur on one level in isolation from the others. "These three levels mutually condition each other" (ibid., trans. emended). Few commentators have added significantly to Gutiérrez's explanation of how the three levels of liberation relate to each other (*see* Manzanera, pp. 169-70, and Oliveros, pp. 311-13).

In particular, the theological level affects the two political meaning levels. Faith alone recognizes the fundamental obstacle to the coming of God's reign, sin (cf. TL 104). Faith also discloses the deepest root and horizon of the aspiration for freedom and dignity which gives rise to the liberation process: the desire for complete communion with God and others.

The gospel also assures us that the triumph of justice and love is not a fanciful dream. If the problem is as grave as sin, the remedy available is as radical as grace and the Holy Spirit. Finally, by inspiring a utopian hope, faith also contributes to the humanization of the liberation process and its goal (TL 153-54).

Gutiérrez's answer to the question of the relationship between salvation and the hope of the poor is that God's reign is partially realized in ambiguous historical events that open out to the complete realization of the reign of God. To the extent that a liberating event represents "a greater human fulfillment," to this extent "the historical, political liberating event *is* the growth of the Kingdom and *is* a salvific event" (TL 104). Christ's work of liberation encompasses the whole of the liberation process, of human life, of history, and gives them their unity and deepest meaning (TL 37, 104, 143).

Challenges and Criticisms

Gutiérrez escapes most of the accusations commonly levelled against the theology of liberation.[47] First, he does not collapse transcendence into creation. No particular historical configuration can be identified with the reign of God in history. He would also do well to stress not only the ambivalence of every society and every human achievement but also their tendency to corruption and the inevitability of their death.[48]

Secondly, neither does Gutiérrez reduce life or the gospel or salvation to politics. The real reductionists are the "spiritualizers" who exclude God's saving action from politics (TL 104). At the same time, when one portrays life as the struggle for freedom, the *way* in which politics touches all of life (as Gutiérrez says) must be interpreted carefully to avoid political reductionism and creeping totalitarianism (Comisión Teológica Internacional, "Declaración," in idem, *Teología de la liberación,* p. 209).

Thirdly, Gutiérrez insists that the reign of God cannot be fully realized before God's final intervention in history. It is important to add to this the astute observation of Jon Sobrino to the effect that God's reign not only relativizes all social orders—as theologians in the North always insist—it also serves to "hierarchize" them and judge them against the ideal and the criteria of the liberation of the poor. Not all social orders are equally distant from the divine utopia (Sobrino, *Jesucristo liberador,* pp. 201-2).

Gutiérrez makes a persuasive case for reading history through the lens of prophetic eschatology, building on the foundation of von Rad's studies, which have stood the test of time. He has little to say, however, about this final victory and the beatitude it ushers in, and he is similarly silent on personal eschatology.

Two other challenges deserve greater attention. The first has to do with the relationship between human and divine action. The second issue is related: Does Gutiérrez have sufficient postmodern critical distance on the Enlightenment's presuppositions about history as a universal process in which humanity passes through successive phases toward ever-greater rationality and freedom?

Divine and Human Action

Gutiérrez's writings of the 70s at times appear to interpret human action in Promethean, or even Pelagian, terms. For Gutiérrez, social praxis mediates salvation.

The affirmation of the single vocation to salvation, beyond all distinctions, gives religious value in a completely new way to human action in history. . . . The building of a just society has worth in terms of the Kingdom, or in more current phraseology, to participate in the process of liberation is already, in a certain sense, a salvific work. (TL 46; cf. TL 32)

Again:

To work, to transform this world, is to become a human being and to build the human community; it is also to save. Likewise, to struggle against misery and exploitation and to build a just society is already to be part of the saving action which is moving towards its complete fulfillment. (TL 91)[49]

Social praxis functions in Gutiérrez's soteriology somewhat as love of neighbor does in Rahner's. For both, one encounters God in the neighbor. For Gutiérrez, to know God is to do justice (TL, Chapt. 10, *passim*). Divine and human action coincide in that genuine love which liberates.

This is sound enough. TL's activism, which characterizes human existence as self-generation through work and praxis, rightly seeks to counter the fatalism of traditional cultures—and the exaggerated preference for contemplation over action in traditional theologies such as Maritain's. However, Gutiérrez's position in TL appears undialectical and in need of a more solid foundation.

Consider, for example, his early reflections on the exodus. Gutiérrez notes that, while it is surely God who liberates here, God does so through human beings (cf. TL 75, 91). The fact that this liberation *creates* Israel suggests to him that the human race generates itself through work and liberating praxis down through history.

It is true, as Gutiérrez also notes, that the Bible desacralizes nature (and perhaps work and technology today, as well). Furthermore, important biblical traditions treat politics as a thoroughly secular affair (von Rad 1:51-53). Nonetheless, the exodus narrative is not the best place to look for secularization—not to speak of self-generation—if that means that human beings are thrown back entirely on their own efforts. The relationship between divine and human action is unusually complex in the Book of Exodus.[50]

In TL, Gutiérrez failed to achieve a synthesis of divine action and human action. His writings of the 70s appeared to celebrate an activism with little appreciation for contemplation or receptivity. He devoted scant attention to the meaning of suffering and impotence.

From the beginning, he stressed the gratuity of God's saving gift and, unlike others, resisted the language of building the kingdom. However, he juxtaposed divine gratuitousness and efficacious action, rather than integrating them.[51] He stressed a performative faith to the neglect of faith as trust (PPH 36-74 and Manzanera, pp. 110-16; *see* Dulles, "The Meaning of Faith," pp. 10-46).[52]

But must not God's collaboration affect our political action? If so, and if "faith appears to us ever more as a liberating praxis" ("Evangelio y praxis," p. 243), then the reverse must also be true: Trust which surrenders to mystery in hope must lie at the heart of liberating praxis. This side of the coin needs stress, especially in cultures of pragmatic efficiency, where liberating praxis means letting go (*see* Neal).

Gutiérrez later addressed these issues with extraordinary depth and eloquence in *We Drink from Our Own Wells, On Job* and *The God of Life*, all of which, significantly, reflect deep appreciation for the traditional piety of the poor. Whereas earlier works spoke of conversion in terms of active love of neighbor (cf. TL 118), *We Drink* calls for that repentance which the "hombre nuevo" always implied (Chapt. 6). While earlier writings stressed encountering God through loving the neighbor (TL 114-16), *We Drink* affirms that only an encounter with God can make disinterested love of neighbor possible (p. 112).

In his book on Job, Gutiérrez locates the struggle for social justice within the context of God's gratuitous love and respect for human freedom.[53] Gratuitousness provides the basis of a Christian contemplation which pervades action and appreciates beauty, prayer, and ritual. Gratuitousness and contemplation ground the "spiritual childhood" of the "poor in spirit" (Matt 5,1) who realize their absolute need for God and are completely available before God (TL 169-71; *We Drink*, pp. 126-27; *On Job, passim; The God of Life*, Chapts. 6-8; cf. Manzanera, p. 163). *The God of Life* calls for evangelical watchfulness (pp. 103-4).

Surely spiritual childhood, contemplation and watchfulness must affect social praxis itself. The pregnant phrase "Christian life is *commitment in the form of an acceptance* of the gift of the reign of God"[54] opens a path for an ethic of social practice which could develop the importance for Christians of nonviolent forms of struggle.

Finally, the depth of Gutiérrez's insights in *On Job* and other later works reflects a deep appreciation for God as *mystery* (*El Dios de la vida*, pp. 5-9; *La verdad*, pp. 11-14), which mitigates an earlier confidence in reason, particularly social science. Later works show a greater sensitivity to absurdity in life, to the suffering of the innocent, to the God of surprises.

God's surprises (or miracles) in history need not constitute spectacular exceptions to the laws of nature, but they happen, and they reveal the limitations of all attempts to explain history. Appreciation of mystery, not mystification or obscurantism, relativizes all ideologies. It brings reason and revelation into right relationship, paradoxically countering dogmatism, whether social-scientific or theological. Revelation transforms reason. Faith does not add to reason in social analysis, much less substitute for it, but it illuminates social analysis; it steers it.

Marx and the Enlightenment

Gutiérrez rejects liberal theologies of evolutionary progress, and his more recent works reassess his earlier optimism about social

transformation in Latin America. His appreciation of the pervasive-
ness of sin in history helps correct "Catholic" tendencies toward irenic
optimism. Nevertheless, when Gutiérrez speaks of Kant, Hegel,
Marx, etc., as "the best philosophical tradition" and the self-generation of humanity as a conflictual conquest of freedom through greater
awareness, we must ask whether he remains captive to the Enlightenment's idea of history as a single process in which humanity passes
through progressive phases toward greater freedom and rationality.
The response begins with an assessment of his use of Marx.

Gutiérrez spelled out his use of Marxist thought only vaguely in
TL. He uses Marxist categories in the spirit of critical neo-Marxism
rather than Marxist-Leninist "orthodoxy."[55] He has recently demonstrated how many "Marxist" concepts in his earlier works derive from
a more common patrimony.

Gutiérrez disowns a full-blown Marxist anthropology (*La verdad,*
pp. 54-55).[56] In TL he affirmed Louis Althusser's conception of Marxism as a science of history, i.e., a social-scientific tool, not a philosophy
(José Carlos Mariátegui and Antonio Gramsci hold similar views).
However, he distanced himself from Althusser's neo-positivist view
of science, rejecting the idea of a radical "epistemological break" that
would deny the utopian elements in the mature Marx. Gutiérrez
argued that a fundamental continuity is evident in Marx's thought:
From beginning to end, Marx seeks to diagnose various forms of
alienation and points the way to their supersession (*Aufhebung*)
through appropriation.[57] Gutiérrez has recently cautioned that he
never adopted the theory of class struggle as the motor of history or
as a political program. Yet Christians must recognize class struggle
as a fact of life to which they must respond in love (*La verdad,* pp.
75-112, 186-88; TL 156-61). Finally, like Marx, he sees theory and
practice, especially liberating political practice (praxis), in dialectical
relationship.[58]

Gutiérrez's critical appropriation of Marxist ideas rests on solid
ground, as the following chapter will further confirm. But does it rest
on the idea that history is a film with a single coherent plot?

In an important essay, Antonio González has not only clarified
Gutiérrez's position but also demonstrated how his central insights
open a path for Christian thought and praxis in postmodern times
("El problema"). González first points out the central concern of Kant,
Hegel and Marx: history's victims become history's *subjects,* transforming the history of oppression into the history of freedom. But in
the face of persistent evil, each of these great thinkers fell into a kind
of determinism. In developing a "theodicy of history," they all came
to appeal in their later thought to a macro-subject of history, whether
Nature (Kant), absolute Reason (Hegel) or productive forces (official

Marxism, if not Marx himself). The macro-subject in each case implies a single plot for universal history; its development implies the actualization of human potentialities. But it leaves little room for creative innovation by free human subjects. In this outlook, all societies are advancing to achieve what Europe has achieved. What is worse, the great Enlightenment figures all considered conflict to be the motor of history and wound up justifying the struggles and horrors of history as the necessary price of historical progress. In the present primitive phase of history, the poor remain victims, not subjects. In this way, the Enlightenment's greatest representatives came to jeopardize the initial project of the Enlightenment itself.

González argues that Gutiérrez does not try to appropriate the emancipatory themes of the Enlightenment the way European political theology does, but rather to speak of God's saving work from the perspective of history's victims, indeed from the victims of the "enlightened" societies (TL 3-12, 110-12; PPH 18, 30-33). "Salvation" surely does not mean "progress" in the modern sense. But this does not mean we must look for salvation on a supernatural plane outside of history or, says González, in the transcendental subject. Rather, we must reread history from the standpoint of the victims of history (PPH 39-42, 136-37) and of "progress," and enquire about the saving work of God *in historical events* from that standpoint. This is where the deepest meaning of history is disclosed, in the dying and rising which is the daily bread of the poor. Among the poor, historical reality imposes the goal of action: that the poor become more and more the subjects of history (TL 17-22, 56-57, 63-68). (This is the concern, of course, of the young Marx as well.) This means that history must be transformed not from above, as the Enlightenment theorists propose, but from below, trusting not in some metaphysical determinism or macro-subject but in the God of the poor, who stands by them in their struggle for life. "History . . . is not the development of potentialities preexistent in human nature; it is rather the conquest of new, qualitatively different ways of being a human person" (TL 22). History thus presents itself as an open task in which God is the first actor, working through human beings. The poor countries ought not consider the rich countries to be humanly more advanced.

We must beware of all kinds of imitations as well as new forms of imperialism—revolutionary this time—of the rich countries, which consider themselves central to the history of humankind. (TL 18; cf. 14)

Perhaps Gutiérrez did not maintain the thorough independence that González's essay suggests, but he did maintain a critical distance on the conceptual tools he borrowed from the Enlightenment. In his use of these tools, he followed the criterion he expressed in 1974:

> Theology does not identify itself with a method of analysis of society, or with a philosophical reflection on the human person. . . . Theology never uses a form of rationality without modifying it in some way. This is characteristic of theology and the whole history of theology proves it. (*La verdad,* p. 94; cf. ibid., pp. 112-25; PPH 98-101; TL xiii; *see* TL 21)

Like Rahner in relation to German Idealism, Gutiérrez borrows Marx's and others' categories critically (*La verdad,* pp. 154-61), even altering them in an effort to make sense of Christian faith within a social matrix characterized by oppression and upheaval, for theory is judged by its ability to illuminate reality.

Gutiérrez's use of Enlightenment concepts at times led him to juxtapose apparently opposing theses, such as total secularity and dependence on God's gratuitous love. Only in his later works has it become clear that his central insights concerning the poor as the locus of God's saving activity (and the theologian's reflections) serve as the key to integrating the tensions. Indeed, it seems to me that no ideology functions as the decisive factor in Gutiérrez's theology but rather the experience of God among the victims and the identity of the God of life who takes their side.

We have already noted how Gutiérrez lacks a thoroughly developed philosophical anthropology. The criticism of Rahner and others on this point holds. On the other hand, it is striking how Gutiérrez devotes far more attention than Rahner or Maritain to interpreting scripture.[59] In fact, his theology often has a confessional, "theologal" quality.[60] This need not render it unscientific. Biblical categories apparently illumine the social reality which Gutiérrez interprets in light of faith.

Concluding Reflections on Three Paradigms

We began this book by describing how today the suffering of the poor challenges Christians to explain their hope. In the last three chapters, we examined three representative Catholic theologians on this question, tracing a fundamental shift in the paradigm used to explain "salvation."

Of the three theologians, Gutiérrez provides the most thorough and satisfactory treatment of the topic. The chief reasons are his starting point, the liberation process, and his constant effort to consider Christian symbols in social terms. He argues from the beginning that God's call is a *convocation* to communion with God and with one another, that the individual is a social being, and that human life is a *political* drama, a struggle for freedom and communion. The basis of every aspiration for, and achievement of, genuine freedom and communion is the liberating action of God.

Rahner's philosophical anthropology affords his reflection a depth that Gutiérrez sometimes lacks. Rahner's starting point is the liberation (the transcendence) of the individual subject. But the subject transcends to God *through* the world, which is above all the neighbor; and in his later, more political period, Rahner made important contributions to the question of Christian hope and social justice. On the other hand, Rahner's relatively irenic understanding of social life and his lack of a political philosophy leave him with less to say about the theological meaning of political liberation.

Both Rahner and Gutiérrez overcome the traditional (Maritainian) distinction of orders conceived as inseparable *parts* of life that correspond to metaphysical distinctions (matter and spirit) and to institutions (church and civilization). Such a conception is really a leftover of the discredited "extrinsicist" theology of grace. Although distinguishing two orders helps Rahner express God's presence to the world by way of both material (creation) and quasi-formal (redemption) causality, the language of two orders suggests a fundamental ontological division in the universe such that God's saving action touches only a part of history.[61] History is one, although we can and must make distinctions within it.

It is legitimate to distinguish the ecclesial from the nonecclesial, cultic from secular, and action from prayer and contemplation. But strictly speaking, after Christ, one distinguishes the secular, or worldly, from the cultic and ecclesial, not from the religious. (One may, of course, speak non-strictly; but then one should be aware of using "religious" narrowly, to refer to "cultic" and "ecclesial.") The all-pervasive presence of grace, at least as an offer, gives a religious dimension of meaning to human life as a whole. In particular, social justice and the liberation of the oppressed is a religious issue in the strictest sense. This by no means precludes the relative autonomy of the nonecclesial order, of reason and politics.

God and grace suffuse history (at least as an offer). God's saving presence touches all of history—although grace manifests itself in vastly different ways. Since this presence of grace is real, however, it would be anomalous not to explicitly celebrate it (in prayer and contemplation) or not to institutionalize its communitarian dimension (church).[62]

There have been political liberations which have not, in the long term, served humanization. Salvation and liberation are not simply identical. Yet neither are they parallel phenomena. There can be no sustained, truly human liberation (or humanization) unless it is part of integral liberation (salvation), that is, unless it is informed by grace. We need not shy away from provocative examples: The reign of God was present partially and ambiguously in the Sandinista revolutionary process, the Enda revolution of the Philippines and the demise of apartheid in South Africa to the extent, and only to the extent, that these represent works of love informed by God's grace.

Salvation always manifests itself historically in some form of liberation. We must understand liberation broadly, therefore, for the paschal mystery of Jesus, which appears as senseless tragedy to eyes without faith, remains the paradigm of God's liberating action for Christians, as the exodus was for Israel. As Gutiérrez's magnificent reflections on Job testify, God's saving work also occurs under conditions which do not, objectively, permit social liberation (*see* Moltmann, *The Crucified God*).

The presence of grace in history is a mystery which cannot be explained with scientific precision. We can only point to this presence with limping analogies and symbols. Gutiérrez's three interpenetrating dimensions of meaning do not offer us a scientific explanation of the relationship between God's saving work and liberating praxis. It is not the last word, but Gutiérrez adds one more classical metaphor to the history of interpretation of God's saving work in the world, one that is especially suited to our time and goes a long way toward clarifying the historic ambiguity of Christian theology concerning "salvation" and the hope of the poor.[63] God's salvation is "integral liberation [which] starting with liberation from sin covers the different dimensions of human existence" (Manzanera, p. 203).

Maritain has offered penetrating and valuable reflections on social philosophy and ethics, and many other topics, which will stand the test of time. We cannot say the same for his paradigm for the relationship of Christian hope to social justice. Rahner and Gutiérrez have shown the direction that Catholic theology must go. The remaining chapters of this book attempt to move farther in that direction.

The following chapter sketches three ways in which development can occur and already has occurred. First, we will consider the challenge to dualism posed by feminist theology and the contribution of Xavier Zubiri and Ignacio Ellacuría to our understanding of transcendence in history.

Second, we will sketch the main lines of a philosophy of liberation, or social theory, to further develop the second level of liberation which Gutiérrez considers the bridge between salvation and political liberation (cf. TL 81-82, 90). Our hope here is to supply some of the philosophical anthropology Rahner finds lacking in theologies of praxis and some of the social theory lacking in theologies like Rahner's. We will concentrate on developing a social understanding of human existence that can better explain the social implications of God's saving activity. Third, the next chapter also reflects on the obstacles to liberation-salvation, especially sin and concupiscence, which liberal and Catholic thinking often understate.

5

NEW BRANCHES FOR AN OLD TREE

In this chapter we consider how the theological tradition can and should develop in order to respond more adequately to the suffering of the poor and so respond in greater fidelity to its own roots. We have already suggested the principal needs and areas of challenge. These will serve as subtopics for this chapter. In this limited space we can hardly do full justice to the seriousness of these themes, but we can outline some of the main lines for future development.

The first task at hand is to consider the challenge of feminist theology and the notion of transcendence in the thought of Ignacio Ellacuría and Xavier Zubiri. Many feel that the tradition has not overcome the dualism which has plagued it for centuries. How can we speak of transcendence without dualism? Feminism, Ellacuría and Zubiri address themselves to the issue. Second, we will outline a philosophical anthropology of liberation which can help us specify how God's saving action addresses society. Third, we will offer some reflections for a theology of salvation in light of the obstacles to liberation and then present our conclusions.

Transcendence without Dualism

No Christian theology can afford to ignore the growing contributions of feminist theology. Catholic theology, especially, suffers from the failure to incorporate the voice of women. In this section, we examine the feminist challenge to overcome dualism, especially as Rosemary Radford Ruether articulates the challenge. We next consider the thought of Ignacio Ellacuría, martyred Jesuit of El Salvador, and his mentor, Xavier Zubiri, who have developed the idea of transcendence *in* history.

The Challenge of Feminist Theology

Insofar as we have shown that God's saving work is the liberation of the victims of history, this study carries us to the threshold of feminist theology. In this respect, Catholic theology can make common cause with feminist theology. But contemporary feminist theology challenges the tradition.[1] Can Catholic theology be feminist, or does feminist criticism invalidate Christian theology?

A Revisionist Theology. For almost 2,000 years, the church and its theology have helped to keep women in bondage. Today it is necessary to take seriously, if critically, the arguments of feminists such as Mary Daly who reject Christian symbolism as irreformably patriarchal and sexist (*Beyond God the Father;* idem., *Pure Lust; Christ*). Proponents of feminist Wicca (witchcraft) and other forms of feminist neo-paganism argue in similar fashion. Daly's work tends toward gnostic elitism, however, and the view that men are inherently evil (Ruether, *Sexism and God-talk,* pp. 229-30). For its part, Wicca and Goddess worship negate Judeo-Christian traditions in undialectical fashion and unself-critically perpetuate female/male, nature/culture dualisms. Although some of these movements deserve serious attention, they also suggest the dangers involved in wholesale rejection of the traditions underlying Western culture (ibid., pp. 38-41). In contrast to these currents, others argue persuasively for a critical reappropriation of Judeo-Christian traditions. Anne E. Carr is one example. Building on the work of H.-G. Gadamer, Carr recognizes that our rootedness in culture implies that all understanding of existence, including theology, is *interpretive* knowledge, occurring in dialogue with traditions. Carr notes that we can create new ideologies (including theologies) but we cannot create religions out of whole cloth. Theology does not create symbols or destroy them; it does not even affirm or deny them. It interprets them.

Carr argues that theology should interpret symbols critically, however, for all symbols are ambiguous and at least potentially enslaving. Traditions distort reality as well as disclose it. Carr accepts Habermas's principle that we must approach our traditions with an "emancipatory interest," unmasking the partial interests which symbols (God the Father) and traditions reflect. One approaches traditions suspiciously, demystifies them, and then, with a view to their liberating potential, revises and reapplies them. The experience of women, says Carr, must guide the whole process (pp. 99-103; cf. Ruether, *Sexism and God-talk,* pp. 21-22). In developing the position outlined, Carr also builds on the work of Paul Tillich and Paul Ricoeur.

In this spirit, feminist biblical interpretation has entered a golden age, critically appropriating the biblical tradition (Trible, *God and Rhetoric;* idem, *Texts of Terror;* Schüssler Fiorenza, *In Memory of Her;* cf. Ruether, *Sexism and God-talk*, pp. 22-37), including the story of Jesus, his praxis, especially his treatment of women, the "oppressed of the oppressed" in the gospels (Ruether, *Sexism and God-talk,* pp. 136-37), and his egalitarian ethic of mutuality and service. Elizabeth A. Johnson has made especially noteworthy contributions to rethinking symbols in the Catholic tradition (*see* Chapt. 5).

The Critique of Dualism. What does this revisionist feminist theology say about salvation in history and society? Our treatment will be brief and incomplete and will serve principally to indicate how feminism addresses the central problem of dualism. No feminist theologian to date has developed as thorough a synthesis on the issues as the three paradigms we have already considered, but Rosemary Ruether, following a generally revisionist path, has probably given the question more thought than any other feminist theologian (Johnson, p. 281n.33, considers Ruether's *Sexism and God-talk* "the most comprehensive reconstructive effort in systematic theology to date" from a feminist perspective).

Ruether believes that androcentrism, rooted in Hebrew thought and aggravated by Greek categories, has distorted "all the dialectical relationships of good/evil, nature/grace, body/soul, God/nature," and human/nonhuman "by modeling them on a polarization of male and female" (*Sexism and God-talk,* p. 37; cf. Chapt. 3, *passim*). Elsewhere Ruether adds the polarities "nature/civilization, sexuality/spirituality, nurturance/dominance, immanence/transcendence, femininity/masculinity" to the list (ibid., p. 52). This results in nondialectical dualisms and hierarchical thinking: one pole dominates the other. Here revisionist feminist theology converges with liberation theology and many of the points argued in this book. At the same time, feminist theology typically goes further and challenges male political and liberation theology in its critique of dualisms. In Ruether's words (ibid., pp. 70-71):

Patriarchal theologies of "hope" or liberation affirm the God of Exodus, the God who uproots us from present historical systems and puts us on the road to new possibilities. But they typically do this in negation of God/ess as Matrix, as source and ground of our being. They make the fundamental mistake of identifying the ground of creation with the foundations of existing social systems. Being, matter, and nature become the ontocratic base for the evil system of what is. Liberation is liberation out of or against nature into spirit. The identification of matter, nature, and being with mother makes such patriarchal theology hostile to women as symbols of all that "drags us down" from freedom....

Feminist theology must fundamentally reject this dualism of nature and spirit. It must reject both sides of the dualism: both the image of mother-matter-matrix as "static immanence" and as the ontological foundation of existing, oppressive social systems and also the concept of spirit and transcendence as rootless, antinatural, originating in an "other world" beyond the cosmos, ever repudiating and fleeing from nature, body, and the visible world. Feminist theology needs to affirm the God of Exodus, of liberation and new being, but as rooted in the foundations of being rather than as its antithesis. The God/ess who is the foundation (at one and the same time) of our being and our new being embraces both the roots of the material substratum of our existence (matter) and also the endlessly new creative potential (spirit). The God/ess who is the foundation of our being-new being does not lead us back to a stifled, dependent self or uproot us in a spirit-trip outside the earth. Rather it leads us to a converted center, the harmonization of self and body, self and other, self and world.

These paragraphs challenge theology to think of liberation in a way that reconciles humanity to (nonhuman) nature. Unlike Maritain and similar thinkers, neither Rahner nor Gutiérrez envisions liberation or transcendence as a flight from matter. Nonetheless, Ruether challenges both to affirm more explicitly that genuine personal and political liberation includes healing our alienation from our bodies and from the earth. For example, if liberation means humane work, as Gutiérrez affirms, this work must respect the earth as friend rather than dominate it as enemy or master. At the same time, while feminists are correct to reject the idea of human dominance over nonhuman nature and presumably the necessity of competition between the two, it is not always clear that they affirm the priority of human life within ecological systems.[2]

Ruether, however, is saying more. She questions the idea of human spirit/transcendence as flight from nature and body and toward God. What is at stake is not only the matter-spirit relation (human transcendence) but the notion of God's transcendence, as well.

The reader may object that Rahner has effectively overcome these dualisms. Carr, for her part, believes that his anthropology and his theology of grace open themselves up for critical appropriation by Christian feminists today (*Transforming Grace,* pp. 110-11, 131-32; see Ruether, *Sexism and God-talk,* pp. 85-86). For Rahner, human beings are conscious self-creating freedom, and God is the Holy Mystery of love, surrounding, sustaining, challenging, and liberating humans, opening them to one another and drawing them forward in history (compare Ruether, ibid., p. 49). Feminist theology can find common ground with Rahner's understanding of the unity of divine and human action and faith as free participation in God's action rather than obedience to external authority (ibid., p. 154).

On the other hand, Rahner speaks the Kantian language of transcendence. God is the horizon of our experience beyond every thing or category. Further, although Rahner insists that the transcendental structures of human subjectivity operate only in and through categorial experience, those structures remain distinct from the categorial. Rahner thus leaves many with the impression that the concrete and categorial is of secondary importance and not to be taken with the utmost seriousness (González, "El problema") and that God, like a Kantian noumenon, comes to us from somewhere beyond history. We need to examine the question of transcendence in greater depth.

Transcendence in History: Ellacuría and Zubiri

Ignacio Ellacuría was president of the Jesuit university in El Salvador where he was murdered, along with five Jesuit colleagues and two Salvadoran women, on November 16, 1989. A theologian and philosopher of Basque descent, he had long collaborated with fellow Basque philosopher Xavier Zubiri (1898-1983). The writings of both are still little known to English-speaking readers. For both Ellacuría and Zubiri, God does not transcend history but rather transcends *in* history.

Zubiri believes that the entire philosophical tradition of the West has been afflicted with a metaphysical dualism based on epistemological error. It has always sharply distinguished the objects of the senses from the objects of intelligence. Sensible objects are material, multiple and changing; intelligible objects formal, unitary and unchanging. According to Zubiri, Kant managed to unite the sensible and the intelligible in the object of experience but was still left with the dualism of knowable phenomenon and unknowable noumenon because, like all his predecessors, he failed to unite sensing and intelligizing in the subject. For Zubiri, human beings are fundamentally *sensing intelligence* (or intelligizing sensibility). Humans find themselves *within* reality, apprehending it by an intelligence that senses. All conceptualizing builds on that primary apprehension. Sensible reality is intelligible reality, and vice versa. There is no noumenon; there is only reality, the object of experience.[3] God, therefore, is to be found *in* reality but transcending in it. Reality could not exist without God. God is not things, but God is in them, "founding" them.[4]

Ellacuría approaches the relationship between salvation and social change as a concrete problem of human action, that is, of relating God's action to ours.[5] In our experience, notes Ellacuría, action is a unity. We must begin from this unity, he says, rather than try to unite two abstract concepts. God intervenes in the only history there is in such a way that human action results, and human beings intervene in history in such a way that God becomes present.

Building on Zubiri, Ellacuría (*Mysterium liberationis* 1:328) insists that transcendence does not mean "separated from or outside history." In accord with biblical thought, we ought to

> view transcendence as that which transcends *in,* as that which physically impels toward *more* but does not remove *from;* as that which pushes something forward, but at the same time holds it. In this conception, when we reach God historically . . . we do not abandon the human, we do not abandon real history. Instead, we sound its depths; what was already effectively present becomes more present and efficacious. God can be separated from history, but history cannot be separated from God. And in history transcendence must be seen more in the relation necessity-freedom than in the relation absence-presence.

For Ellacuría, humans do not transcend to a God outside history but to a God who transcends things within history. God is not any thing; but God is to be found in, not outside, of reality. Ellacuría arrives at this understanding of transcendence because, like Zubiri, he holds that all things, and especially life and history, are the external shape (*plasmación*) of God. "Each thing, according to its limits, is a limited way of being God" (ibid., p. 359).[6] Therefore Ellacuría can speak of the "great history of God" which envelops so-called secular history and that history of salvation and revelation formally recognized as such in the Bible and by the church. It is the history of the "cosmic-historic Christ" in whom everything is converging. Ellacuría understands this all-encompassing process in the first place as the struggle between grace and sin in history, and only in this way as "the supernatural" perfecting the natural.

What are we to make of "transcendence *in* history"? Perhaps we should ask what it would mean to speak of God, or anything else, "outside" of history or "outside" reality. If we agree that the expression is virtually senseless, then we have little alternative to speaking of transcendence within history, if we wish to speak of transcendence at all. "Transcendence in history" suggests quite well a God hidden and revealed in the depths of reality.

Perhaps Rahner's critics fail to appreciate how he has modified the Kantian concepts he has appropriated. Perhaps his insistence that transcendental structures operate only in the concrete and categorial and his understanding of God as horizon to our experience amount in the end to what Ellacuría and Zubiri intend when they say that God transcends from within the depths of reality. Recall that Rahner spoke in his last years of God as the most inner entelechy of history (*see* O'Donovan, "Journey into Time," p. 624). In that case, however, Rahner's Kantian language would seem at least insufficient, at least for communicating this understanding, especially given the risks of unduly restricting God's saving activity to human subjectivity.

In the following section, we develop an argument—missing in all paradigms considered so far—for the social and political nature of human existence, and thus of human fulfillment. Because grace transforms reality in Catholic theology, this will affect the way we understand salvation.

Zoon Politikon

Introduction

In traditional Catholic theology, grace perfects reality ("nature"). Christian hope is, therefore, a truly human hope. Precisely *because* God is all-transcendent, the divine self-bestowal is complete *human* fulfillment.[7] If salvation answers to the deepest human needs, then how we understand salvation will depend in part on our understanding of the human condition.

As we have seen, however, the grace theology of Western Christianity has always had difficulty thinking about salvation in social categories. Traditional Catholic soteriology relates God's saving action directly to persons, not to social relations or institutions. It relates grace to society only indirectly through moral action. This individualistic approach to grace, says Leonardo Boff, "is based on an erroneous conception of the human being" (p. 141). Therefore, this section argues that human beings are social and political animals in a stronger sense than traditionally affirmed. We will show that human beings *constitute* themselves as human only in society, and they are fulfilled as humans only in society. Our arguments should provide the conceptual tools we need to speak about social relations and institutions—about politics in a broad and rich sense—which is something that Aristotelian Thomism has never been able to do satisfactorily. Not only should this allow us to affirm that salvation is a new community, a clearer understanding of social relations should enable us to specify (if somewhat generally) *how* grace (God's saving action) is related to social relations (and not just persons). The third section of this chapter will nonetheless criticize efforts to interpret salvation too much in terms of structural change—or in terms of worldly success.

Beyond Traditional Views. In the traditional Aristotelian-Thomist paradigm, the person is "constituted a person, made for God and eternal life, before he is constituted a part of the city" (Maritain, PCG 75-76). The human being is certainly a *zoon politikon,* essentially social, first, because humans need culture and community to survive and to develop and, second, because, as spirits, they have an innate drive to communicate in love and knowledge with others. In this tradition, however, human nature is given prior to social life and is only accidentally affected by it. A preconstituted human self experiences the need for others and desires to enter into social relations.

Both Rahner and Gutiérrez interpret the human condition—and hence salvation—in more strongly social terms than this. It is in and through their interaction with nature and with others that human beings, both individually and as a species, come to be what they are. "Human nature" is not changed in merely accidental ways through this interaction, as though it were *merely* a matter of developing innate potential. Rather, who-we-are is transformed, created, through work and social interaction.

As we saw, however, Rahner argues for a strong sense of sociality on the basis of the a priori transcendence of spirit toward other persons and the interrelatedness of all things, that is, on the basis of transcendental anthropology and a metaphysical cosmology of internal relations. Rahner also appeals to the authority of Scripture and Christian dogma. These arguments will not convince everyone. We can hardly fault those who demand a more empirical account of human sociality, especially since the absence of such an account prevents Rahner from specifying *how* God's saving grace is related to society.

For his part, Gutiérrez appeals 1) to the biblical teaching of solidarity and God's *con*vocation and 2) to the Hegelian-Marxist idea of self-generation through interaction with nature and others. But Gutiérrez offers little philosophical or social-scientific basis to supplement a rather weak appeal to Scripture on this point.

The next section examines how a stronger sense of sociality has recently been persuasively argued in several areas of thought.

Convergence in Contemporary Anthropology. At the end of the twentieth century, diverse currents of thought concerning the human condition have been converging. Studies of the human being from different perspectives increasingly take action as their starting point, and they insist on the constitution of the self and the world in terms of interaction with other selves.

German idealism long ago recognized how the person appropriates an identity and achieves self-realization (freedom) by interacting with the social world. Marx took up this concept and materialized it: Human beings constitute themselves through work and social interaction.

Evolution theory greatly stimulated this general line of thought when it affirmed that species develop (Lamark) or at least survive (Darwin) by adapting to their environment. This inspired reflection on the emergence of human characteristics—freedom, language, rationality—as means to address survival problems. Biologists and zoologists took up the challenge of explaining the difference between humans and other animals and how the former emerged as a species. The mid-twentieth-century school of philosophical anthropology, associated with names such as Arnold Gehlen and Helmuth Plessner, built on their work.

Meanwhile, also inspired by Darwin, American pragmatists like Dewey and Mead worked to solve fundamental philosophical problems from the standpoint of action directed to real-life problems, including adaptation to a social environment. In a different spirit, Maurice Blondel (*L'Action,* 1893) also developed a philosophical anthropology based on action.

In this century, philosophy has taken a fundamental turn toward language, itself the product of social interaction. The linguistic turn has culminated, after Wittgenstein and Austin, in the revalorization of language's pragmatic dimension. The social nature and constitution of the person has also been stressed in the phenomenology of Martin Buber (*I and Thou,* 1923) and E. Lévinas (*Totality and Infinity,* 1961).

The philosophy of Xavier Zubiri reflects this general line of thought. Zubiri has incorporated some of its fundamental insights in a "materialist" metaphysic which holds great promise for the development of a philosophy and a theology of liberation.[8]

Besides a great respect for empirical data, the more recent thinkers in all these currents share an understanding of human beings as fundamentally social actors and communicators rather than individuals who aspire to contemplate. They are convinced that the best way to understand the human condition is from the standpoint of interaction with a social environment. By examining the work of four figures who share this general outlook, we can see why.

Grounding Sociality: Four Recent Approaches

Clifford Geertz. In some well-known studies, anthropologist Clifford Geertz has argued that culture is indispensable for any truly human existence. According to Geertz, the study of human evolution reveals a period of overlap during which cultural forces interacted with biological factors in the shaping of *homo sapiens*:[9] "The innate, generic constitution of modern man (what used, in a simpler day, to be called 'human nature') now appears to be both a cultural and a biological product" ("Growth," p. 67).[10] Geertz draws from this the following conclusion:

> Most bluntly, it suggests that there is no such thing as a human nature independent of culture. Men without culture . . . would be unworkable monstrosities with very few useful instincts, fewer recognizable sentiments, and no intellect: mental basket cases. As our central nervous system . . . grew up in great part in interaction with culture, it is incapable of directing our behavior or organizing our experience without the guidance provided by systems of significant symbols. . . .Without men, no culture, certainly; but equally, and more significantly, without culture, no men.
>
> We are, in sum, incomplete or unfinished animals who complete or finish ourselves through culture. ("Impact," p. 49)[11]

Since culture ("Tools, hunting, family organization, and, later, art, religion, and 'science'") was ingredient to the somatic development of *homo sapiens*, it is "therefore necessary not merely to his survival but to his *existential realization*" ("Growth," p. 83, emphasis added). Geertz's thesis is that, apart from the social interaction which constitutes culture, there can be no functioning identity, no personality, no consciousness or communication, no intelligence, no meaning—no human person. Human beings are essentially social; their identity and distinctive way of operating, their "essence," is constituted in interaction with culture.[12]

Peter Berger and Thomas Luckmann. The "incompleteness" of the human being at birth is confirmed by the biological and zoological work of Jakob von Uexküll and Adolf Portmann, which Plessner and Gehlen have interpreted philosophically. The well-known treatise by sociologists Peter L. Berger and Thomas Luckmann, *The Social*

Construction of Reality, [13] summarizes the results of this work. Berger and Luckmann (following von Uexküll) point out humanity's "world-openness," the fact that a human being's "relationship to the surrounding environment is everywhere very imperfectly structured by [its] own biological constitution." The human organism develops in part outside the womb after birth in interaction with its environment. "In other words," Berger and Luckmann write, "the process of becoming man takes place in an interrelationship with an environment." Not only the survival but also "the direction of . . . organismic development" of the human infant "is socially determined." From this they conclude that

> there is only human nature in the sense of anthropological constants (for example, world-openness and plasticity of instinctual structure) that delimit and permit man's socio-cultural formations. But the specific shape into which this humanness is molded is determined by those socio-cultural formations and is relative to their numerous variations. While it is possible to say that man has a nature, it is more significant to say that man constructs his own nature, or more simply, that man produces himself. (pp. 47-49)

Berger and Luckmann combine these insights with George Herbert Mead's theory of the social genesis of the self through the mediation of roles and identity by "significant others." For Berger and Luckmann, not only does the biological organism develop to completion in interrelation with nature and culture, the *self,* too, "as a subjectively and objectively recognizable identity" is shaped and emerges in the same process of environmental interaction: "The same social processes that determine the completion of the organism produce the self in its particular, culturally relative form" (p. 50).[14]

Within a framework of interaction, humans "produce" themselves, say Berger and Luckmann, not in a solitary Promethean effort, but by means of what is "always, and of necessity, a social enterprise." The human person is essentially and irreducibly social:

> Solitary human being is being on the animal level (which, of course, man shares with other animals). As soon as one observes phenomena that are specifically human, one enters the realm of the social. Man's specific humanity and his sociality are inextricably intertwined. *Homo sapiens* is always, and in the same measure, *homo socius.* (p. 51)

John Macmurray. John Macmurray set forth a comprehensive theory of the social nature of human existence from a more strictly philosophical perspective in his Gifford Lectures of 1953-54 (*Form of the Personal*). Macmurray criticizes the theoretical standpoint of the dominant philosophical tradition of the West, especially the starting point of modern philosophy, the "I think." He argues instead for the primacy of the practical in philosophical knowledge and for the "I do" as a philosophical starting point. In the spirit of pragmatist philosophy, therefore, he begins with the self as agent.[15]

However, if one begins, not with the thinker-observer but with the agent-participant, one begins with persons-in-relation, not the isolated individual.

> The idea of an isolated agent is self-contradictory. Any agent is necessarily in relation to the Other. Apart from this essential relation he does not exist. But, further, the Other in this constitutive relation must itself be personal. Persons, therefore, are constituted by their mutual relation to one another. (*Persons in Relation,* p. 24; cf. pp. 86, 209)

Macmurray shows that human beings are not equipped with innate drives that are "sufficiently definite to fulfill [their] biological function." As a result, "all purposive human behaviour has to be learned" from others. From the beginning, therefore, the human infant "lives a common life as one term in a personal relation." The child "needs the Other in order to be himself" (ibid., pp. 48, 50, 98).

This is not only true of the infant, however. One develops in maturity not simply by growing *out* of these interpersonal relationships but rather by transforming them. In time, the total dependence of the infant becomes (ideally) the mutual interdependence of the adult (ibid., pp. 66, 105, 107). The new circle of the others becomes wider, and many relationships take an indirect form (ibid., p. 67, etc.); but it remains true that the person is a term in a network of personal relationships.

> Thus human experience is, in principle, shared experience; human life, even in its most individual elements, is a common life; and human behaviour carries always, in its inherent structure, a reference to the personal Other. (Ibid, p. 61)[16]

In other words, "we need one another to be ourselves" (ibid., p. 211; cf. pp. 70, 119). For Macmurray, human beings can only be human in the first place by being-in-relation; they can only be fulfilled or "complete" by being-in-relation in particular ways (ibid., p. 105).

Xavier Zubiri. Finally, Zubiri grounds a similar analysis of the human condition within a metaphysical framework. (For Zubiri, *metaphysical* refers not to what is trans-physical but to the formal structure of reality.)

Zubiri rejects the idea that persons are subjects prior to their activity, or substances underlying their operations, or, first of all, consciousness (as in modern philosophy). They are rather psycho-biological organisms, animals, who deal actively (*habérselas*) with reality.[17]

In the process of evolution, notes Zubiri, "higher" animals developed a measure of independence with respect to stimuli until, with the human being, a qualitatively new way of operating emerged: not just pure sensation (as with other animals) but not intelligence sharply distinguished from sensation, either. What developed was sensing intelligence, or intelligizing sensation. Intelligence does not apprehend mere stimulus; it apprehends reality (Zubiri, *Inteligencia sentiente,* Chapts. 1-3).

Whereas pure animal sensation receives stimuli passively, sensing intelligence (human beings) engages reality actively. Developing Zubiri's insights, Ellacuría stressed that humans' biopsychological structure forces them to confront (*hacerse cargo de*) reality. This enables them to assume (*cargar con*) it in responsibility (not simply contemplate it) and actively transform (*encargarse de*) it (Ellacuría, "Fundamentación biológica," p. 422).

For Zubiri, human reality is social reality. Reality in general is transcendental (*Inteligencia sentiente,* Chapt. 4). That means that all reality is not only dynamic and open to "essential" change, but that each reality "refers to" other realities and to reality as a whole. Human beings, by their biopsychical nature, are especially open to reality; they are biopsychically *turned toward* others of the same species (*Sobre el hombre,* pp. 193-98). We always find our lives "interfered" with by others from the beginning; and these other humans humanize (or dehumanize) us in our mutual interaction. Humans apprehend this turning-to-others not as a mere stimulus but as a highly complex and infinitely variable reality called society. Society becomes community when the others are recognized as other "I's" like myself. Human reality, both personal and social, does not just change with time; it "becomes" in the course of history (ibid., Chapt. 4).

Geertz, Berger and Luckmann, Macmurray and Zubiri offer four persuasive and convergent efforts to interpret the human condition as essentially social, in the sense of "constituted as human through social interaction." These thinkers share with many others the view that "*Homo sapiens* is always, and in the same measure, *homo socius.*" They agree with Fichte that "Humans become human only among humans" and that "If human beings are to exist at all, there must be several" (cited in Landmann, p. 219, trans. emended). Feminists, incidentally, have welcomed and further developed this thinking as truer to human, and especially women's, experience and subversive of patriarchy and the dominant understanding of human beings as isolated, competing individuals.

If human beings are social in such a strong sense, and if grace perfects the human condition, then salvation is surely a social matter. In what sense? On the basis of what we have seen so far, even from a traditional standpoint, we ought to ask about the way grace relates, not simply to human individuals—the almost exclusive focus of the Catholic theology of grace—but to the social constitution of the self. The importance of this question becomes clearer when we consider the political and moral dimensions of the constitution of the self. These are implicit in Karl Marx's treatment of sociality.

Sociality in Karl Marx

For Marx, like Hegel, nothing individual is understandable apart from the whole of which it is a part (Ollman, esp. Chapt. 3; *see also* Lukás, Chapt. 1; Unger, pp. 125-33). This includes human beings, whose sociality is a consistent theme throughout Marx's writings, although just how this was to be understood changed from earlier to later works.[18] In the *1844 Manuscripts* we read, "It is above all necessary to avoid postulating 'society' once again as an abstraction confronting the individual. The individual *is* the *social* being."[19] According to the sixth Thesis on Feuerbach, "The human essence is the ensemble of social relations" (Marx and Engels, p. 122). Again, "The human being is in the most literal sense of the word a *zoon politikon,* not only a social animal, but an animal which can develop into an individual only in society" (cited in Ollmann, p. 105, trans. emended).

Marx holds human beings to be essentially social in this way not only because he sees them as *related* to the world but also because he *identifies* them with their activity. "My *own existence* is a social activity" (*1844 Mss.,* p. 158). "As individuals express their life, so they are. What they are, therefore, coincides with their production, both with *what* they produce and with *how* they produce" (Marx and Engels, p. 42; cf. 63-64). Self-realization ("objectification") occurs in the first place in relation to other human beings (*1844 Mss.,* p. 157).[20] "Activity and mind are social in their content as well as in their *origin;* they are *social* activity and social mind" (ibid).

The social activity *par excellence* is work—production. Production is the prime analog of human activity, in relation to which all others are defined.[21] In this activity, human beings are "generated" in interaction with their environment. In the first place, "Circumstances make humans just as much as humans make circumstances" (Marx and Engels, p. 59, trans. emended; *see also* the third Thesis on Feuerbach, ibid., p. 121). Since, however, the circumstances themselves have been created by human beings (ibid.) and since human beings relate actively to their surroundings, humans produce themselves: "By thus acting on the external world and changing it [through labor, a human being] at the same time changes his own nature" (cited in Avineri, p. 81). "The worker produces capital and capital produces him. Thus he produces himself" (*1844 Mss.*, p. 137; *see also* pp. 138, 157. Cf. Marx, *Preface and Introduction*, p. 3). As a result, consciousness is "a social product" (Marx and Engels, p. 51).

History is thus the story of the transformation of human nature.[22] Full humanity is still to be realized, and this can only come about when, under appropriate social conditions, social life-activity will be a genuine appropriation of its object through free, conscious activity (*see 1844 Mss.*, pp. 154-55).

Under capitalism, humans do not realize ("objectify") themselves in labor because the *social relations* of labor rob them of the fruits of labor and distort human activity. Therefore humanity comes to be, not only by transforming nature, but also by transforming society. The becoming of persons and humanity as a whole is therefore a *political* problem.

In the following subsection, we will develop our own understanding of the political character of the human condition. Then, in light of that, we will point out some limitations of Marx's social theory and their importance for a theology of salvation.

Recognition and "the Political"

As we have seen, persons, and humanity as a whole, emerge through interaction with their environment. Human beings shape their world and are shaped by it. In what sense?

Freedom in the World. To be human means to be in the world in a distinctive way. It means belonging to the world, like other animals, and being subject to its conditions. But it also means being able to set the world over against oneself and, unlike other animals, exercise a degree of freedom with respect to it.[23] We are conditioned freedom, freedom under pressure. Freedom with respect to the environment is necessary for the survival of the human animal and for its self-realization. Self-realization means not only freedom *from* mere response-to-stimulus but also freedom *for* responsible engagement with the world. Responsible engagement is fundamentally love, identification with the interest of others, especially those in need. But we need to spell all this out in greater detail.

Being persons (both survival and self-realization) depends both on how we deal with the world and how it deals with us. The world, which is first of all other persons, can personalize or depersonalize us, even destroy us. It is important to reflect on how the world *recognizes* us and calls personality forth. "Self-consciousness," wrote Hegel, "*is* only by being recognized" (p. 229). Our self-realization as persons depends crucially on how the world recognizes us.

Recognition has an objective dimension (or, better, precondition). I always find myself already located in a society which maintains me in an objective social situation, with or without my consent. It leaves me unemployed, hungry, without options or free to excel in sports or to thrive generally. Society (concrete persons, personally or via institutions) pressures us and profoundly conditions our free action. On the other hand, recognition refers more properly to how society subjectively *interprets* and *evaluates* us and our situations. Society not only profoundly conditions where I am; it conditions *who* I am. It reaches to the center of the person to condition the drama of the formation and realization of the self.

Society recognizes someone *as* . . . accepts someone *as*. . . . Recognition is not merely the acknowledgment of an identity but the assignment of one. To some extent, recognition objectifies the person recognized, even as it leaves the person more or less free to overcome the objectification.[24] Specifically, being human means being assigned multiple *roles* (Berger and Luckmann, p. 132). I am male; I am a carpenter; I am a responsible mother; I am a poor student; I am on public assistance; and so on. Society, the source of all meaning, communicates to me what it *means* to be male, a carpenter, a responsible mother; it tells me—all of us—the *significance* of being a poor student or on public assistance.

A person internalizes roles, modifies them, grows in and out of them, exercising a degree of freedom in determining what roles mean and who one really is.[25] Society provides the raw material with which one fashions one's identity. "Significant others" (themselves creatures of and representatives of their environment) provide the most important elements of the self during infancy and early childhood. In the course of life, new roles confront, and affirm or challenge, a person's socially mediated personality (Rasmussen, pp. 20-24).[26]

All this presupposes the profoundly uncomfortable dependence of individuals on their environment for food, work, love, and an identity which depends on a shared world of meaning. Both life itself and identity are fragile, dependent and frequently threatened.[27] We have no choice but to belong to a society which constantly treats people like objects. We are forced to struggle with these pressures and, in doing so, we frequently call society into question.

In Hegel's classic description of the master-slave dialectic, the master has assigned the slave a role and, thereby, an identity which the slave has interiorized. By interacting with the environment, first through labor and later in social interaction with the master, the slave can overcome the interior contradiction of his being, freeing himself *from* external definition and *for* a form of self-generation in a less constricted form of interaction with the world (Hegel, pp. 229-40).[28]

Survival and material well-being are obviously a social and political problem. Hegel's parable illustrates that personal identity and self-realization also, far from being a private, wholly interior affair, is a practical political matter. It is practical. The slave challenges society's subjective labeling by practically transforming his objective situation. The self is transformed by transforming its environment. Although Hegel's story is interpersonal, it is a political drama. It is not simply that slave and master stand for groups as well as individuals. More important, challenging society's labels means challenging its structures, for roles and their meaning mediate public *institutions.*

> The roles *represent* the institutional order. . . . Only through such representation in performed roles can the institution manifest itself in actual experience. . . . To say, then, that roles represent institutions is to say that roles make it possible for institutions to exist, ever again, as a real presence in the experience of living individuals. (Berger and Luckmann, pp. 74-75)[29]

Individuals (parents, spouses, etc.) who mediate roles and identity are socially constituted bearers of institutions. The roles they assign are neither arbitrary nor fabricated by individuals. They represent and embody social institutions and are the means by which those institutions exist "as a real presence in the experience of living individuals."

Not only survival and physical well-being, but also becoming who one is and must be—humanization—is a practical *political* matter. It is a problem of freedom in the context of social institutions, all of which, "by the very fact of their existence control human conduct. . . . This controlling character is inherent in institutionalization as such" (ibid., p. 55).

"The Political." To say that becoming a person is a political matter does not mean that human existence is reduced to politics, but that the interior and interpersonal dimensions of human life are inseparably bound up with the political dimension and colored by it. The personal is political. The master-slave parable illustrates how the issues of power, the struggle for freedom, and conflict pervade life.

We therefore use *political* here in a sense that differs from ordinary modern usage. This wider meaning does not merely represent a retrieval of the classical Aristotelian notion of the political—although it also does that in part. The dominant modern understanding of politics as an orientation to power (Weber) tends to separate itself from morality (Machiavelli), to consider its task one of proper technical administration of government, regulation and calculation of strategies. The classical notion, by contrast, conceives of politics as inherently moral, as having to do with the realization of the good through the exercise of prudence and as a matter of social interaction that cannot be reduced to technical control (Fiorenza, "Political Theology," pp. 143-45). We must retrieve these factors of the classical understanding of the political.

But both the social constitution of the self and modern history require a still broader understanding of politics. In contrast to the classical doctrine, the new understanding of politics presupposes that human fulfillment is a matter of achieving *freedom,* especially a freedom for *mutuality.* Classical political theory stresses order and harmony and permits mutuality only among equals, presupposing that a few are born to rule over a majority destined to serve and to obey (TL 30-31). By contrast, speaking about human fulfillment in terms of freedom and participation enables us to express the fact that the majority is in a situation of dehumanizing oppression. The language of conflict and liberation replaces the lyrical appeal for harmony and order. Once we understand human existence in terms of domination and oppression, conflict, freedom, and mutuality, "the political" becomes a dimension that embraces the whole of human life and the arena in which human fulfillment is achieved.

Freedom and Love. We insist, however, on freedom *for* mutuality. The foregoing reflections draw on liberal Enlightenment themes which accent freedom *from* constraints to the frequent neglect of freedom *for* commitment. Too many supposed radicals fail to move beyond liberal individualism at just this point. In reality, authentic human freedom is at once freedom *from* constraints and *for* commitment. This is not pious idealism but hard-nosed realism grounded in the biophysical facts of the human condition.

Since humans lack an instinct apparatus capable of responding to stimuli in an appropriate way, they must transcend mere response to stimulus simply in order to survive (to say nothing of flourishing). In a first break with animal narcissism, they must learn to set the world over against themselves, size up their situation, and respond to it. Independence of mere stimulus necessarily entails responsible engagement with the world. (Subhuman animals do not experience a world with time and meaning; they experience only stimuli.) Freedom and engagement are two sides of a single coin which constitute the distinctive human way of being in the world. Freedom from internal and external constraints *is* freedom *for* responsible engagement. Failure to achieve this double freedom means, to that extent, stagnating in subhuman existence, responding to stimuli and dominated by fear. As we shall see in the following chapter, Jesus invited people to break the chains of fear by means of what he called "faith" ("Fear not, you of little faith"). This freed them to respond to the world with love.

Humanization is therefore a process that overcomes the tyranny of the egocentric impulse for self-preservation characteristic of animals, not by destroying it but by supplementing it with more enlightened self-interest and altruism which develop through engagement with the world.

The mutual entailment of freedom and engagement is crucial. Human animals can become free to engage the world only to the extent that they become free from mere stimuli; but they cannot free themselves from mere stimuli unless they engage the world responsibly. This engagement is fundamentally love. Here Christian revelation illumines the data of science and day-to-day experience. Both demonstrate that people who fail to love abuse, and lose, their freedom to subtle forms of slavery (greed, lust for power, etc.). They find themselves mired in new and refined patterns of stimulus and response. They regress to animal-like behavior dominated by fear. Genuine freedom is the capacity to give oneself. Authentic freedom and love grow correlatively, not in competition, as liberal individualism supposes. Human self-realization is simultaneously growth in freedom and love. There is no greater love or freedom, no greater measure of humanity, than giving one's life for others. Those who lose their selves striving for their neighbor's freedom are those who find themselves and are truly free.

Grace and the Social Condition. According to the traditional soteriology, grace perfects the human condition, but grace relates directly only to individuals. Grace saves individuals. Contemporary theology, such as Rahner's, for instance, argues that these individuals are social beings and that salvation is not only new individuals but also a new community. Our more empirical argument reinforces that thesis by showing that human beings are social beings in a very strong sense and constitute themselves and fulfill themselves through social interaction.

At the same time, we have shown that persons form their identities in essentially *political* struggles to overcome dehumanizing and objectifying social relations. This allows us to be more specific about how grace (God's saving action) relates to the social order. We have tried to solidify the basis of Gutiérrez's second meaning level of liberation, providing a more empirical grounding than liberation theology commonly does.

If this is the human condition, and if grace perfects human reality, then salvation occurs in the sociopolitical drama of humanization and as the most radical form of human liberation. God's gift is utterly transcendent and gratuitous, surpassing anything we can plan or discern about human fulfillment. Yet this gift, which cannot be reduced to any particular social configuration, *is* human fulfillment and transforms the material and social conditions in which it is received. Because human life is social and political, so is salvation. Salvation could no more prescind from being-in-relation than from being embodied.

Although the traditional theology of grace does not speak this language, we shall see in the following chapter that the Bible does speak of grace in these terms, and in striking ways we have not yet examined. It poses as central the question of how God's saving action (grace) relates to social relations. The answer is that God rejects master-slave relations and offers human beings a new way to live in communion. The Bible condemns as sin the ways in which (as we have seen) society objectifies and depersonalizes; and it calls liberation from this sin "salvation."

Meanwhile, assuming that salvation takes place in the drama of human liberation, we need to beware of interpreting this uncritically according to prevailing ideologies.

Salvation and Liberation

Human animals are truly human to the extent they give themselves in love. Therefore, salvation occurs when this happens. However, it occurs, not after the pattern of evolutionary progress, but after the pattern of cross and resurrection, which is the fate of those who love. In speaking of liberation and salvation in history, it is easy to forget the complex reality of the person or understate the historical weight of death, failure and sin. First we return to Karl Marx.

Marx as "Technocrat"

Marx socializes and materializes Hegel's master-slave parable. Human beings are the ensemble of social relations; they are society. They overcome alienating external definitions and achieve "self-activity" only by transforming social conditions, in particular, by abolishing private control of the means of production. Here again, human fulfillment is the self-generation of persons-in-relation through liberation in the political arena (Marx and Engels, pp. 92-95).

Recent scholarship has shown that, for Marx, this self-generation takes place through reciprocal interaction between persons and their environment. On the other hand, Marx always understands human activity (and human existence) first of all from the perspective of humanity's relation to nature in productive labor. It is what we have called a *techne* relationship. The human being is *homo faber* (*see* Avineri, Chapt. 3). Following the Newtonian and Industrial revolutions, Marx, like many of his contemporaries, interprets this as technical control and domination[30] to the neglect of a receptive, passive relation to nature in respect and appreciation for it and conscious of belonging to it. Marx's stress on productive labor as the prime analogue of human activity tends to overflow into social relations[31] with the danger that the distinctiveness of human beings' relations with one another can become obscured (*see* Habermas, *Knowledge and Human Interests,* Chapt. 3). This raises the dangerous prospect that history as a whole might be treated as an object of technical control. We then confront the future as so much raw material for conquest in a way that threatens social life as well as the nonhuman environment (*see* Alves, *Human Hope;* idem, *Tomorrow's Child*).

Human life is more than unilateral activity, not to say technical control. It is social interaction and receptivity. Above all, if the reign of God is a gift, then a faith praxis which "takes up the reins of history" must integrate contemplation and a spirit of gratitude into action, especially in opulent societies which reward the effort to control the future—and to control others.

New Persons and New Social Relations

Reality is richer and more complex than the enlightened spirits of the nineteenth century supposed. So much so that we can speak of God transcending in the depths of reality (Zubiri). Marx was a pre-Freudian Enlightenment thinker—and an atheist—with insufficient appreciation for this depth and complexity, especially in the internal life of the person. Marx identified human beings with their activity and their social relations and attributed human misery almost exclusively to external causes.

By failing to appreciate the complexity and depths of the person, Marx exaggerated the ease with which human beings can become free by changing external conditions. As a result, he exaggerated the ease with which those conditions could themselves be changed, because, as he well knew, there can be no separation of exterior and interior change. The two are internally related.

Structural change, and perhaps technical progress, are necessary for humanization, but they are not enough. We (especially men) are dazzled, at times obsessed, by power and struggles to get and keep it. Still, taking and maintaining governmental power is not the decisive factor for social change, much less for humanization, to say nothing of salvation. Institutional change, generally, is less important than new persons and new social relations. Justice and community *can* happen. Tyrants can fall. History teaches, however, that profound change for the better rarely occurs and never lasts without conversion and heroic virtue. New persons and new social relations are decisive factors for real change and humanization.

There are no more "Winter Palaces" in the world. Even if there were, they could be retaken, because today's technology has provided the powerful of this world with an overwhelming advantage in contests of violence. In addition, absolutizing the taking of power dehumanizes generous revolutionaries and de-natures just causes. Yet, even if this were not true, we would still give priority to new social relations and new persons (Brackley, *People Power*).

The Sandinistas' 1979 *"toma de poder"* in Nicaragua, and their electoral defeat in 1990, pale in importance alongside the new social relations and persons who have emerged in the course of the revolutionary process. The taking of power was reversible, the deeper changes much less so. Something similar could be said about the new social relations emerging among repopulated refugees in El Salvador—and among South Bronx residents for whom "taking power" has little meaning. Deeper and more lasting change occurs where people break with individualism to serve the community, where they develop a critical awareness, where women and men begin to collaborate as equals and local communities organize for mutual assistance to secure their rights or develop cooperative enterprises. This is politics in the broad sense, micropolitics, or horizontal politics (Brackley, *Organize!*). It is what Gutiérrez called the second level of liberation— new persons in new social relations building qualitatively new communities. Revolution from "above," even if possible, is rarely worth the cost. What the world needs is nonviolent revolution from "below." There are grounds for hope. As history closes the door to state revolution, it seems to be opening the door to popular organizations in civil society. In recent decades, formal and informal nongovernmental organizations have burgeoned worldwide: groups of trade unionists, women, students, environmentalists, human rights advocates, neighbors and cooperativists (*see* González, "Orden mundial"; Gorostiaga, p. 51). This is perhaps the key locus of social change in the world today. These organizations—some local, others international—and not governments are the chief promoters of human rights and the defense of the environment.

We cannot afford to be naive. Structural change is important. Popular organizations, new social relations and new persons thrive with difficulty in societies which structurally punish cooperation and reward selfishness. Furthermore, populist micropolitics faces macroobstacles—oligarchies, governments, national and international finance. It is therefore necessary to work for structural change both locally and nationally. It is also necessary for local popular organizations to make allies with nongovernmental organizations capable of defending local initiatives against their predators. In tandem with the flourishing of local organizations, one of the signs of the times which has emerged at the end of the century is the growth of a *global civil society* with transnational nongovernmental organizations capable of defending local groups.

New persons and new social relations: That is where humanity—and salvation—is realized, as people grow in love and work for community. As Vatican II states, "temporal progress" is not the same as the growth of God's reign (GS 39), not when temporal progress is understood as technical control and institutional change as such. Progress in love and justice—new persons and new social relations—is another matter, however. That is the eruption of God's reign in history.

Inertia and Evil

Structural change is not enough partly because of sin and personal and social inertia. New democratic governments must contend with old authoritarian habits and egoists of today and tomorrow—and with sin in general. Although Christ has won the decisive battle in the struggle against evil, the forces of sin have clearly waged an impressive war to stave off final defeat. The reign of God in history faces the active resistance of sin and the passive resistance (inertia) of concupiscence. We must appreciate the nature of both in order to apprise what God's reign, and we, are up against.

The previous section demonstrated concretely how "society" objectifies persons and stifles their development. This is social sin. As Gutiérrez says, sin is the radical alienation present at the heart of every situation of injustice. It is also "an interior personal fracture" (TL 103).

The postbiblical tradition has generally considered particular sins, actions or omissions, to be the prime analogue of sin. From personal sins we come to understand habitual sin (vice) and original sin, etc. Perhaps we should question this schema.[32] In the New Testament, sin (not sins) is a trans-personal, death-dealing enterprise. Jesus confronts the anti-reign of Satan and the demons. In the Pauline writings, sin is an alien force which overtakes human beings, enslaving them and leading them to death. So, too, the "sin of the world" and "the world" itself in Johannine writings. In other words, sin is a massive death project which opposes God's project of abundant life. Humans inherit a sinful world and always already participate in it (original sin), further collaborating through particular sins. But sin is an organized enterprise with a logic, a definite dynamic. Who or what is behind this project? Traditional theology answers "Satan" (cf. 1 John 5,19) and with Ephesians: "We are not contending against flesh and blood, but against the principalities, against the powers, against the world rulers of this present darkness, against the spiritual hosts of wickedness in the heavenly places" (Eph 6,13).

It is all too easy to dismiss this view of sin as apocalyptic myth. We need to question our own nominalistic thinking which is part of an individualistic culture incapable of appreciating evil as a transpersonal death-dealing project. If we do not wish to identify the subject of this project as a personal Satan, we must at least guard against the failure to recognize the scope and power of evil (Peck).

The sin enterprise enlists persons and institutions in its service; it is the massive structural injustice that divides humanity and produces tens of thousands of unnecessary deaths each day. While it is true that this enterprise and the structures of death have no real life apart from personal sins, the collective enterprise of sin is more than the sum of personal sins (John Paul II, *Sollicitudo rei socialis,* 35-37).

If sin is a massive enterprise, then, as the quote from Ephesians suggests, it is not sufficient to simply do good and *avoid* evil, an insufficient concept of morality the church has promoted for centuries. The world is a battlefield between two opposing enterprises, and there is no neutral ground on a battlefield. If we do not oppose evil, we stand accused as its accomplices. As Martin Luther King insisted, we must do good and *resist* evil. Here "Christ above culture" Catholicism needs to borrow a page from H. R. Niebuhr's "Christ against culture" model.

It is also important to integrate an understanding of personal guilt, forgiveness and justification into a theology of salvation, integrating important elements of the motif of "Christ and culture in paradox."

Like sin, inertia, or homeostasis, is a more important factor in history than we usually suppose in working for justice and community. Christian faith recognizes the profound depths of this inertia in the form of concupiscence,[33] present not only in the interior of the person, but also in the "ensemble of social relations."

Because of sin and concupiscence, the struggle for freedom and justice will never be finished in history as we know it. While some regimes are closer to God's reign than others, every achievement in history stands under God's judgment as ambiguous, limited, and sinful.[34]

Because of the scope and power of both sin and concupiscence, it is crucial to account for defeat and locate the Cross at the center of any theology of salvation.

Failure and Defeat. Persons emerge and fulfill themselves in the struggle to transform into real community a social world which objectifies people. Tragically, history reflects the presence and power of sin: Success seems to be the exception in this struggle. History often appears to be more the story of the defeat of freedom than the story of freedom's conquest. It is the history of suffering. It would be hard to show that this is any less true in modern times than before (Metz, *Faith in History,* Chapt. 6). This calls into question any attempt to identify the history of salvation, pure and simple, with the history of freedom understood in purely political terms, even in our broad understanding of politics. Because of sin, the history of freedom has often been a history of the kind of utter defeat that is senseless apart from the resurrection of the dead which is a *creatio ex nihilo* (ibid., Chapt. 7).

If salvation occurs within the process of historical liberation, it occurs in apparent defeat as well as in triumph. It occurs for those who toiled in mines and on hillsides and wasted away in institutions, but who refused to surrender their humanity. It occurs for those who have died struggling for a society they will never see but who managed to build new human relations in the cracks of the national security state. It occurs for those for whom only faithful endurance is possible. Salvation is for them, too, not because it utterly transcends or prescinds from human fulfillment—it does not—or because salvation does not occur in historical liberation—it does—or, finally, because salvation can only occur when human beings fail or are rendered powerless, or when all human effort is vain—for this perverts the meaning of the Cross. Rather, salvation occurs in defeat as well as in victory because human fulfillment occurs that way and because God is a God who brings victory out of defeat and life out of death. Dying and rising, cross and resurrection mean that the human good itself, self-realization, takes place in a life of faith and love which inevitably clashes with its social environment but rises from defeat, brokenness, and death. This is where salvation occurs, because it is in a struggle of this kind, against the sin-enterprise, that human liberation is achieved. The struggle for freedom is itself an exercise of genuine though incomplete freedom when it must reconcile itself for a time to what it cannot change.

This does not mean that history must continue to be the history of suffering and injustice. Inertia and sin abound. Because evil is so radical, things are generally much worse than we are prepared to acknowledge. But grace abounds even more. If we can allow the suffering of others to touch our hearts, we have a chance to see that things are also much better, more hopeful than we dared suppose. Those who give their lives for freedom and real community and for the God who makes all things new will put no limits on what God can achieve through human beings in history.

Conclusions

We began this chapter by considering the feminist challenge to dualism in Christian theology. Following the suggestive insights of Zubiri and Ellacuría, we undertook an analysis of the human condition without having recourse to Kantian transcendental categories. Our approach does not obviate the transcendental questions: What a priori conditions make such a human animal possible? We may still wish to ask and answer this question. But we found that the more empirical approach of contemporary philosophy provided important insights for explaining humanization in terms of liberation for communion.

Different approaches to the human condition confirm, even when they disagree on other points, that human beings are social beings in a much stronger sense than Western thought has generally supposed. We need others not just to survive and grow, but to be persons in the first place—to have consciousness, intelligence and freedom. We develop as persons only by interacting with others. Therefore, since salvation is the ultimate fulfillment of human personhood (*gratia perficit naturam*), it is and must be essentially social. Salvation is a new community.

More specifically, human fulfillment takes place through interaction with an environment which threatens to depersonalize. This makes human fulfillment a political struggle for freedom from constraints and for commitment (ultimately, love). Therefore, salvation takes place within this struggle for liberation in history, not principally in the quest for political power in the narrow sense, but in the broad sense of the struggle for freedom and community within the context of all kinds of human institutions (*gratia vincit peccatum*).

This fulfillment, and hence salvation, does not occur chiefly through technical mastery. It is integral liberation which embraces all of human life—social, personal and political—healing the antagonism between humans and nature, women and men, God and world. It is a gift which one waits for and receives with gratitude in the midst of human effort. Only God can overcome the radical forms of inertia and sin.

God's salvation is a revolution in the heart of history at the deepest core of our lives together. (God does not bring a salvation from outside history, but from within its depths.) The obstacles are so great and the transformation so profound that salvation characteristically takes place as a rising from failure and death, a healing of brokenness and defeat. Because it is so thorough and depends on the cooperation of free human beings—a cooperation which is its goal and precondition—God's revolution is a slow and painful process.

As we complete this critical appraisal of Catholic theology, we are left with a need to connect our findings with the witness of the Bible. We have claimed that traditional Catholic theology does not adequately explain the relationship of God's saving action (grace) to human social reality. All the more reason, then, to pose to the Bible the basic question of this book and of our times. As we shall see, the Bible speaks to us of how God (and grace) relates not only to individuals but also to their social relations.

The following chapter examines Jesus' announcement of the reign of God. Did he understand this as the liberation of the poor? a political hope? a new community? His proclamation both affirms and challenges the tradition. Jesus reveals a God who rejects oppression and offers the possibility of living together in communion.

6

JESUS AND THE REIGN OF GOD

Introduction

In this book, we chose to break into the hermeneutical circle at a particular point, namely, with the modern experience of massive injustice and the desire to overcome it. We then traced and evaluated the recent paradigm shift in theological responses to the challenge that injustice poses to Christian hope. In taking this approach, we have neglected the Bible. While a systematic theology could hardly proceed this way, the purpose of this book is to assess Catholic thinking about salvation in the face of poverty and oppression. Now, however, we must allow the Bible to address the topic on its own terms and question contemporary Catholic thought about it.

Of necessity, we have to examine only select traditions of the Bible, and the results will be tentative, pointing the way for future work. Even so, this limited effort throws light on what we have seen so far.

Dualism in Biblical Interpretation

The effort is also necessary because so many use the Bible to deny that salvation in Christ embraces the material (as well as spiritual) dimensions of life and to deny its social and political dimensions. They claim that salvation in the New Testament does not have to do directly with material conditions or social relations (still less with politics and economics) but rather with the human spirit, the spirit of the individual, above all. This is how many mistakenly understand Jesus' statement "My kingdom is not of this world" (John 18,36). It is what Augustine meant when he claimed that the promises of temporal blessings in the Old Testament are fulfilled by spiritual blessings in the New. We could multiply examples, including more recent ones

(*see* Brown, *Theology in a New Key,* pp. 82-83). Ahistorical reductionism challenges us to reflect more deeply on what the Bible says about
salvation and the poor.

A Focus: Jesus and the Reign of God

Since the subject is highly complex, we must focus carefully. This
chapter will concentrate principally on the reign of God in the earliest
traditions about Jesus.

Why this focus? In the first place, Christian theology considers
Jesus the key to interpreting Scripture as a whole. What we discover
about him and his ministry sheds light on other biblical traditions.
In addition, Jesus does not reveal just one message among others. As
the Word, his person reveals God in a unique and definitive way. In
fact, Jesus' announcement of God's coming reign, or kingdom, is really
a declaration that God is coming as king. The reign of God manifests
who God is. This is theology's central question, after all, the theme
that governs all other propositions, including what salvation means
for the poor.

We also choose this focus because the proclamation of the coming
reign of God was the most central motif unifying Jesus' teaching and
ministry.[1] It brings us to the heart of his message. Thirdly, the coming
reign, or kingdom of God, suggests a salvation with social and
political overtones. Finally, in our post-Enlightenment times, historical truth, the facts, has pride of place in argumentation. In this
cultural context, the truth about the historical Jesus, or the closest
we can get to it, is crucial to any credible witness the church and
theology can hope to give.

Preliminary Notes

We need not review the history of life-of-Jesus research and its
thorny methodological issues here.[2] It is important to be clear, however, about what the findings of this textual and historical study
might mean for theology today (*see* Schillebeeckx, pp. 71-76; Cook).

By focusing on the earliest Jesus traditions and stressing their
importance, I do not intend to imply, as some contend today, that they
necessarily have greater authoritative weight for Christian belief and
practice than later traditions do. Neither do I intend to use the
earliest Jesus traditions in fundamentalistic fashion to argue what
salvation means in the New Testament as a whole, much less what
it means for us today. But what the early Jesus traditions say about
salvation does throw light on the rest of the New Testament, and

theology must take these traditions with utmost seriousness, especially in our post-Enlightenment context.

In the interest of brevity, I will devote little time here to arguing against positions I disagree with.

Finally, most scholars today believe that we can say something about what Jesus taught and what he did. We can even speak of a growing consensus about a core of teachings and actions (*see* Sanders, pp. 1-2; Borg, p. 15). It comes as little surprise, however, that no consensus has been reached about the social and political meaning of Jesus' message.

In this chapter we present in concise form what the best tools available enable us, and oblige us, to say about the salvation Jesus proclaimed and what it meant, and might mean today, to the victims of history.

God Comes as King

In speaking about the reign, or kingdom of God, Jesus drew on a symbol with deep roots in Israel, but he also invested it with new meaning. The expression "reign (or kingdom) of God" in Jesus' message refers principally to the activity God exercises as king. It means God's active sovereignty or governance (*see* Meier, *A Marginal Jew* 2:240). Indeed, the reign of God is first of all the coming of God in power; it is therefore the manifestation of God (Chilton). The expression "kingdom of God" does not primarily refer to a place or realm. "Kingdom of heaven" (frequent in Matthew) is an exact equivalent for "kingdom of God." Here "heaven," as frequently in the New Testament, is simply a circumlocution for the divine name.

Jesus always used the expression "reign of God" to refer to the final and definitive, or *eschatological,* intervention of God which was to end the "old age" of wickedness and signal the dawning of the "new age" of righteousness (Jeremias, *Theology,* pp. 101-2; cf. p. 100). God's reign does not come peacefully, however, for God comes as king to vanquish the forces of the "old age" who contest God's reign. Jesus' exorcisms, especially, liberate individuals as part of the wider liberation of Israel and the whole world from the thrall of Satan. In his ministry, Jesus clashes with both human and demonic representatives of this anti-reign (*see* ibid., pp. 93-96).[3]

Secondly, Jesus used "reign of God" to denote not only God's *kingly activity,* but also the "space" ruled by God and the *blessings of the new age.* In this sense, Jesus speaks of "entering the kingdom" (Matt 5,19; Luke 13,28-29; Matt 11,11; etc.).[4] Finally, in Jesus' teaching, the reign of God is both a present and a future reality. God's final saving action

had begun in his ministry; more important still, its full consummation was in the near future. Jesus contrasted the first fruits—as
mustard seed, leaven, seeds—with the much greater reality that is
expected—bush, leavened dough, harvest. The future victory is already present in germ.[5]

But what kind of salvation does God's kingly activity bring? What
are the blessings described symbolically as a great treasure, a pearl,
new wine, a new garment, a harvest, a wedding feast, risen dough, a
distribution of wages—for those who lack such things and long for
them?

The God Who Delivers the Poor

The Beatitudes

The logical place to begin is with programmatic sayings, that is,
sayings which describe the kingdom and the mission of Jesus as a
whole. We might consider, for example, the inaugural proclamation
of Mark 1,14-15, or the longer version in Luke 4,16-21, where Jesus
identifies himself with the bearer of good news to the poor, announcing liberty to the captives and the oppressed. Or we could study Matt
11,5 par., where Jesus describes for the Baptist's delegation what he
is doing and saying. On the other hand, not all trace these sayings
back to Jesus himself. It is preferable, therefore, to begin with a
programmatic text which no one doubts goes back, in some form, to
Jesus and which, in fact, is more revealing than the others. That text
is the beatitudes.

In his monumental study of the beatitudes, Belgian scholar Jacques Dupont argued that Jesus proclaimed God's coming vindication
of the poor and afflicted in Israel after the manner of the ideal king
of the ancient Near East, not because the poor were righteous, but
because God is righteous and merciful. Dupont's interpretation of the
beatitudes is steadily becoming the prevailing interpretation (cf.
Schlosser, p. 449n.91), but few scholars have drawn the necessary
conclusions for their overall portrait of Jesus.

In the first volume of his three-volume work, *Les Béatitudes,*[6]
Dupont reconstructs a plausible approximation of the earliest form
of the beatitudes. It reads like this:

> Happy the poor,
>> because the Reign of Heaven is theirs.
> Happy the afflicted,
>> because they will be consoled.

Happy those who hunger (and thirst),
    because they will be satisfied.
Happy will you be when they hate you and exclude you,
    etc. . . . (*Béatitudes* 1:343)[7]

Dupont then shows that the beatitudes concerning the poor, the afflicted, and the hungry evoke the ensemble of oracles of Second Isaiah, announcing God's long-awaited coming as king to console (deliver) the materially hungry and the socially oppressed (ibid. 2:96-97).[8]

The beatitudes are central to the rest of Jesus' ministry. He consoles the afflicted (Luke 2,25; 23,51; Mark 15,43) and frequently refers to God's satisfaction of the hungry and thirsty at the eschatological banquet (Luke 12,37; 14,15-24 par.; Matt 8,11 par.; etc.). His reply to the Baptist's delegation (Matt 11,5) echoes the beatitudes and evokes the oracles of consolation (ibid. 2:96).

These oracles refer to a group (or groups) who are at once poor, hungry and afflicted. Therefore, unless we wish to spiritualize the hunger and the tears, we must agree that the poverty is material (ibid. 2:35-44, 120). The beatitudes therefore proclaim that the poor will rejoice ("laugh") at the arrival of the "kingdom," for it means the end to their poverty and hunger. Jesus pronounces the poor "happy," not because they are virtuous, and certainly not because they suffer, but because their misery will soon end. (In Matthew's beatitudes, on the other hand, the poor in spirit are the humble who trust completely in God.)

Further evidence confirms Dupont's crucial conclusions. First, throughout the Bible, "the poor" most often refers to the economically deprived and socially oppressed. Even when passages in the later prophets and psalms use "the poor" to designate the poor in spirit and the persecuted pious, this extended meaning presupposes rather than supplants the primary one (cf. Hoppe).[9] Second, the Semitic parallelism of the beatitudes also confirms that we have a single group of poor. Their material hunger and tears interpret their poverty for us, just as their coming satisfaction and laughter interpret the kingdom for us. Third, Jesus does not call the attention of John's delegation to cures of spiritual leprosy or spiritual blindness (cf. Mt 11,5); neither therefore is he announcing good news to the spiritually poor.

Besides this internal textual evidence, however, there is a more fundamental theological reason why Jesus must have announced concrete liberation to the socially oppressed. It has to do, in the final analysis, with the identity of Yahweh—as reflected throughout Israel's traditions.

Yahweh, the God of the Poor

For Dupont, the key to understanding the beatitudes (and, by implication, the gospel) is the identity of the God who comes. The primitive beatitudes (unlike Matthew's) speak less of the conditions for entering the kingdom than of the God-king who comes. They speak not about human dispositions but about God's dispositions. Who is this God, and what are God's "dispositions"?

Yahweh, the Liberator-king. Dupont shows that Second Isaiah—and Jesus, too—proclaims the saving action of a God-king who acts in the tradition, widespread in the ancient Near East, of the just king who delivers the defenseless from their oppressors (*Béatitudes* 2:54-65). The gods, too, often fulfilled this role, especially when human kings routinely failed to do so.

While these traditions were widespread, there was a difference in Israel. The defense of the weak was central to the covenant with Yahweh. In addition, in contrast to Israel's neighbors, this defense of the poor was more than a simple demand for action; the entire social order fell under Yahweh's judgment. The torah judged policies and institutions in Israel. The king was not author of the law but was rather subject to it. The prophets' denunciations of the king and the powerful are without parallel in the ancient Near East. In Israel, the God Yahweh first of all assumes the responsibility to insure justice for the defenseless, while the king (and other Israelites, as well) exercises this responsibility as agent of Yahweh, the just king—indeed, Israel's only real king.

As king, therefore,

> God is the protector of the orphan and the poor; he does justice to them against those who oppress them by profiting from their weakness. By so acting, God shows himself "just": this does not mean that he repays the merits which those who suffer have acquired by pious conduct—of this nothing at all is said. (Ibid. 2:73; cf. pp. 65-67)[10]

God does not take the side of the poor because they are good but because God is good and compassionate to those who suffer. When the kings of Israel and Judah failed utterly to fulfill the role of the just king, the prophets projected the manifestation of God's royal justice into the future (ibid. 2:73-77, 82-84, 89).[11] It was this manifestation that Second Isaiah, and Jesus, announced.

The reign of God means "righteousness" (*sedeq*) and "peace" (*shalom*) because these are the priorities of the God who comes as king. Justice is central to Yahweh's identity and so to his reign.

Sedeq, mishpat, sedaqah. [12] Everywhere in the Hebrew scriptures *hesed*-and-*emeth* (*hendiadys*: steadfast loving-kindness) characterizes God as one who acts to do *sedeq, sedaqah,* and *mishpat* (what is right and just) and so to bring about *shalom*. Israel sings to Yahweh:

> Righteousness (*sedeq*) and justice (*mishpat*) are the foundation of your throne;
> Loving-kindness (*hesed*) and faithfulness (*emeth*) go before you. (Psalm 89,14)[13]

But the Jewish scholar Eliezer Berkovits has remarked:

> It is doubtful that among the many ideas of the Hebrew Bible any have suffered more from misunderstanding, and often biased misrepresentation, than the concepts of *sedeq, mishpat,* and *s'daqah.* (p. 340)

We can scarcely exaggerate the seriousness of this judgment if we recall that these three words are central to the meaning of the kingdom of God and express the highest values in the Hebrew Bible.

Sedeq is the highest and most comprehensive expression of what is valuable, right, and fair in the community. It is the Good. In Israel, *sedeq* means justice for the oppressed. *Sedeq* is not justice in the Western sense, however: proper conduct measured by the abstract demand to render to each person his or her due. *Sedeq* is rather the central concept governing all *relationships*. It means setting things right between people and living in accord with what specific social relationships require. That is why it means vindicating the oppressed (von Rad 1:370-83; Berkovits, p. 247; Walsh, pp. 4-5, 31-32).

Sedeq subsumes *sedaqah, mishpat, hesed*-and-*emeth,* and *yeshuah* (deliverance, salvation). After *sedeq,* the most important values in the Hebrew Bible are *mishpat* and *sedaqah*, which also have to do with the fulfillment of responsibilities within relationships,[14] indeed setting wrong relationships right by showing compassion to victims. Thus, in contrast to Western justice, there is no tension between biblical justice and compassion (*rahamim*). *Sedeq, mishpat* and *sedaqah* each has its distinctive nuances and can mean uprightness in general, but the important point is that they all have to do with social relations and share a core meaning richly expressed by their constant appearance together in various constellations. The core meaning they share is the defense of the weak, the vindication of the victim, the liberation of the oppressed. This is essential to Yahwism. It expresses, in fact, the "values" and intentions with which Yahweh acts. It expresses the meaning of "kingdom of God": "*Sedeq* and *mishpat* are the foundation of your throne" (Ps 89,15a = 92,7b); "A powerful king who loves *mishpat* . . . you execute *mishpat* and *sedaqah* in Jacob" (Ps 99,4).

Finally, the fruit of *sedeq, mishpat,* and *sedaqah* is *shalom,* the state of peace, security, and economic prosperity described so beautifully by the prophets.[15] *Shalom* designates the complete happiness to be expected when at last Yahweh comes to fully establish his reign (Gross 2:648-51).

These reflections imply three consequences for us. First, the Bible speaks of a God who is preoccupied with *social relations,* including the way these are institutionalized within Israel. This ties the present reflections to those of the previous chapter and alerts us to the importance of social relations in the message of Jesus.

Second, and more important, *sedeq, mishpat,* and *sedaqah,* along with *hesed* and *emeth,* are not only central to the ethos of Israel but reflect *who Yahweh is:* the one who defends the weak and frees them from the oppressor. Yahweh is the *go'el* (redeemer, vindicator) of the oppressed. This is not a "part-time" concern of Yahweh's or a secondary characteristic. This is what distinguishes Yahweh from the other gods (Ps 82).[16] This means that, no matter how "secular" an affair (from the standpoint of analysis and tactics), social justice is a quintessentially *religious* issue in Israel, indeed, the central religious issue.

Finally, it is impossible to conceive of God's kingdom or reign without the liberation of the poor and oppressed, without social relations of *sedeq* and *shalom.* Liberation of the poor stands at the heart of the symbol "kingdom of God." It belongs to its "core meaning."[17]

Therefore when Jesus drew from Isaiah's oracles of consolation, with their good news to the poor and afflicted, to explain God's coming reign, it would have been impossible for him to use these in a less-than-concrete sense. He would have been proclaiming the coming of another God and starting another religion in radical discontinuity with the Old Testament.

Blessed Are the Poor of Galilee

What did this proclamation mean to the people of Jesus' day? Most commentators balk at the common-sense proposition that the "poor" (*ptochoi*) to whom good news was announced (Luke 6,20; Matt 11,5) were precisely the crowds (*ochloi*) of common people whom the gospels identify as Jesus' actual hearers. They seem to assume that the poor were a minority group in first-century Palestine. The evidence suggests, however, that the masses of Galilee whom Jesus addressed suffered far more economic distress and social marginalization than we used to suppose (*see* Riches, Chapt. 4; Mealand, Chapt. 1; Schottroff and Stegemann, Chapts. 1 and 2; Oakman; Goodman; Theissen).[18]

Poverty in Galilee

Palestine in Jesus' day consisted of a small group of rich households and the great mass of the poor, with perhaps a small middle class in between. Conditions were especially severe in Galilee (Mealand, pp. 4-5. Cf. Goodman, Chapt. 3, and Theissen, pp. 41-43). The great mass of peasants endured severe hardship. They were subject to landlessness, debt, unemployment, heavy taxes,[19] hunger and malnutrition, to which the sickness recorded so often in the gospels may be related.

The beatitudes announce that God's coming reign reverses their fortunes. Increasing numbers of scholars believe that the announcement in Luke 4,19 of the year of God's favor refers to the opening of the final Jubilee Year, when debts would be cancelled and each family would receive back its ancestral lands, as Leviticus 25,8-17 had prescribed (Beasley-Murray, pp. 85-91, 270; Lohfink, "The Kingdom of God"; Borg, pp. 136-37). The beatitudes (and woes) declare that "the last shall be first and the first last" (Matt 20,16; cf. Matt 19,30 = Mark 19,30; Luke 13,30) (Schottroff and Stegemann, pp. 24-25).

All of this, of course, raises serious questions. How does this revolutionary proclamation square with other elements central to the message of Jesus? Is "the poor" an economic category alone? Does Jesus sanctify a social class—or glorify poverty? Is there something meritorious in poverty in itself? Is the reign of God no more than having and consuming material goods? or social revolution? And what about the conditions for entering the kingdom and the need for a response on the part of individuals? What about repentance and the forgiveness of sins? Finally, if Jesus proclaimed an end to poverty, must we not admit, as we look around us 2,000 years after his coming, that he was deluded?

Facing these questions seriously transforms the traditional understanding of Jesus' message and sheds light on our conclusions in the previous chapters.

Poverty Is a Social Relation

If God's sovereign rule abolishes poverty, does it mean no more than bread for the hungry—mere material abundance? Hardly. Poverty, of course, does mean a lack of goods. In fact, *ptochos* (the word for "poor" in the gospels) suggests serious want, even destitution (ibid., p. 16; Crossan, pp. 266-74). The Bible understands poverty realistically, however—as a matter of *social relations* first of all. The various Hebrew expressions for "the poor" denote not only a lack of possessions (a *techne* relationship), but also a social (*praxis*) relationship: contempt, inferiority, oppression, and violence. The poor are victims of the rich. Even though the woes may well not come from Jesus himself, they throw into relief the fact that rich and poor are not isolated groups of haves and have-nots. They stand in social relation.

"Woe to you who are full now. . . . Woe to you who laugh." What is wrong with satisfaction or laughter? we ask. Nothing. The point is not that there is something wrong about enjoying life. The point is that the rich (like "Dives") are living it up while the poor (like Lazarus) die of poverty (Luke 16,19-31).

Some believe that God's reign means material abundance in the Old Testament and merely interior blessings in the New. False. In both testaments it means new relationships between God and humans and among humans themselves. Therefore, it also means abundance. In both testaments, God comes as king to do *mishpat* and *sedaqah* and to establish *sedeq* and *shalom*. These are matters of *social relations*. Therefore Jesus says to the poor: "Seek first his reign and his justice and all these things shall be yours as well" (Matt 6,33).

Are the Poor Better?

If God sides with the poor against their oppressors, does this mean the poor are morally superior? Is there something meritorious in poverty and suffering? Does God hate the rich?

These questions miss the mark. The Bible sees nothing good or meritorious in poverty.[20] As we saw, when Jesus announces deliverance to the poor, neither the goodness of the poor nor the goodness of poverty are at issue, but the goodness of God.

The advantage of the poor at the time of the establishment of the reign of God finds its explanation, then, not in the justice or piety of these privileged ones, but in the justice of God, that

justice which God wants to manifest in making himself their
defender and their savior. (Dupont, *Béatitudes* 2:89)

Some poor *may* be more just or more submissive to God than their
violent oppressors. The point, however, is not that the poor have opted
for God but that God has opted for the poor. God takes their side
because they suffer injustice, and God is compassionate (ibid. 2:34,
49). The key here is not the subjective dispositions of the poor but
their objective oppression. The point is "the dispositions of God" (ibid.
2:15).

From this standpoint, attempts to find something meritorious in
the attitude of the poor smack of "works-righteousness" thinking,
with God rewarding some individuals for their dispositions rather
than liberating them for justice's sake, that is, out of gratuitous
compassion (*hesed, charis*) for the suffering.

Here as elsewhere, and in contrast to individualistic grace theology, the Bible relates "grace" directly to social relations. God comes
to judge and change everyone and everything, including social relations.

Neither does Jesus' God hate the rich. God loves everyone. But we
must force ourselves to think in terms of social relations. The point
is God's *option* for the poor in the face of a concrete and contingent
social situation, a social relation, that God finds abhorrent and that
the kingdom replaces. (I cannot agree with those who speak of God's
preferential *love* for the poor as though this were equivalent or
preferable to "option." Perhaps God does have a preferential love for
the poor, but that is another issue.)

But the poor are frequently as wicked as the rich, someone will say.
How can the kingdom be for them?

When a mother sees her younger child beaten by her older child,
she takes the side of the victim, regardless of the latter's behavior
and even though she loves both. That is how Jesus says God operates
(*see* Johnson, pp. 181-82). God responds to the objective injustice
regardless of the "goodness" or "badness" of the victim.

Today this would mean that God takes the side of the worker
abused at the factory. But when the worker returns home and abuses
his wife, God takes the side of the wife. This shows that being a victim
—like the abusive worker—does not automatically entitle one to
"enter" the kingdom. Jesus requires a response from his hearers.
They must break with the past (repent: Mark 1,15) and accept the
possibility and obligation of "kingdom living."[21]

Sin and Status

Forgiveness of personal sin was central to Jesus' ministry. Besides the poor, Jesus—and God—was gathering a second group of outcasts—the sinners.

The Sinners

First-century Jews expected God's coming to vindicate the poor and oppressed. The whole Old Testament spoke of that. But if God's option for the poor was understood, his option for sinners was not.

> There is nevertheless one category of disinherited ones which appears to secure [Jesus'] solicitude even more [than the poor]: the sinners, those rejected by a society officially dominated by the demands of the religious law.

Once again, the reason for this option is not the dispositions of the sinners (obviously) but the dispositions of God (Dupont, *Béatitudes* 2:219, 220; cf. Chapt. 5 *passim*). The explanation is grace, God's compassion for the suffering, for "sinners" in the gospels refers to social outcasts. For Jesus, Yahweh is a compassionate father who is gathering the outcasts—the poor, yes, but sinners, too—replacing the *social relationships* which separate not only rich and poor but also "righteous" and sinner.

Jesus' dealings with sinners—for example, his table-fellowship with tax collectors—were certainly offensive to many, if not downright subversive.[22] He (like John) required that the "righteous" also repent. He rejected the use of torah observance to sharply distinguish the righteous and the wicked.[23] From this perspective, the issue of ritual purity also has social implications.

Impurity

We cannot be sure of the social significance of ritual impurity in the Galilee of Jesus' day or even of Jesus' position on the matter (Riches, pp. 104-6, 128-29; Sanders, Chapt. 9; cf. Jeremias, *Theology*, pp. 204-11; Merkel, pp. 137-41). Nevertheless, purity regulations, too, even if not morally obligatory, probably contributed to status stratification, creating second-class Israelites in the eyes of some.

In Galilee, purity rights and sabbath observation probably served to distinguish first-class Jews from Hellenizers and Gentiles.[24] Such practices reflected a priestly theological outlook which Sadducees, Essenes, and Pharisees all shared. This outlook failed to stress, as did the prophets, the frequent conflict between cultic observance and compassion toward those in need (Riches, pp. 67-77; Borg, Chapt. 5). The risk here was to give greater importance to ritual observance connected to cult in the Jerusalem temple (the chief symbol of national identity) than to the vindication of poor Galilean peasants and those in need generally (Riches, p. 118).

For his part, Jesus summarized the torah in the *two* great commandments (Matt 22,40) and the Golden Rule (Matt 7,12). God is more concerned with compassion toward the needy than with ritual observance (Matt 9,13; 12,7). One's relationship with God depends on one's social relationships.

The Community with No Outcasts

Jesus' treatment of sinners and ritual issues falls within the broad context of his attack on self-exaltation and status-stratification in general: God's reign belongs to insignificant children (Mark 10,14-15). Jesus criticizes self-promotion (phylacteries), taking the highest places (Luke 14,7-11), and leaders, both religious (Matt 23,5-12) and political (Luke 22,24-27), who dominate others. Leaders must be servants of all (Mark 9,35), for those who exalt themselves will be humbled (Luke 14,11; etc.). To love "enemies" meant to love people considered wicked outcasts (Riches, pp. 133-35).[25]

We can only understand the unity of Jesus' message if we grasp its social significance: God (with Jesus) is establishing a new community, a people of God for the new age. God's reign brings new social relations (*see* Nolan, Chapts. 8 and 9). Therefore it means food for the hungry, consolation for the afflicted and friendship for outcast sinners.

Small wonder Jesus focused greatest attention on *the poor* and *the despised sinner*, who stand for all the outcasts.[26] His message is a unity. God comes as compassionate ruler to abolish a society divided into rich and poor (Luke 6,20-26; Mark 10,23-27) on the one hand and "righteous" and "sinner" on the other. The solution to the one problem is for the rich to share their belongings with the poor, as Zacchaeus did; the solution to the other is for everyone to recognize they are sinners, accept forgiveness, and forgive others.

"The poor" stands for other outcasts, as well, indeed for all outcasts: Jesus' healings help reintegrate *the sick* (especially the leper) and the *possessed* into the community (Mark 1). His enhancement of the status of *women* is particularly striking.[27] He apparently rejected the authoritarian patriarchal household of his day. The new community is to be a family of mothers, brothers and sisters (no earthly father!) (Mark 3,31-35 par. Matt 23,9; cf. Mark 10,29-30; Schüssler Fiorenza, *In Memory of Her,* Chapt. 4; Crossan, pp. 299-302; Borg, pp. 133-35).

Neither can there be a new community if *children* (Mark 9,36-37 par.; Mark 10,13-16 par.) and *the simple and uneducated* (Matt 11,25-27) continue to be devalued.[28]

Finally, in God's time, *Gentiles* will enter the kingdom. Meanwhile, Jesus shows an openness to both Samaritans and Gentiles.[29] The divine compassion for suffering and degraded persons is the key to Jesus' message: God is raising up the lowly and gathering all into a new community with no outcasts or second-class citizens. As we have stressed throughout this book, salvation is a new community. So, too, for Jesus. God offers to all the possibility to live together in a new way, requiring only that each accepts this gift and assumes the kingdom behavior which God makes possible.

But new ages and new communities threaten old ones.

Jesus and Politics

Jesus did not seek power. He was not the warrior-messiah many expected to liberate Israel from Rome. He and his group adopted neither the strategy nor the tactics of resistance fighters. It is undeniable, nonetheless, that Jesus had political expectations. The powerful had good reason to perceive the good news for the poor as bad news for them.

The political import of Jesus' ministry follows from his understanding of God's partiality toward the poor and the outcast. Replacing unjust relations entails both new persons (conversion) and a new social order where the politics of service replaces the politics of domination (Mark 10,42; Luke 13,32).

This hope was for all Israel, not some sectarian conventicle. To the consternation of his enemies, Jesus stirred the masses. He was not simply a teacher, but the founder and leader of a renewal movement.[30] He was gathering a new people of God and probably expected God to reconstitute Israel with a new covenant (Jer 31,31): The social order will be transformed (or replaced). The Twelve will "judge" the tribes of Israel (Matt 19,28; *see also* Matt 20,20-28).[31] The destroyed temple will be replaced. The earth will be renewed.

However, Jesus did not view national restoration in terms of war against the Romans. He rather sized up the situation like a new Jeremiah. While his contemporaries expected God to destroy the Romans, Jesus foresaw the destruction of Jerusalem at the hands of the Gentiles (Borg, pp. 161-63; Nolan, pp. 17-19, 86). Why? Because of the infidelity of Israel, especially its "shepherds." This time the trouble was not the worship of Astarte or Baal but of Mammon. As it always had been, the problem was again the trampling of the weak.[32] Like the prophets of old, Jesus recognized there could be no national security without social justice—and no authentic temple worship, either.

Jesus' protest in the temple—where economic, social, and religious power converged—in the spirit of Jeremiah (cf. Jer 7) probably served as the immediate provocation for his death.[33] But it climaxed an entire ministry of provocation (Sobrino, *Jesucristo liberador,* Chapt. 7). Jesus announced a new age in which the last will be first, the first last; for God exalts the humble and humbles the mighty. He denounced the pretensions of the "righteous" and ritually pure; he undermined traditional family authority; above all, he declared that God was now taking up the cause of the poor and outcast and was about to institute a new social order: no more poverty, no more hunger. He may have proclaimed the debt release and land reform of the Jubilee year. All this would not only threaten the Jewish establishment but surely arouse the Romans, as well.[34] Thus, although Jesus was not an insurgent, there was good reason for the Jewish leaders to present him to Pilate as one and for the Romans to formally execute him as one.

The Final Consummation

Jesus apparently expected divine intervention to establish the reign of God soon.[35] Just *what* he expected is hotly debated. As we saw, Jesus accepted that current of apocalyptic thought according to which God's coming as king provoked conflict with the reign of Satan, a conflict which, according to the usual understanding, would soon reach a crisis point before the God's reign should arrive (Matt 23,32; Luke 22,53). Persecution would try the faith of those who welcomed God's kingdom. Jesus apparently foresaw at least the destruction of Jerusalem by the Romans (to say nothing of wider catastrophe or angelic participation) should Israel fail to accept God's mercy as Jesus proclaimed it. Following resurrection and judgment, however, God's reign would usher in the fullness of life, possibly in a restored nation of Israel, but in any case, a new social order—a new world—in which Gentiles would also share (*see* Jeremias, *Theology,* pp. 127-31, 241-49).[36]

Matter and Spirit

Jesus did not await a future kingdom in heaven to be inhabited by souls.[37] He surely shared the belief of most of his contemporaries in the resurrection of the dead (Sanders, p. 237),[38] but this meant the whole person. The gospels know of no anthropological dualism and have no doctrine of the immortality of the soul. When Jesus speaks of saving one's *psuche* (Mark 8,35), he means enjoying the fullness of life God intended for human beings. The life in question is always the life of the body, of the whole person; the *psuche* never exists independent of the body. On the other hand, this life is more than mere health and wealth, for it is always lived in relationship to the Author of life. So, in the Bible, "Salvation is always salvation from anything that might hamper the development of this life, whether it be death and sickness or unbelief and sin."[39] God saves *the whole person.*[40]

"Thy Will Be Done on Earth"

Besides this biblical "materialism," the bulk of evidence suggests that, for Jesus and the synoptic gospels, if not the New Testament as a whole, God's kingdom comes to earth. "Thy kingdom come; thy will be done on earth" (Matt 6,10).[41] All prophetic and much apocalyptic literature agree on this point. "The meek [*'anawim*] will possess the earth" (Matt 5,5; cf. Ps 37,11).[42] With the coming judgment and resurrection, the rupture with the old eon will be complete. Still, for Jesus, and in contrast to eschatological traditions we know, the new eon was beginning in his ministry— even before the total rupture—as a seed which will produce abundant harvest, as leaven fermenting the whole mass. "The reign of God is (already) among you" (Luke 17,21). There would be continuity between what the disciples experienced in the present and what the kingdom would come to be in all its fullness.[43]

This hardly divests the kingdom of its transcendence. Although the reign of God will happen in history, life will be radically transformed, not just reformed. It will not be history just as we know it. "They will be like the angels" (Mark 18,25), experiencing no death or need for reproduction. Patriarchs will rise from the dead and dine with Gentiles in what can only be a "new world."

Such expectations surely tax the modern mind and saddle us with a burden of interpretation for today. But we must clearly distinguish our interpretation from Jesus' message. While he does announce the end of the age, nowhere does he announce the "end of history" or the "end of the world" or the "end of time" or a kingdom "outside time."

Those who characterize Jesus' expectations in these terms incur a heavy burden of argumentation they rarely assume.

Most argue that the crucifixion and resurrection, the delay of Jesus' return, and the location of Christian communities outside Israel quickly transformed Jesus' more earthly kingdom into a more "spiritual" one in later New Testament texts. While there is some truth in this, I believe commentators often exaggerate the spiritualizing of early Christian eschatology. We cannot pursue the issue further here, but most evidence suggests the early church shared Jesus' hope for a new community of bodily persons in a transfigured world.[44]

Unfortunately, the new world did not arrive as Jesus seems to have expected.

Divine and Human Action: Faith

Up to now, we have failed to address one question posed earlier. If Jesus proclaimed God's deliverance of the poor, was he not mistaken? Almost two thousand years have passed since he pronounced the beatitudes, and we would be hard pressed to affirm that the liberation has occurred in the sense he expected. It gives some comfort, however, and a starting point in the search for answers, to realize that Jesus and his disciples faced fundamentally the same questions as ourselves: "Where is your God?" "O Lord, how long?"

The way he understood the relationship between divine and human action in his own ministry throws light on the situation with which the delay of the kingdom presents us. But first we must put to rest a common misunderstanding that would allow us to escape too easily from the challenge posed by this question.

The Poor Will Not Always Be with You

Did not Jesus predict "The poor you will have with you always"? And does this not call into question the understanding of God's reign presented here? It would, but in fact, as quoted, the text crassly mistranslates the Greek original of Mark 14,7 par. in a way that has spawned warped interpretations for centuries. Whether or not some form of the saying in question goes back to Jesus, the gospels do not say "The poor you *will* always have with you." The Greek (and most modern translations) reads, "The poor you always have with you," in the *present* tense (*echete*). The sense is: As a matter of fact, "the poor you have around you all the time"; therefore, "whenever you will, you can do good to them; but you do not always have me." In the text,

Jesus makes a factual observation about the poor, not a prediction. Although the poor are around all the time, Jesus soon will not be around; so, the extravagant anointing of his feet is a fitting "good work."

Our interpretation makes it unlikely that the text refers to Deut 15,11: "For the poor will never cease out of the land." Even there, however, verses 4-5 of the same chapter read: "But there will be no poor among you . . . if only you will obey the voice of the Lord your God." In other words, in Deut 15 poverty is the fruit of sin. Jesus (and "Mark") also surely believed that the definitive coming of God's reign would end both sin and poverty. Recalling Deut 15, 4-5, the author of Acts notes that poverty disappeared in the first Christian community: "There was not a needy person among them" (Acts 4,34).

Faith: Accepting God's Gift

Jesus' expectation of God's intervention hardly precluded human action. The action required was love, love which speaks the truth, denounces lies, heals and gathers the outcast, embraces enemies and, in Jesus' case, organizes a renewal movement. Jesus insisted, however, on a decisive first step, or fundamental posture, called "faith."

He apparently saw God's intervention as *already* beginning ("I saw Satan fall like lightning" [Luke 10,18][45]), but God would not reign by force. God would work through human beings. People could either refuse God's offer of the kingdom or accept it. Acceptance, or "faith," allowed the power of God to work through believers. Faith was what turned the power of God loose.

Jesus saw the power of God at work, beginning to transform the world, not only in his healings and exorcisms, but also in those from whom he evoked faith ("Your faith has saved you!" [Mark 5,34 par.; 10,52 par.; Luke 7,50; 17,19]). The realization of God's reign in Jesus' table fellowship with the disciples implies a certain fusion of divine and human action, including the disciples' action. Their mutual forgiveness mediates God's forgiveness (Matt 6,12). Many sayings (Luke 9,62; Matt 7,13-14; Mark 7,15; 10,15; Matt 5,44-48) seem to link the experience of the kingdom with a human response (Perrin, *Jesus and the Language of the Kingdom,* p. 54; cf. pp. 160, 168, 196; Jeremias, *Theology,* pp. 230, 254; Beasley-Murray, Excursus 2).

You of Little Faith

However, the evidence suggests that the crowds who marveled at Jesus' preaching and his healings generally failed to accept his message of repentance and unselfish love. "Then he began to reproach the cities in which most of his deeds of power had been done, because they did not repent" (Matt 11,20; cf. 11,16-19 par.). Jesus demanded a "faith" which meant breaking with egoism and accepting the new way of life. But this faith seems to have been a rare commodity, perhaps to Jesus' own surprise: "generation without faith" (Mark 9,19 par.), "you of little faith" (Matt 6,30 par.; 16,8 par.; 17,20; cf. Mark 6,6.52; 8,21; Matt 8,26 par.; 14,31 par.). He hurled these imprecations especially at the disciples. They, too, failed to muster the faith which the moment demanded.

In some ways, they had reasons to doubt. Jesus' ragged band of followers (Acts 1,15 speaks of 120 in the upper room) and some exorcisms hardly looked like the "kingdom of God" people expected. Jesus had announced the liberation of the poor (Luke 7,22b; cf. 4,18-19; 6,20); but the present signs of the kingdom were more humble and personal healings (Luke 7,22a). Opponents demanded a sign from heaven that he was the awaited one (Mark 8,11-12 par.; etc.). Even John the Baptist seems to have doubted.

Jesus responded to doubters with the parables of the mustard seed, leaven, the seed growing slowly: These humble healings and unassuming tactics are only the beginnings of the spectacular blessings which God will soon reveal (see Jeremias, The Parables of Jesus, pp. 149-51; Beasley-Murray, pp. 124-25).

The poor response probably frustrated Jesus and may have provoked a crisis for him (see Sobrino, Christology, pp. 41, 58-59, 68; idem., Jesucristo liberador, pp. 259-62; see also Dodd, Chapts. 7 and 8). He might well have been tempted to overcome the apparent failure by responding to popular appeal for spectacle, to the cry for bread (alone), or even the clamor for a traditional political leader (they were like sheep without a shepherd, Matt 9,36).[46] In that case, the temptations (Matt 4,1-11) and Jesus' ministry as a whole present him continually rejecting the usual demagogic means to win followers and usher in the new community.[47]

This crisis of meager results may have led Jesus to curtail the healings. He probably directed more attention to the small group who did follow him; and in Jerusalem he eventually dramatically confronted the powerful who opposed his message. But otherwise, he seems to have clung to his original strategy of demanding a personal response in faith to God's coming reign.

What was this faith that Jesus demanded?

The Meaning of Faith

For Jesus, faith means relying totally on God, placing oneself entirely in "the Father's" hands.[48] But faith is not passive; it is no opiate. It rather removes the fear and worry which paralyze action, especially in the face of opposition and insecurity. "Do not be afraid; only believe!" (Mark 5,36; Luke 8,50; cf. Matt 8,26; Mark 4,40; Luke 8,25). It refuses to doubt deliverance (Matt 21,21), even in the face of overwhelming odds. It counts on God's power to erupt *in* the doing (and waiting) to supply where human effort lacks (Matt 13,44-46; cf. Mark 6,45-52; Luke 5,1-11). Anyone who has experienced this way of life among the poor has sensed the extraordinary power of such faith to inspire action and perseverance under trial. Faith alone—faith in action—brings about the future.

Faith expects results—surprises—in the form of deliverance in concrete situations of sickness, hunger, mental affliction (possession), injustice. In the healing stories, faith does not invoke a magical power which suspends the laws of nature but a power which transforms a situation from within[49] (much as the traditional theology of grace suggests). Jesus said it could move mountains (Mark 11,22-24 par; Matt 17,20; Luke 17,6), that all things are possible for it (Mark 9,23).

Faith is not a private matter. First, it comes from contagion, in the encounter with another believer, like Jesus who evoked it: "Your faith has saved you!" Second, faith represents the power to establish the new community and the social, economic, and political conditions it requires—in the face of the "anti-reign" of the dying age.

In one early tradition Jesus urges the *poor* not to worry about what to eat or wear and not to fear those who could only kill the body. In another, he exhorts victims to turn the other cheek and bless those who cursed them, and all to freely give to those in need without hope of return (Luke 6,27-36; 12, 22-34).[50]

Lohfink is probably right when he suggests that God's reign arrived precisely where such faith and love thrived, in the communities, for example, like those to whom Paul and the others wrote their letters. It is perhaps because these communities eliminated poverty from their midst through sharing that we hear relatively little in the epistles about caring for the poor. "There were no poor among them" (Acts 4,34).[51]

The radical character of faith as a new way of being suggests at how deep a level God works change. The coming of God's reign transcends institutional change—although it must include it. Faith points to the transformation of persons' and communities' entire way of being in the world. It goes to the root of existence, of persons, of history. It points to new human beings, a new creation. This is probably why God's has proven to be a slow revolution. It respects human freedom. This, I believe, is largely why Jesus patiently stuck to the low road of service which eventually demonstrated to him and later New Testament writers that the reign of God manifests itself efficaciously only in cross and resurrection, what theology calls the Paschal Mystery in which all are invited to share.

The Great Delay

God's revolution can be refused. Our reflections suggest that we can trace the Great Delay of the social transformation Jesus expected to the Great Refusal—to "believe" in this synoptic sense. In that case, however, *if* this faith is possible today for human beings, then God still offers unlimited possibilities for the kingdom to come "soon." That undercuts much of the pessimism and reliance on force (deterrence) characteristic of Christian "realism" of both left and right. This realism is commendably clear-eyed about selfishness and sin but unrealistic about the power of God to bring about changes in history.[52] It is also important to remind those who affirm, rightly, that the reign of God is wholly God's initiative that God works through human beings (including atheists) with "faith" during this extended wait of ours.

This reflection on faith in the Jesus-tradition has obviously moved us beyond historical inquiry about Jesus and into his meaning for us today. We can separate exegesis and hermeneutics only in limit cases. Faith and discipleship in Jesus' ministry speaks to faith and discipleship today.

Conclusion: The Reign of God Today

Jesus announced that God was beginning a social transformation in Israel. The poor are special beneficiaries of God's saving action, not because they are good (much less because misery has value in itself), but because God is good and takes compassion on the suffering. There will be no more poverty, hunger, or tears. Not that God's reign means only bread. God's is an "integral" revolution which includes the heart, the body, new social relations, a new social order. God's coming in power means a community with no outcasts or devalued members, a community of *sedeq, mishpat, sedaqah, shalom.*

God's reign therefore embraces outcast sinners, all sinners (including oppressors), with the offer of forgiveness.

The fundamental reason the reign of God means what it means is to be found in the identity of the One who reigns: the God of *sedeq* who will no longer tolerate abuse of the weak and who comes with compassion (*hesed*) on behalf of the poor and sinners.

This God comes to save the whole person, and not to bring us to an ethereal heaven or to outer space, but to transform this world into, or replace it with, a new sky and a new earth, raising the dead that they might share abundant life.

The offer of a new way to live together can be refused. God will bring about the new world by working through those who accept the divine amnesty in "faith" in order to assume the kingdom way of life.

At this historical distance, we can appreciate Jesus' frustration that God's revolution is painfully slow. The faith which accepts God's working and the human love which channels it seem as hard to come by today as in Galilee 2,000 years ago.

What does the reign of God mean today, especially for the poor? What does Jesus' ministry and message say to that? We have constructed a hypothesis, partial and tentative, about Jesus.[53] Nonetheless, because Jesus is the same yesterday, today, and forever (Heb 13,8), believers need to allow such images of the historical Jesus (our best tries) to help them hear the risen Christ today in the *kerugma* proclaimed in the churches and in the world. How can the historical Jesus we have "discovered" serve faith today? I can think of three ways.

In the first place, our findings should contribute to understanding later New Testament traditions themselves. Naturally, these must speak for themselves; but when we interpret them, we must be aware of the traditions from which *they* developed, traditions which are part of their literary environment, lest we make unwarranted assumptions—for example, excessively "spiritualizing" Christian hope in later texts.

In the second place, and of greater importance for our time, our findings help us rule out theological appeals to Jesus which fail to account for his proclamation as the elimination of poverty and injustice and the establishment of a community of basic equality. No one who wishes to base a theology on New Testament traditions can ignore Jesus' own social and material expectations. In fact, today's situation requires that the liberating and egalitarian elements of the reign of God Jesus proclaimed take precedence over regressive or less appropriate New Testament traditions in the development of today's theology and pastoral practice. This is more obvious in some cases ("Slaves obey your masters" [1 Pet 2,18] and "Let women keep silence in the churches" [1 Cor 14,34]) than in others ("Anyone who resists the authorities resists what God has appointed" [Rom 13,2]). History demonstrates that any theology and pastoral practice that is faithful to the Gospel has always developed through the selection and creative use of those traditions of the past which best served the needs of the present. In fact, the Bible itself came to be in just this way.[54]

In the third place, our image of the historical Jesus can help us write the Gospel according to Us—for our time.[55] *Today* the words and (much more) the actions of Christians must proclaim that God's saving gift is abundant life in a community with no outcasts or despised members.

We can agree with Perrin and Bultmann that Jesus' proclamation of the kingdom expresses an "understanding-of-existence" (*see* Perrin, *Jesus and the Language,* pp. 10-12, 36; Bultmann, pp. 51-56), or a "way of being-in-the-world" (Tracy, *Blessed Rage,* pp. 214-23) and that today, too, we can and must re-present Jesus' proclamation as the possibility of a new way of being-in-the-world. However, we must present God's offer—as Jesus in fact did—as a new way of being-*together*-in-the-world.[56] The self-offer of God, in and through our concrete situation (as Rahner would say), confronts us today as the offer of a new way to live together.

God's reign presents itself at the same time as a way of being-together-*against*-the world. God's reign clashes with the anti-reign, with its principalities and powers, its unjust systems, institutions, and human agents (Sobrino, *Jesucristo liberador,* Excursus 1). As Sobrino says, human society (let us say, Western civilization) is not only *not yet* God's reign; it is *certainly not* God's reign. It is rather dominated by injustice, lies, and violence and in direct conflict with God's reign.

Jesus spoke about God's reign, which meant, first of all, about *God.* This symbol of "God's reign" means many different things in different times and places (Perrin, *Jesus and the Language, passim; see* Meier, *A Marginal Jew* 2:240-42). But there are limits to the flexibility.[57] More than anything else, the identity and fidelity of the God of the Bible impose these limits. Faithful re-presentation of Jesus' message today—especially in a world where poor children die preventable deaths every day—must build on the core meaning of that symbol: The "reign of God" refers to the activity of the divine *go'el,* the liberator, who takes the side of the poor and the weak, not because of their merits or even their faith, but because they suffer and God is just and compassionate. Any faithful re-presentation of Jesus' message today must include this social and political message of liberation—not because we must repeat the message in the same words in each epoch or because God is completely unchangeable, but because the God of Jesus remains the compassionate and faithful God of *mishpat* and *sedaqah.*

7

GOD'S REVOLUTION

Once More, the Three Paradigms

For all its denial, our age, like none before, knows how endemic injustice is. We know that torture is almost routine in many countries and unnecessary death a daily occurrence everywhere. We are aware of massive poverty, sexual and racial discrimination, and environmental crisis, and we know they are human creations. Today more than ever, the cry of the poor challenges Christians to explain what the gospel means for the victims of history.

Christian theology has made recent progress in spelling out the relationship between Christian hope and social liberation. We have seen that the Catholic tradition has emancipatory potential. It can and must speak of salvation as the liberation of the poor, even if salvation is more than social liberation and not every liberation is God's work.

But we have a long way to go, as the ambiguities and contradictions in official church documents demonstrate. Some of these documents reaffirm, and others backtrack on, the Latin American bishops' statement at Medellín that "the divine work is an action of integral liberation and human development at every level."

We examined the roots of this "disputed question" by tracing a paradigm shift in three representative thinkers, Jacques Maritain, Karl Rahner, and Gustavo Gutiérrez, all of whom continue to exercise great influence in and beyond the Roman Catholic community.

We studied how each paradigm construes the relationships between nature and grace (secular and salvation history), matter and spirit, divine and human action, and how each understands the social character of the human condition and eschatology.

146

The Traditional Paradigm

Maritain articulates the classic pre-Vatican II paradigm. He distinguishes the temporal and spiritual orders in order to unite them, presenting God's grace as necessary for any integral achievement of social justice.

The traditional paradigm radically distinguishes human liberation from salvation, however. Social justice prepares for salvation and results from actions inspired by grace, but social justice is not salvation, not even one aspect of it. The temporal common good is a purely natural good. Salvation in history, on the other hand, is a matter of individual persons and of the church. Therefore, overcoming injustice and building community in history is not what God—and God's church—is chiefly about. The church has a principal religious task, entrusted mainly to the clergy, of directly promoting the ultimate supernatural goal of salvation and a secondary secular task, entrusted to the laity, of directly promoting justice in the world. What God redeems in society travels a historical path "parallel" to that of the church, to converge with it in the reign of God. However, the concrete fruits of human enterprise will not themselves share in that final victory.

The Aggiornamento Paradigm

We criticized Maritain's (largely implicit) theology of grace. He held a modified version of the "extrinsicism" opposed by *aggiornamento* theologians. For their most important representative, Karl Rahner, God's self-offer constitutes the "horizon" of human existence, so that salvation embraces every dimension of existence, interior and exterior, material and spiritual, personal, social, political. No really human good, including social justice, fails to partake of the ultimate human good. In that case, we argued, one can speak of salvation in three senses: justification, or the indwelling of the Holy Spirit; moral acts (love); and the fruits of these (justice, peace). Rahner considers every truly human good to be graced, a partial and ambiguous manifestation of God's reign, a blessing of salvation. We later saw that Jesus, too, used "reign of God" to refer to the blessings which God's saving activity brings about.

The traditional paradigm also suffers from an inadequate appreciation of human sociality and characterizes the dynamism of human spirit as a movement away from matter and toward intransitive activity. These are two sides of a coin: If the self transcends from matter to God, it realizes itself by transcending away from others.

Aggiornamento theology, represented by Rahner, has a stronger understanding of the social character of human existence—and of salvation. First, because of the unity of the cosmos at every level, grace and salvation overflow the individual, traveling the lines of created mediations to the others. Secondly, the idea that the human person (spirit) actualizes itself in interaction with the world overcomes both matter-spirit dualism and individualism at a stroke. The person transcends to God by transcending, in love and freedom, into the world of others. Since, as Rahner puts it, the divine self-bestowal and human transcendence together constitute the deepest drama of history, secular and salvation history are coextensive and interpenetrating. Divine and human action fuse in a unique form of causality. To accept God's gift of a new way to live together is to assume the task it requires. Finally, Rahner's anthropology gives the fruits of human labor and social forms, transfigured, a place in the final victory of God.

On the negative side, liberal theologies of the North, like Rahner's, typically understate the weight of social sin. In addition, even when they strongly affirm sociality, they usually lack a solid social theory which could help them diagnose social sin and point toward realizable, contingent utopias. This perpetuates the traditional inability of grace-theology to relate God's saving action effectively and directly to society.

The Liberation Paradigm

Whereas the *aggiornamento* paradigm starts from the liberation of the average (abstract) individual, liberation theology begins with the widespread injustice suffered by the poor majorities, especially in the poor South, and with movements of liberation. Liberation theology recognizes that institutional liberation is not enough. As Gutiérrez insists, structural change must be part of a deeper process in which new persons and new social relations arise. These utopian notions bridge the theoretical gap between structural liberation and salvation.

For liberation theology, as for Rahner, salvation embraces all human beings and the whole human being. But with Gutiérrez, salvation language is social from the start: God *con*vokes to *com*munion. The deepest meaning of history is liberation from sin and for communion with God and others. There are not two histories parallel and converging, but one process of liberation, with its progress and reversals, within which one must distinguish levels of meaning. From this standpoint, talk of two orders is misleading. For liberation theology, therefore, as already for Rahner, the secular good—social justice—is a religious concern in the strict sense.

In contrast to irenic liberal theologies, however, liberation theology has a deep appreciation for social sin and conflict. It locates the grace-nature relationship within a grace-sin dialectic. The ability to name sin gives this theology greater historical concreteness. Salvation is the deepest meaning of liberation from historically specific sin. Salvation takes its social and political character from the concrete forms of social and political sin of a given time and place. We experience partial realizations of God's reign in ambiguous historical liberations.

On the other hand, we need to hear more from theologians like Gutiérrez about the transitory nature of all human achievement and its tendency to corruption. Moreover, although Gutiérrez's rich reflections on Job and spirituality show a deep appreciation of the implications of faith for chronic setbacks in the struggle for freedom, these reflections beg to be integrated into the theology of the threefold liberation process, a formulation which is rightly becoming a classic metaphor for the relationship between salvation and political liberation.

Gutiérrez's reflections on eschatology (promise and fulfillment) illuminate historical experience. But he says little about the final outcome of history, a fact which reflects in part his lack of a well-articulated anthropology. Rahner's anthropology leads him to appealing hypotheses, in general agreement with the New Testament, about the continuity between the struggle for justice and the final victory of God.

Moving Forward

Examining the paradigm shift suggested directions for further development, some of which we pursued in Chapter 5. First, we saw how feminist theology challenges male theologians to think of liberation less in terms of flight and to think of communion, the goal of liberation, more in terms of healing and reconciliation with body, nature and earth. Ellacuría's and Zubiri's understanding of the human person and of God's transcendence *in* history may do a better job of overcoming dualism than Rahner's transcendental anthropology.

Secondly, our study of the paradigm shift left us with the need to articulate a better understanding of the social character of human life. In fact, from many different perspectives, contemporary thought confirms that human existence is social in a stronger sense than the dominant thinking in the West has affirmed: Human beings constitute themselves in social interaction and in work. Humanization occurs as they struggle to overcome mere stimulus and dehumanizing social relations in order to be free to love and to live in communion. In that case, salvation occurs in that struggle.

These and other factors lead us to criticize the way traditional theology frequently over-values contemplation, especially as flight, and under-values social praxis. On the other hand, we must be wary of the hyperactive conceptions of human being and action common to modern ideologies. While human beings forge themselves in sociopolitical interaction, this interaction humanizes when it integrates transitive action with receptivity, contemplation and gratitude.

Neither is salvation the same as evolutionary progress. As exodus was for Israel, Jesus' paschal mystery serves for Christians as the fundamental pattern for liberation. Salvation typically occurs in the midst of failure and defeat and as a resurrection from the dead. That is what it takes for a new society with new human beings, for a new community which emerges more from "below" (from the powerless) than from "above." God even saves in situations which do not, objectively, permit social liberation.

The radically social character of the human condition explains why "technical" relations are less central than "praxical" (social) relations. We can understand neither work nor poverty nor liberation correctly if we interpret them primarily in terms of *techne*. The liberal (or even classical) focus on the individual reduces work to a relationship with nature, political liberation to structural change, and poverty to a lack of things. In this way, work, political liberation and property relations are "materialized" and removed from the "order of redemption." Individualism fails to perceive that work, liberation and poverty are first of all questions of social relations (*praxis*) and as such affairs of the human spirit. Injustice, which is a lack of love, is a spiritual issue. It is therefore through social relations that divine Spirit transforms work, structures, and property relations—something Jesus saw with consummate clarity.

The God of the Bible

The Bible speaks about a God who is love (*hesed, agape*) and who does *sedaqah* and *mishpat*—who sets free the oppressed—and establishes *shalom. Sedeq, mishpat,* and *shalom* govern right *social relations.* They undo wrong social relations to create community. As virtues, they are central to Yahweh's identity and, as values, to Yahweh's "reign."

Liberation, new persons in new social relations, a new community: This *is* salvation. In this integral sense, social justice, however "secular" in its tactics and strategy, is the quintessential *religious* question, the central preoccupation of Yahweh.

These are the roots of Jesus' announcement of God's coming as king. When he proclaimed God's reign, he meant that God was coming to free the poor and oppressed from their material and social chains— not because the poor are righteous but because God is righteous (*saddiq*) and shows mercy to the oppressed.

This is the social meaning of grace: God's gratuitous option in favor of victims, God's rejection of unjust social relations and offer of life in genuine community. In God's name, Jesus was gathering Israel's outcasts into a new community of equals. This meant life in its fullness in a transfigured world. It meant a moral and social revolution for Israel, in which the nations would one day share. The socioreligious powers of the day perceived this project as a threat, and they killed Jesus for his fidelity to it.

Jesus saw God working through human beings who have *faith,* a basic life-stance that overcomes fear and allows God to build community by means of the human praxis of love.

Jesus' hope was transcendent: It was the active presence of God in the world; it was the new age of the resurrection. But the evidence suggests that no matter how transcendent, the new world he expected to reign was a sociopolitical reality.

What does this mean for believers today? It means that when God's project finally triumphs over the counter-project of death, then, whatever form it takes, this triumph will mean life shared together in a new world. In other words, Christian hope answers to the sufferings of history and to the deepest longings of human beings for life and community. Finally, there is an intrinsic connection between the struggles and achievements of human beings and the promise of revelation.

The Church in the Divine Revolution

Our conclusion, then, is that God is working an integral revolution, a revolution at every level of human (and nonhuman) being: personal (and impersonal), interpersonal, social, economic, political and ecclesial. The reign of God confronts us in and through our everyday experience in all its concreteness and ordinariness. It confronts us as the offer of God's self-communication, which is at the same time the offer of a new way of being-together-in-the-world.

Liberation in history is a partial and ambiguous (sinful and grace-ful) mediation of salvation, but genuine liberation points ahead to a final, definitive consummation. The advance of God's reign is not easy to chart (Luke 17,20-23). Yet the reign of God is among us, and its protagonists and victors are more often than not the victims of this world.

We speak of "revolution" because the transformation is both radical and conflictual. God's revolution (*res novae*) makes all things new (Rev 21,5); it is a new creation (2 Cor 5,17; Gal 6,15), a new earth and sky—a new world—where justice dwells (2 Pet 3,13; Rev 21,1).

More than others, this revolution demands personal conversion, the death of the "old self" and the birth of the "new human being" (Eph 2,15; 4,22-24; cf. Rom 6,1-11). Real conversion manifests itself in sacrificial love and new social relations of mutuality and equality between women and men, adults and children, workers and profes-sionals, people of different races and sexual orientations. But new social relations require the support of economic, political, and cul-tural institutions—a new social order which makes it easier for people to love their neighbor (Peter Maurin) and which no longer punishes generosity and rewards selfishness.

Institutions, in their turn, function within social systems. If com-munism has failed as a social system, "real existing capitalism," especially the neoliberal variety, has hardly proven itself a viable framework for community. We must not only protest and resist the new world disorder, but also build, from "below" and locally, viable alternatives, seeds of an economy of solidarity and community that can meet basic needs and in which those who depend on the means of production can hold the managers of the means of production accountable, democratically.[1]

Like other revolutions, God's revolution is conflictual and subject to setbacks. The form of this world—its injustice, disrespect for the poor, and reliance on violence—is passing away (1 Cor 7,31), but not peacefully. If Christ transforms culture (Niebuhr), the transforma-tion is not modern evolutionary progress. Irenic, world-affirming Catholic theology needs to come to terms with what sectarian "Christ-against-culture" Christianity affirms in agreement with the New Testament: The world fiercely opposes God's grace.[2] The gospels portray the mortal clash of two kingdoms: A project for life encounters a project for death. Every social "order" rises on the bones of its victims and resists justice with violence. God's revolution counters this with the "violence" of nonviolent resistance and truth-telling.

The demand for conversion and the low road of nonviolent sacrifi-cial service make this a slow and painful revolution, despite all its flashings-forth of grace. And yet it is a joyful revolution because of the efficacious presence of God and the assurance, often half-conscious, of final victory.

If the sectarians, Augustine, and Luther can teach Catholic theology about sin and conflict, they frequently fail to appreciate the efficaciousness of grace in history. It is true that things are much worse than we ordinarily imagine; but they are also much better. While sin and concupiscence abound, God's grace abounds all the more. A hard-headed "Christian realism" which takes account only of pervasive sin but denies God the ability to change both hearts and society is not realistic enough about the power of God in history. In the face of relentless evil, Christians expect God's surprises to erupt in history. Catholic theology has traditionally detected these—the presence of the future—in the lives of the saints. It needs to recognize them also in Gandhi's liberation campaigns, the U.S. Civil Rights movement, the women's movement, the fall of tyranny in East Germany, the Enda Revolution in the Philippines, the repopulated communities of El Salvador and in social transformation in Haiti and South Africa.

To say that God liberates all humanity by taking the side of the oppressed means that those who abuse the poor must sooner or later answer to God for them. It also means that the final victory is assured. As Martin Luther King used to say, "the arc of the moral universe is long, but it bends towards justice," and "truth crushed to earth will rise again."[3] To say that God takes the side of the poor implies, finally, that those who claim to believe in God and follow Jesus must assume the cause of the poor, which is the cause of all, and the destiny of the poor as their own.

The Church's Role

At the close of the twentieth century, it is difficult to see far into the future. But it is not difficult to hear the cry of the poor (and women and other marginalized groups) growing more insistent. History's victims are waking up in ever greater numbers, and they will not easily fall back to sleep again. Their cry will, or should, set the church's agenda for as far ahead as we can see. Theology and practice which respond to that cry is no passing fashion. A church that fails to respond will be irrelevant to the next century.

God's revolution faces obstacles in the church. Besides our more obvious vices, perhaps the greatest is the lack of faith, as Jesus understood it. But there is also the failure of Christians to engage in nonviolent resistance of the "culture of death" and the failure of the church to consider the promotion of justice as a central and nonnegotiable aspect of its mission.

Paul warned against not resisting, but rather conforming to this *saeculum* (Rom 12,2). It is all too easy for the church and the institutions it promotes to fall into such naked secularism and try to cover it with a sacramental fig leaf. This secular*ism* of Rom 12,2 corresponds to sin on the Pauline sin-grace axis (old age vs. new age).

Treating the promotion of justice as a central religious issue, however, is the farthest thing from such secularism. As the bishops' synod declared in 1971,

> action on behalf of justice and participation in the transforma-
> tion of the world [are] a constitutive dimension of the preaching
> of the gospel, or, in other words, of the Church's mission for the
> redemption of the human race and its liberation from every
> oppressive situation.[4]

Think of the countless times that the church has negotiated a truce with tyranny in order to practice its sacramental ministry in peace. There can be no fullness of Christian life without Eucharist, but there can be no Christian life at all without commitment to justice.

Action on behalf of justice is no secondary task ("ethics, pre-evan-gelization") for the church. The Bible speaks to us of a God who gets upset when little people are pushed around. This is not a spare-time or secondary concern of God's, but the central concern. This is who God is: the liberator (*go'el*) of the poor. Sin is injustice, and salvation is the fullness of life in community. Therefore, social justice is a religious issue in the strictest sense. It is not a merely secular ethical imperative deriving from a message about the salvation of individu-als.

"Religious" and "secular" (orders of redemption and creation) are not mutually exclusive. Strictly speaking, "secular" contrasts with "cultic" and "ecclesial," not with "religious" (although we commonly speak nonstrictly and use "religious" to mean "cultic" and "ecclesial").

Social justice, in particular, is at once a secular and religious matter. Human affairs, politics, and reason enjoy a relative inde-pendence with respect to the church and revelation. (This secular*ity* affirmed by Vatican II follows from the Thomist understanding of "nature," or creation, as enjoying inner consistency and a certain independence with respect to grace.) But, at the same time, the saving work of God's grace embraces *all* of historical existence—personal and psychological, social, cultural, economic, and political—to trans-form it. We must therefore affirm the relative autonomy of the world and of the struggle for justice and at the same time recognize that justice is a strictly religious issue.

Insofar as justice is a secular affair (in its tactics and strategy), the laity undertakes this struggle. However, as a religious issue (God's project for the world), social justice goes to the heart of the church's mission and engages the church as a whole and its organizational structure.

The church does not have two missions, one primary and one secondary. It has a single *integral mission* as beacon and sacrament of God's integral revolution. This mission has different aspects, but they all serve the one purpose of announcing and realizing God's reign. Changing social institutions is simply one important part of the struggle for justice (a less-important part than new persons and new social relations) and hence of the church's mission, which includes all the "material and spiritual works of mercy" and the devotional life. Ministry of the Word, sacramental life, prayer and worship are all necessary to nourish and celebrate the historical-transcendent process whereby God fashions new persons in new social relations. The ministers and official representatives of the church community, who exercise a prophetic ministry of Word and sacrament, ought to function, as Herbert McCabe once put it, as chaplains to God's revolution.

A credible and faithful ministry of the Word, grounded in deeds, requires denouncing specific injustice and announcing hope in particular situations. A church which practices this will reap a rich harvest of persecution and martyrdom—the seeds of future growth, not only of the church, but, more importantly, of that reign of God which—as the Preface for Christ the King says— is "a reign of truth and life, a reign of holiness and grace, a reign of justice, love and peace."

NOTES

INTRODUCTION

1. Ignacio Ellacuría, "The Historicity of Christian Salvation," in *Mysterium Liberationis: Fundamental Concepts of Liberation Theology,* Ignacio Ellacuría and Jon Sobrino, eds. (Maryknoll, NY: Orbis Books, 1993), p. 251.

2. "Of the three principal driving forces [straining ecosystems], the growing inequality in income between rich and poor stands out in sharpest relief" (Postel, p. 5). The other two factors are population growth and economic production. For the statistic on women in poverty, *see* United Nations, "Integración social," p. 1.

1. SALVATION AND SOCIAL JUSTICE AS A *QUAESTIO DISPUTATA*

1. The order of creation is relatively autonomous (GS 34, 36, 39, 41, 59, 67). Here, as elsewhere in Vatican II, the bishops reject the "extrinsicist" theology which confines the supernatural work of grace to the meta-empirical level of personal existence. The bishops relegate the more dualistic language of Pius XI and Pius XII to footnotes. Cf. GS 42 n.90 and GS 58 n.129, which one should interpret in light of GS as a whole.

2. "What must be aimed at," writes Paul VI by way of summary, "is integral humanism. And what is that if not the fully-rounded development of the whole person and of all persons?" (42). The expression "integral humanism" derives from Jacques Maritain who had already influenced Vatican II's notion of the "integral vocation" and destiny of human beings.

3. Like GS, PP distinguishes the "Kingdom of Heaven," which the church establishes on earth, from the relatively autonomous political order (13). It likewise distinguishes the fulfillment of "nature," which it styles "personal and communal development," from the "further perfection," which is salvation (15-18).

4. Transformed by love through faith and baptism, the Christian "seek[s] out a new, more profound relationship with God, one's fellow human beings, and created things" (Med., "Justice," 4). The bishops consider the dynamism toward transformation and development in Latin America to be "an obvious sign of the Spirit" who conducts the history of people toward their destiny. This dynamism for transformation leads not only toward more effective control of nature (a *techne* relationship) and personalization and community (*praxis*), but toward an encounter with God. God labors in history to save the whole human being, body and soul. Just as Israel experienced the saving power of God in the Exodus, Latin Americans experience the same saving God in the integral development described by Pope Paul in PP 20-21 (Med., "Introduction to the Final Documents," 4-6).

5. Ibid., "Education," 6; emphasis added. The originality of the formula "integral salvation" expresses well the fresh approach of Medellín to the ancient question of the relationship between grace and the world.

6. Ibid., "Catechesis," 4; cf. ibid., 17. "In the search for salvation, we must avoid the dualism which separates temporal tasks from the work of sanctification" ("Justice," 5). "All creation is grafted onto the saving design that includes all humankind" ("Liturgy,"

4). "All liberation is an anticipation of the complete redemption of Christ." All "growth in humanity" brings us closer to salvation ("Education," 9).

7. In this sense one interprets "The Church links human liberation and salvation in Jesus Christ, but she never identifies them, because . . . not every notion of liberation is necessarily consistent and compatible with an evangelical vision" (35). Any liberation which lacks a transcendent ground, motive and goal carries the seeds of its own destruction. Ibid.

8. According to 480, the *"positive* echoes" (emphasis added) of Medellín's elucidation of integral humanism were taken up by EN and by Pope John Paul II, whose address at Puebla also alludes to "incorrect interpretations" of Medellín (*see* John Paul II, "Opening Address," in Eagleson, p. 57.) The next paragraph continues: "But there are different conceptions and applications of liberation. . . . They contain points of view that can hardly be brought together satisfactorily. The best thing to do, therefore, is to offer criteria that derive from the magisterium and that provide us with the necessary discernment regarding the original conception of Christian liberation" (481).

9. Christ liberates human beings from sin *and all its consequences* (187, 1194) which include injustice, of which sin is the root (70, 517, etc.). In the spirit of EN, evangelization should serve integral liberation (343-344, 362, etc.).

10. Soon after the release of this document, the Vatican imposed an 11-month silence on Brazilian theologian Leonardo Boff; shortly before that, Peruvian Gustavo Gutiérrez barely escaped censure by Peru's bishops, whom Vatican officials had pressured to act. Gutiérrez was summoned to Rome to defend his theology.

11. The first instruction accused unnamed liberation theologians of denying the distinction between salvation history and profane history (a charge the second Instruction failed to repeat), for they radically secularize the reign of God, absorbing it into history and equating it with the liberation movement, understood in Marxist terms (Instruction I: IX, 3; cf. X, 6). In this spirit, the first Instruction concludes by quoting Paul VI's *Profession of Faith* of 1968:

> We profess our faith that the Kingdom of God, begun here below in the Church of Christ, is not of this world, whose form is passing away, and that its own growth cannot be confused with the progress of civilization, of science or of human technology, but that it consists in knowing ever more deeply the unfathomable riches of Christ. . . . (Instruction I: "Conclusion")

Note here the common tendency to contrast salvation (Instruction II, 23) with "progress achieved in the fields of the sciences, technology and economics" (21), that is, *techne,* without clearly spelling out salvation's relationship to progress in love and justice.

12. The "supernatural order of salvation and the temporal order of human life" are two distinct, if inseparable, "spheres" (80).

13. Sin is the root of all forms of slavery. Cf. also Instruction I, "Introduction"; cf. VI, 4; X, 7.

14. "The salvific dimension of liberation cannot be reduced to the socio-ethical dimension, which is a consequence of it" (71; cf. 99; compare Instruction I, "Introduction" and IV, 13).

15. Even before the second Instruction was written, Juan Luis Segundo argued that the first Instruction was based on a hidden theology which not only distinguishes but separates the social-and-secular from the interior and transcendent in contrast to the teachings of GS. *See* Segundo, *Theology and the Church.*

16. RM 11. The pope cautions elsewhere against completely secularizing "Kingdom" or of separating it from Christ and the Church (cf. RM 17-18, 83).

17. In addition: God offers in Christ "the experience of a complete liberation which goes to the root of all evil, namely sin" (RM 23; cf. RM 28 on the work of the Spirit and RM 59).

18. It is noteworthy that the paragraphs containing this creative language (14-16) make no reference to papal or conciliar documents but only to Scripture.

19. Gustavo Gutiérrez, for example, often called "the father of liberation theology," characteristically refers to God's saving work as liberation leading to communion with God and others.

20. This book will only discuss the nature of the social good itself insofar as this is necessary to elucidate its relationship to "salvation." For my own view, *see* Brackley, *Etica social,* esp. pp. 116-120, 159-65, 273-85.

21. St. Augustine, *City of God,* XVIII, 11; XIX, 27; XI, 15. This remains true even though Augustine was the first to relate the work of grace to a theology of God's providential guidance of history. *See* Markus; Gilkey, pp. 159-75.

22. Cohn; Williams. German idealism later drew on concepts deriving from mysticism that grounded forms of millenarian hope for the future.

23. Viviano (Chapt. 3) attributes this in part to skittishness caused by the raging controversy over Joachim of Fiore's inner-worldly ideas of the kingdom.

24. Scripture plays a secondary role in this book, which chiefly intends to evaluate Catholic thought on a particular issue. Methodologically, we enter the hermeneutic circle at the point where experience and praxis challenge theology. This challenge should send us back to Scripture in order to reformulate theology and then to renewed praxis. *See* Segundo, *Liberation of Theology,* p. 9.

2. THE TRADITIONAL PARADIGM OF JACQUES MARITAIN

1. As with Maritain's understanding of the state, human rights and the whole range of subjects related to social philosophy and ethics, his conception of the relationship of Christianity to society continues to deeply influence Catholic thought. Pope Paul VI, for example, declared himself a "disciple of Maritain," whose thought is reflected in the encyclical *Populorum progressio* (*see* Kernan, pp. 172-75).

2. "I shall be a socialist and shall live for the revolution" (*Notebooks,* p. 8). This is a new translation of Maritain's *Carnet de notes.* Maritain claimed in 1954 that he actually became a socialist at the age of "thirteen or fourteen" (ibid., p. 7).

3. Maritain's half-hearted affiliation with *L'Action Française,* at the urgings of his conservative spiritual director, Père Humbert Clérissac, caused him acute embarrassment in later years. On this stage of Maritain's career, *see* Doering, Chapt.1.

4. This is a strictly *theological* problem. As a Christian philosopher, Maritain uses the work of theologians and official (magisterial) Catholic teaching "instrumentally," as he says, frequently without providing a great deal of theological grounding of his own (*see* *Science and Wisdom,* part 2. For a briefer treatment, *see* McCool, "Jacques Maritain," pp. 383-85).

5. In a letter to William Nottingham in 1964, Maritain described IH as the definitive expression of his political philosophy (Nottingham, p. 93). The earlier works of social philosophy are *Le primauté du spirituel (The Things That Are Not Caesar's),* 1927; *Religion et culture (Religion and Culture),* 1930; *Du régime temporel et de la liberté (Freedom in the Modern World),* 1933.

6. Cf. *Religion and Culture,* pp. 19-23; *Scholasticism and Politics,* Chapts. 1 and 2; PCG, pp. 90-105.

7. Along with others, Nottingham rightly notes "Maritain's failure ever to take Protestantism seriously" (p. 27; cf. p. 100; cf. McCann, p. 58n.60).

8. Maritain's most thorough critique of Marxism can be found in *Moral Philosophy,* pp. 209-60.

9. Concerning the new human being, *see* IH 93-94 and PCG 98.

10. On the importance of this critical consciousness or *prise de conscience,* cf. also IH 231; *Religion and Culture,* pp. 16-17.

11. "Existentially considered . . . man is at once a natural and a supernatural being" (IH 10). Cf. *Scholasticism and Politics,* p. 225. Of course, the orders are not identical with nature and grace themselves. "If we accept the data of Judeo-Christian revelation," writes Maritain, "we shall have to distinguish between two orders—the order of nature and the order of grace; and between two existential realms, distinct but not separate—the world on the one hand, and the Kingdom of God, the Church, on the other" (*Philosophy of History,* p. 37).

"Grace and nature, first, Maritain sees as the most important of the opposites which have to be reconciled. All the other important pairs follow logically from this first: faith and reason, the speculative and the practical, contemplation of God and the understanding of the world" (Fowlie, p. 56).

12. On the notion of an order, in general, *see Freedom in the Modern World,* pp. 77-79; Anderson, "Role of Analogy," pp. 98-101. The temporal and spiritual orders are each multiplicities of diverse elements: institutions (church and state), persons (clergy and laity), perhaps even actions (sacred and secular), etc., belonging to one or the other order, sometimes depending on the perspective from which they are viewed (in some respects, the church and the clergy belong to the temporal order, as well).

13. They are "supra-temporal goods of the natural order," even though they already belong to "the order of the absolute" (PCG 62-63, including note 33; *Distinguish to Unite,* p. 256). The human spirit also transcends the temporal order.

14. It is "as a spiritual totality" that the person "is referred to the transcendent whole" (PCG 61; cf. IH 9).

15. Spirit is the ontological principle of personality (*Freedom in the Modern World,* p. 48; cf. PCG 25-33; *Moral Philosophy,* p. 452).

16. Spirit is subsistent form (PCG 25, 31) and as such is nonmaterial: The world of being consists "of things known by the senses (the sensible or corporeal world) and of things invisible and spiritual, accessible to reason alone" (*Introduction to Philosophy,* p. 177).

17. We should not suppose, however, that Maritain subscribes to a Platonic dualism. Human beings are one composite substance, "flesh animated by a spirit" (PCG 26; cf. pp. 25-33; *Introduction to Philosophy,* pp. 176-77).

18. "There is a spiritual, metaphysical order beyond sensible nature . . . and it is above all the mechanism and all the laws of the world of bodies. To this order belongs what is in the most hidden recesses of personality. . . . As such, a spirit is no part of this universe . . . it emerges above the whole created universe (both sensible and supra sensible)" (*Distinguish to Unite,* p. 256).

19. Its material conditions include all "public commodities and services" such as roads, economic and political structures, schools, and so on (PCG 52). The moral dimension includes the development of both speculative and practical activities (IH 95-96; cf. p. 133). The common good embraces the goods of culture, such as "the body of just law, good customs and wise institutions," and also "the sum or sociological integration of all the civic conscience, political virtues and sense of right and liberty" (PCG 52). Maritain once characterized the "natural end of the world" as threefold. First, "the conquest of autonomy for mankind" in the face of natural forces and social enslavement; second, "the development of . . . spiritual, self-perfecting activities . . . especially knowledge"; third, "the manifestation of all the potentialities of human nature" (*Philosophy of History,* pp. 125-26).

20. Cf. IH 216-17; 133-34, 137, 148-49, 176-77, 254; *Neuf leçons,* pp. 36-40; *Science and Wisdom,* pp. 128, 221n.1; St. Thomas Aquinas, *Sum. Theol.,* 1a2ae, 65, 2.3. "*Bonum honestum*" refers to a moral good of (free, virtuous) human action (rather than the merely "ontological" good proper to all that exists). It is the "substantial" good, the good-in-itself, desirable for itself, as distinct from the "useful good" (a means to what is good-in-itself) and the "delectable" good (a result of possessing it).

21. *See* IH *passim,* which from the thirties on inspired, in Europe and Latin America, leaders of Christian Democratic parties—very many of whose actual policies, I am sure, Maritain would disown.

22. Again, "Culture and civilization," he writes, "have a specifying object—the earthly and perishable good of our life here below—whose proper order is the natural order . . ." (IH 97-98).

23. In a famous essay, Maritain distinguishes two "planes" of activity corresponding to the two orders. (*See* Appendix, "The Structure of Action," in IH 291-308 and also *Scholasticism and Politics,* Chapt. 7.) The first includes actions "of liturgical or sacramental life, of the work of the virtues or of contemplation, of the apostolate or of the works of mercy." The second includes "action of the intellectual or moral order, scientific and artistic or social and political" activity. Any action, "if it is right [is always] *turned toward God as its final end,* [even though] its direct determining aim [is] goods which are not eternal life, but which concern . . . the things of time, the work of civilization or of culture" (IH 291-92; emphasis added). Cf. also IH 124 and *Science and Wisdom,* p. 128 n. 2.

In my judgment, these references show how the division of actions into spiritual and temporal (even with the so-called "third plane") illustrates the weaknesses of the broader distinction of orders. In particular, as our chapter on Rahner will show, there can be no human action genuinely directed to the true temporal good which is not also directed to eternal life.

24. "The Church *is* the kingdom of God begun, the kingdom of God in the 'peregrinal, militant, crucified' state (Ch. Journet)" (IH 101).

25. Maritain identifies a nonpolitical "Eastern" version of the third error, as well (*see* IH 104).

26. What Maritain calls "rich temporal means" are too laden with matter to achieve a spiritual objective (*see Freedom in the Modern World,* pp. 176-78; "Religion and Culture," pp. 223-26).

27. The Latin comes from the hymn "Crudelis Herodes" in the old Divine Office for Epiphany. Maritain translates: "For He does not take away mortal kingdoms Who gives the kingdom of Heaven: He confirms them" (*Not Caesar's,* p. 79).

28. "Christianity has a primary object which does not pertain to the terrestrial order and which has nothing to do with the temporal structures of this world" *(Moral Philosophy,* p. 216).

29. The quotations appear in the same sentence with no indication that two different points are being made.

30. The reader can consult the standard commentaries. The chiastic structure of Jesus' dialogue with Pilate (*see* Brown, *The Gospel According to John, XIII-XXI,* pp. 858-59) confirms the stress on *origin.* John 18,33-38a corresponds structurally to 19,9-11. Brown notes that both treat kingship and power. They do so in terms of origin. John 18,36 corresponds structurally to 19,9: Pilate "said to Jesus, 'Where are you from?'" Cf. John 17,11.16: Jesus' disciples, too, are in the world but not "of" it in this sense.

31. "That state which is called 'the state of pure nature'" is one "in which, as a matter of fact, man has never been established" ("Immanent Dialectic," p. 71; cf. IH 10 and "Religion and Culture," p. 221).

32. Cf. IH 112. In Thomist philosophy, right action depends both on right knowledge and a right-ordered will. The pursuit of the temporal good requires assistance for both. On the level of practical knowledge, revelation must assist reason; on the level of practice itself, grace must assist the will.

33. Maritain made extraordinary contributions in just this area. *See Science and Wisdom, passim,* and the concise account in Nelson, "Moral Philosophy Adequately Considered," pp. 139-60. This article also contains a good summary of Maritain's exposition of the acquired and infused virtues, which we will soon treat.

34. The human person "as a spiritual totality referred to the transcendent whole, *surpasses* and is superior to all temporal societies. . . . A single human soul is worth more than the whole universe of material goods. There is nothing higher than the immortal soul save God" (ibid., p. 61).

35. Maritain's explanation of the Thomist theory of the virtues can be found in *Science and Wisdom,* pp. 210-16 and *Scholasticism and Politics,* pp. 225-28. Cf. IH 22n.4. *See Sum. Theol.,* 2a2ae, 23, 8. According to St. Thomas, a person without supernatural charity is like a sick person. Such a person can do good things—as a sick person can walk—but not consistently or well (ibid., 1a2ae, 109, 2; *Science and Wisdom,* pp. 150-51; *Philosophy of History,* pp. 142-44). Maritain's insistence on the need for charity to realize the temporal good breaks with the "naturalist" tendencies of many in the Cajetan school of Thomism (*see Science and Wisdom,* pp. 145-47, 153).

36. Cf. *Religion and Culture,* p. 30. "The order of redemption . . . should vivify to its most intimate depths the order of terrestrial civilization, or of the temporal" (IH 292; cf. IH 25, 74, 291, etc.).

37. "Under the influence of charity and infused moral virtue the act of acquired virtue which is intrinsically natural becomes supernatural *quoad modum finalitatis suae superioris* and meritorious of eternal life" (ibid., p. 216n.2). On merit, *see Sum. Theol.,* 1a2ae, 114.

38. *Sum. Theol.,* 1a2ae, 19,7, *sed contra.* The will directs action to its end according to the will's intention. Maritain, *Neuf leçons,* p. 41.

39. "But what will come after time is prepared by time. The kingdom of God constitutes the final term which the movement of history prepares and to which it leads" (IH 102; cf. p. 111n.10).

40. *See Philosophy of History,* p. 45. The downward movement of history is due to the "passivity of matter" which degrades and dissipates over time "the energy of history springing from the spirit and from human freedom" (p. 47). On Maritain's philosophy of history, *see* Brooke Williams Smith.

41. "The kingdom of God is not meant for earthly history, but . . . it must be enigmatically prepared in the midst of the pains of earthly history" (*Christianity and Democracy,* p. 44).

42. Thomistic philosophy understands both growth in virtue and civilization analogously to the cultivation of a field which "means inciting nature by some human labor to produce fruits which nature left to itself would have been incapable of producing" ("Religion and Culture," p. 217. In this sense, like moral virtues (or vices), social relations and structures—institutions—are social *habitus.*

43. "Friendship stands a concomitant, as it were, of perfect beatitude" (*Sum. Theol.,* 1a2ae, 4, 8 ad 3).

44. Maritain quotes Francisco de Vitoria to the effect that "neither grace, nor faith, nor hope, nor any other supernatural forms reside immediately in the whole community" (cited in PCG 86n.45). But see below what Maritain says about the church as person.

45. "In beatitude we shall be deified by intellection. But this very vision will be the crowning effect of love" (*Distinguish to Unite,* p. 323).

46. Cf. *Sum. Theol.,* 2a2ae, 188, 8. *See Distinguish to Unite, passim.* Jacques and Raïssa Maritain show how St. Thomas proves the superiority of contemplation by drawing on eight reasons to that effect from Aristotle (*Prayer and Intelligence*).

47. PCG 15; cf. ibid., pp. 15-20, 26-29, 59-61, 73-75, 80-85; *Freedom in the Modern World,* pp. 50-54. In the temporal order a person is more a part of society and a means to an end (the common good); in the supernatural order, however, each person is a "whole" and an end in her/himself (ibid., p. 17n.7). Maritain's conception of the individual and society met with intense criticism within Thomist circles. *See* McCool, "Jacques Maritain," p. 401.

48. "The metaphysical tradition of the West defines the person in terms of *independence,* as a reality which constitutes a universe unto itself, a relatively independent whole" (ibid., p. 40, emphasis added).

49. Today few theologians equate church and kingdom the way Maritain and many contemporaries did *(see* Küng, *The Church,* p. 96, etc.; McBrien, p. 58, etc.). Avery Dulles's objections *(Models of the Church,* pp. 109-11; cf. p. 106) to depicting church as a thoroughly intrahistorical, the kingdom as a completely posthistorical, reality need not lead to identifying the two once more.

3. THE *AGGIORNAMENTO* PARADIGM OF KARL RAHNER

1. The reader can compare Rahner's synthesis with those of Henri DeLubac, Hans Urs von Balthasar, Juan Alfaro, Edward Schillebeeckx and Eulalio von Baltazar in Duffy. Most would agree with Duffy that, while some have pointed to areas where Rahner's position should be extended, no one has clearly superseded his nature-grace synthesis.

2. According to H.-E. Mertens, the actual creator of this schema was the Jesuit Robert Bellarmine (1542-1621) *(see* Mertens, "Nature and Grace," p. 246). For alternative suspects, *see* Duffy, p. 74n.19.

3. For a fuller discussion of these issues, *see* briefly, Mertens, "Nature and Grace"; Duffy; and McCool, *Unity to Pluralism,* Chapt. 9. *See also* DeLubac, *Mystery of the Supernatural;* Rahner, "Nature and Grace," in TI 4:165-88. In this chapter, from here on, all works cited are Karl Rahner's unless otherwise indicated.

4. Rahner characterizes "the order of redemption and grace" as "everything which appertains to the concrete existence and practical putting into action of 'grace' as the actualization of 'redemption' " (ibid., p. 41). This is roughly equivalent to Maritain's spiritual order. Maritain's temporal order, civilization, fits inside Rahner's order of creation, which embraces creation as a whole.

5. "If we want to formulate the relation of the supernatural to the natural order, we can equally well speak of the redemptive order within the created order or of the created order within the redemptive order" (ibid., p. 52).

6. The school of Cajetan tended to characterize this *potentia obedientialis* as a mere nonrepugnance for grace on the part of a "pure nature" regarded as a closed, relatively self-contained system *(see* "Nature and Grace," pp. 167-68, 173). Rahner breaks with this notion in the spirit of Maréchalian transcendental Thomism. He develops the conception of *potentia obedientialis* as an "ontological alert" for the supernatural in his book *Hearers of the Word. See also* "Nature and Grace," pp. 185-88.

7. Maritain does not articulate his position thoroughly in relation to the two orders. I present his sketchy remarks on these issues here so that the reader may compare his position with Rahner's.

Maritain adopted a Cajetanian understanding of *obedientia potentialis* when he wrote *Distinguish to Unite.* "Grace orders us to the vision of the Divine Essence . . . whereas, by nature, we are ordered only to a knowledge of being in general. . . . Doubtless by our very nature as reasonable beings, we are *capable of being proportioned* to the Divine Essence as an object of [our] vision. But we *are so proportioned* by grace. . . . And that is completely supernatural. This capacity of being proportioned to grace is nothing but our soul's obediential potency with regard to the first Agent" *(Distinguish to Unite,* p. 256). DeLubac criticizes Cajetan's position, noting that St. Thomas *(Sum. Theol.,* 1a2ae, 113, 10) clearly states "naturaliter anima est gratia capax" *(Mystery of the Supernatural,* pp. 181-85). The quotation from *Distinguish to Unite* falls under the same criticism.

Years later, as criticism of the dominant school mounted, Maritain alluded to the debate. Acknowledging that, for St. Thomas, intelligence desires to know its object and the cause of things "unveiled and in itself," Maritain rejected the idea that natural "intelligence aspires to the vision of the divine essence, as if specified by this object, as the only truly real knowledge." Nonetheless, humans have "a natural desire, which is not exactly of ourselves but of a transcendental element within us, to pass beyond the human condition. . . . We have no right to have [such desires] granted; if they are granted to some extent it is only through grace. . . . They are not specific (connatural) aspirations of human nature, but only metaphysical (transcendental) aspirations of a transcendental element within us. Truly speaking, it is only in God . . . that these aspirations find their fulfillment" (Maritain, *Scholasticism and Politics,* pp. 15-16, 133-34; cf. pp. 121, 123). Moving further from Cajetan, in this passage Maritain acknowledges "transcendental" aspirations which are "not exactly of ourselves."

8. In Rahner and Vorgrimler, we find this succinct description of the supernatural existential: "Underlying the concept of the supernatural existential is the following fact: antecedently to justification by grace, received sacramentally or extra-sacramentally, man is already subject to the universal salvific will of God, he *is* already redeemed and absolutely obliged to tend to his supernatural end. This 'situation' is not merely an external one; it is inclusively and inalienably precedent to man's free action, and [it] . . . is a real modification of man, added indeed to his nature by God's grace and therefore supernatural, but in fact never lacking in the real order" (pp. 163-64). Therefore, "Our actual nature is *never* 'pure' nature. It is a nature installed in a supernatural order which man can never leave . . ." ("Nature and Grace," p. 183); and "pure nature" refers simply to a theologically necessary "remainder concept" ("Concerning the Relationship," pp. 313-15; cf. "Nature and Grace," p. 185.)

9. *See* "Nature and Grace," p. 183; cf. *Foundations,* pp. 126-33. On the distinction between salvation considered objectively and subjectively, *see* "Salvation," pp. 426-27. Duffy (pp. 104-6) helpfully suggests understanding the supernatural existential in terms of covenant. All human beings stand under the (new) covenant, and this alters their situation radically compared to what it would otherwise be.

10. Maritain's critical realist epistemology builds on the insights of Cajetan and John of St. Thomas. With Aquinas, Maritain holds that all knowledge derives ultimately from sense experience. (On Maritain's critical realism, *see Distinguish to Unite,* Chapt. 3.) But the natural dynamism of the mind, and thus of spirit, is away from matter, since being, the object of knowledge, is intelligible in proportion to its immateriality (ibid., p. 34). The highest form of knowledge is metaphysics, which explicitly knows being as such (intuited implicitly in all conceptual knowledge) via the "third degree of abstraction" (ibid., pp. 35-46). Finally, supra-conceptual mystical contemplation is the highest activity of the human spirit—inferior natural contemplation of the act of existence itself and contemplation of God through supernatural charity. On natural mysticism, cf. Maritain, "Natural Mystical Experience," Chapt. 10. On supernatural mysticism, *see* Maritain, *Distinguish to Unite,* Chapt. 8.

11. In the Incarnation, "God lays hold of matter . . . precisely at that point of unity at which matter becomes conscious of itself."

12. "Order of Redemption," p. 41. Similarly, there cannot "be any human, responsible putting of nature into action which" does not amount "to a Yes or No to grace" (ibid.).

13. *See Spirit in the World,* part 2, Chapt. 4. Although he argues in transcendental fashion (a la Fichte) that human experience presupposes that human beings are spirits of free transcendence, Rahner rejects the idealism of both Kant and Fichte by arguing, with Thomas, that this transcendence takes place in and through a *conversio ad phantasma,* the spirit's (intellect's) turning to objective data presented by human sensibility. The identification of spirit's being with its operations reflects Hegel's influence. However, I believe all Rahner's "idealist" expressions must be located within the framework of his vision of the emergence of humanity from within the evolutionary process. Cf. *Foundations,* pp. 178-203.

14. The human spirit "penetrates into matter in order to become spirit" (*Rahner Reader,* p. 56). "The body is already spirit. . . . Bodily existence is the concrete existence

of the spirit itself in space and time. Physical nature or the nature of the human body . . . is the self-expression of the spirit reaching out into space and time" (ibid., p. 84). "Man, strictly speaking, according to the clear doctrine of Thomism, is not composed of a soul and a body, but of a soul and *materia prima*" ("Theology of the Symbol," p. 247).

15. Drawing on Hegel, Rahner developed a theological ontology which grounds the original unity of matter and spirit prior to any distinction (*see* "Theology of the Symbol"): "For Christian theology and philosophy it is to be taken for granted that spirit and matter have more in common than they have differentiating them." Since human beings "are the self-transcendence of living matter, then the history of nature and of spirit form an intrinsic and stratified unity" (*Foundations,* pp. 182, 187). Matter is " 'frozen' spirit." Assumed by spirit, the human body is "a limited moment in the achievement of the spirit itself. This is valid then even of the rest of the material world, particularly since this must be conceived from the start as the environment and as the broadened corporeality of the spirit" ("Unity of Spirit and Matter," pp. 168-69).

16. On this point perhaps Rahner differs not only from Maritain, but from Aquinas, also. *See Sum. Theol.* 2a2ae, 23, 1 ad 1.

17. Here Rahner appropriates insights of Fichte and Hegel in interpreting Aquinas's thought. Rahner accepts the possibility of basically natural psychological states which could mediate the experience of grace immediately, that is, without categories. Such an occurrence would be rare and hardly normative for spirit. Neither would such mysticism necessarily indicate a more intense life of grace. "Mystical Experience," pp. 90-99. Cf. "Experience of the Spirit and Existential Commitment," TI 16, p. 28, and "Religious Enthusiasm and the Experience of Grace," TI 16, 43.

18. "Every natural created entity is ordered to this grace in such a way that it cannot . . . achieve the completion required by its own nature, except as integrated into the supernatural order of grace" ("Order of Redemption," p. 50). Maritain: The "common good of the city . . . does not preserve its true nature unless . . . it is subordinated . . . to the order of eternal goods and the supra-temporal values from which human life is suspended" (PCG 62; *see above,* pp. 36-37).

19. Rahner speaks of "truth, life, light, peace, joy" in these terms ("Salvation," p. 428). Created grace is itself a result of the divine indwelling ("Some Implications").

20. Such acts "are God's doing in such a way that in them it is really given to men to act, and so to act as really to convey salvation to others in the Mystical Body of Christ, though the scope and the manner of it remains hidden within God's governance of things" ("Significance of the Individual," pp. 91-92). This is a special case of the symbolic nature of all reality, symbolic in the sense of making present what it signifies (cf. "Theology of the Symbol" and Buckley).

21. What we have argued here is that the language of salvation, of God's gift, can and should be extended to include the moral good and the usable and delectable good, which result from the indwelling of the Holy Spirit. *See above,* Chapt. 2, note 20.

22. In its treatment of social reality, wrote Metz, existentialist and transcendental theology, including Rahner's, manifests a typically bourgeois preoccupation with interpersonal relationships. They deal poorly with political responsibility, with the Third World—and with Auschwitz. *See* Metz, *Faith in History,* pp. 60-70, 154-78.

Metz asked, concerning Rahner's theology: "Is there not danger that the question of salvation will be made too private and that salvation will be conceived too worldlessly, breaking too quickly the point of the universal historical battle for man?" (Metz, "Foreword," pp. xvii-xviii). Metz asked further whether transcendental theology undervalues eschatology. He would later stress God's apocalyptic interruption in history in contrast to the historical eschatology Rahner develops in later works (*see* Metz, *Faith in History,* pp. 169-79; idem, *The Emergent Church,* pp. 34-47, etc.; cf. Tracy, "Response to Fr. Metz," pp. 184-87).

23. Rahner summarized the relationship between his theology and Metz's critique as follows: "Metz's critique of my theology (which he calls transcendental theology) is

the only criticism which I take very seriously. . . . Insofar as the critique of Metz is correct, every concrete mystagogy must obviously from the very beginning consider the societal situation and the Christian praxis to which it addresses itself. If this is not sufficiently done in my theory of mystagogy . . . then this theory must be filled out. However, it is not therefore false. For it has always been clear in my theology that a 'transcendental experience' (of God and of grace) is always mediated through a categorical experience in history, in interpersonal relationships, and in society. If one not only sees and takes seriously these necessary mediations of transcendental experience but also fills it out in a concrete way, then one already practices in an authentic way political theology. On the other hand, such a political theology is, if it truly wishes to concern itself with God, not possible without reflection on those essential characteristics of man which a transcendental theology discloses. Therefore, I believe that my theology and that of Metz are not necessarily contradictory" (Rahner, "Introduction," pp. ix-x). Guenther has persuasively argued the correctness of this statement. Leo J. O'Donovan ("Orthopraxis") takes Rahner's critics to task for failing to recognize how Rahner's thought opens into political theology.

24. Love ("a free self-present act") is the light of all knowledge; "knowledge is but the luminous radiance of love" (*Rahner Reader,* p. 40). "In the heart of knowledge stands love from which knowledge itself lives . . . knowledge and love constitute originally the one basic stance of the human being, so that neither can ever be understood except as turning into the other, as grasped in function of the other" (ibid., p. 41). The transcendence of freedom is equally fundamental; and "Freedom is always the freedom of a subject who exists in interpersonal communication with other subjects" (*Foundations,* p. 65).

25. "The true and proper surrounding of man is his personal environment. This environment of persons is the world through which man finds and fulfills himself (by knowledge and will) and . . . gets away from himself. . . . The act of personal love for another human being is therefore the all-embracing basic act of man which gives meaning, direction and measure to everything else. If this is correct, then the essential a priori openness to the other human being . . . belongs as such to the a priori and most basic constitution of man and is an essential inner moment of his (knowing and willing) transcendentality." Everything else that is human "is a moment, presupposition, initial stage or result of" loving communication with the neighbor ("Reflections," pp. 240-42; cf. "Experience of Self," p. 127).

26. Maritain wrote: "To bestow oneself, one must first exist . . . as a thing, which subsists and exercises existence for itself. Such a being must exist . . . eminently, in self-possession, holding itself in hand, master of itself. . . . the metaphysical tradition of the West defines the person in terms of independence, as a reality which, subsisting spiritually, constitutes a universe unto itself, a relatively independent whole within the great whole of the universe, facing the transcendent whole which is God." Such a substance, because it is a "person, . . . of its essence requires a dialogue in which souls really communicate" (PCG 39-42).

27. *See* "Reflections," p. 243-48 and, especially, "One Mediator," p. 183; cf. "The Church's Commission," p. 304. An image can help. God, who is completely unlike any entity, can pass through entities to us directly, the way water drenches us when it passes through a sponge.

28. Obediential potency for grace is precisely transcendence toward the neighbor to be loved (ibid., p. 243).

29. "In the last years, [Rahner's] fundamental correlation is not simply between God and humanity but rather between God as the world's most inner entelechy and the whole history of humanity" (O'Donovan, "Journey into Time," p. 624).

30. History, however, "remains ambiguous in its empirically observable external expressions, and the 'occurrence' of grace is just as hidden as the material character of its acceptance. The thesis of the kingdom of God as 'the world'" is implied by 1) the reality of grace and justification outside the visible church community, 2) the insepa-

rability of material and formal morality, and 3) the unity of the love of God and the neighbor (ibid.).

31. "The Church is not identical with the kingdom of God. It is the sacrament of the kingdom of God," that is, the community which both symbolizes and effectively mediates that transcendent reality ("Church and World," p. 239).

32. Sound anthropology implies that "it is not just the final 'mind' of man . . . which enters 'eternal life,' but also the result of his concrete action in the body and the world, though in an unimaginable transformation (1 Cor 15, 51f.)" ("Salvation," p. 437; cf. p. 424). "That which endures is the *work* of love as expressed in the concrete in human history" ("Theological Problems," p. 270). The all-embracing reach of grace implies: "With the church fathers one might not only say, 'What is assumed [by God], is redeemed,' but also '*Everything* is assumed and thereby everything is redeemed without having to perish' " ("Christian Understanding," p. 243). In his last years, Rahner remarked that "it may be that an end to physical time is not implicit in Christian eschatology at all"—although such a view clashes with his own understanding of human freedom ("Profane History," p. 6; cf. p. 9; O'Donovan, "Journey into Time," p. 639). Freedom means that through categorical decisions humans fashion ("dispose of") themselves as well as the world with definitive results for both *(see* "Theology of Freedom").

33. Cf. "Profane History," p. 12. "Over history stands the cross. Even in this world every ascent is always paid for with a decline" (ibid., p. 13).

34. "The sole 'tradition' which Christianity has acquired on the way is the command to hope in the absolute promise and . . . to set out ever anew from the social structures which have become petrified, old and empty" ("On the Theology of Hope," p. 259; cf. "Marxist Utopia," pp. 59-68).

35. For a comprehensive summary and appraisal of Rahner's works from 1976 until his death, much of it unavailable in English, *see* O'Donovan, "Journey into Time," pp. 621-46.

36. God sustains the evolution of the material world as an analogous process of self-transcendent development toward and into spirit. In this case—although we cannot imagine how—matter, too, will share in the consummation of personal history (ibid., pp. 284-89; cf. "Natural Science," pp. 52-55).

37. "A soteriology which is modern in the right sense should not allow itself to be posed the false dilemma that it has to choose between 'self-deliverance' and 'rescue.' Redemption is of course in all respects the free action of God on man, caused by nothing outside God—especially as salvation is God himself. But when the basic relationship between God and the world is correctly viewed, excluding any anthropomorphic 'synergism,' the action of God appears as the possibility and dynamism of the action of the world, which thus moves in self-transcendence to its fulfillment. . . . World history may well be regarded as humanity's self-liberation from self-alienation. History in this sense takes place in moral action made possible by God's action, as a moment of a rightly understood self-redemption of man, given to mankind by God as its task" ("Salvation," p. 437; cf. "Christian Understanding of Redemption," pp. 240-41).

38. The present experience of grace is already a deficient mode of the beatific vision ("Some Implications," pp. 334-37; "The 'Commandment' of Love," pp. 439-59; etc.). On quasi-formal causality, *see Foundations,* pp. 120-21. It is a more intimate relationship than what Maritain describes in saying "sanctifying grace is an inherent quality, an 'entitative habit' " (Maritain, *Distinguish to Unite,* p. 255).

39. For an overview of Rahner's dependence on German idealism and criticism within the Thomist camp, *see* McCool, "Introduction"; Francis Schüssler Fiorenza, "Introduction."

4. THE LIBERATION PARADIGM OF GUSTAVO GUTIÉRREZ

1. By the early eighties, the majority of the world's Catholics were to be found in Africa and Latin America. By 1988, 9.1 percent were in Africa and 42.4 percent in Latin America (*Catholic International* 2:6 [March 1991]:270).

2. The reader who wishes to study the origins of Latin American liberation theology has a wealth of material at her or his disposal. The most recent brief introductory overviews in English include Berryman, *Liberation Theology*; Boff and Boff, *Introducing Liberation Theology*; idem, *Liberation Theology*; Gibellini; Planas. Good earlier introductions include Brown, *Theology in a New Key*, which offers a fine introduction to Gutiérrez's earlier thought, and Míguez Bonino, Part 1. This book and Alves, *Human Hope*, represent important early Protestant contributions. Hennelly, *Liberation Theology*, provides the broadest and deepest account of the history of liberation theology available to the English reader. A fine account of the genesis of liberation theology, emphasizing the work of Gutiérrez, is provided in Spanish by Oliveros. Rich documentation from the earliest period can also be found in Peruvian Bishops' Commission for Social Action, *Between Honesty and Hope*. For the historical events behind the rise of this theology, see Berryman, *Religious Roots of Rebellion;* Lernoux, *Cry of the People*, which treats repression of the church in Latin America in the mid-sixties and seventies; and more recently, idem, *People of God.* More detailed overviews available in English include the early work (which addresses European political theology, as well) of Fierro and more recently McGovern. Haight, *An Alternative Vision,* synthesizes a more universal liberation theology. Cf. Hennelly, *Theology for a Liberating Church;* Chopp. An encyclopedia of basic concepts has recently appeared: Ignacio Ellacuría y Jon Sobrino, eds., *Mysterium liberationis;* abbreviated English ed., *Mysterium liberationis.* From a more critical standpoint, *see* Novak; and Comisión Teológica Internacional, *Teología de la liberación.* From a social-scientific standpoint, *see* Sigmund; Christian Smith. From a Marxist critic, Kee.

3. For biographical comment on Gutiérrez, consult Brown, *Gustavo Gutiérrez,* Chapt. 2, and Ellis and Maduro, Part 2. In Spanish, *see* Manzanera, p. 13. Manzanera's book stands out as the most comprehensive and detailed commentary on Gutiérrez's works from his earliest contribution in 1960 until 1978.

4. This is, after all, the central notion of Christianity (TL 83). References to the Spanish original of TL are from *Teología de la liberación: Perspectivas.* Unless otherwise indicated, all works referred to in this chapter are by Gutiérrez.

5. "Theology from the Underside of History," PPH, Chapt. 7, esp. 191-93, 212-14. Cf. PPH 36-37, 50-51, 57, 92-93, etc. "For the proclamation of the message to invite hearers to discipleship means starting with the daily life and questionings of the hearer of the Word, as well as with the mental categories with which the hearer tries to understand his or her life experiences" (*La verdad,* p. 122).

6. In LP (1st ed., 1968), Gutiérrez characterized theology as "critical reflection on the presence and activity of the Church" (LP 11). LP represents a revision of a series of talks given in 1964. By 1968 ("Hacia una teología de la liberación" [Montevideo: MIEC-JECI, 1968]), Gutiérrez had developed the above methodological principles. After 1971, he insisted that a theology of liberation must not only reflect *on* liberating praxis, but *from* praxis (PPH 60, etc.). Such was the challenge presented by the work of Brazilian theologian Hugo Assmann who entitled his 1973 collection of essays *Teología desde [i.e., "from"] la praxis de la liberación* (*Theology for a Nomad Church*). On Gutiérrez's use of "praxis" in different periods, see Manzanera, pp. 72, 311.

7. *See* "Introduction to the Revised Edition: Expanding the View," TL xxx. On the variety of the forms of suffering, *see On Job,* esp. p. 131n.25. On contemplation and practice as the first step, *see El Dios de la vida,* pp. 6-9 (*see* the greatly expanded 1989 edition, *The God of Life,* p. xiv); *On Job,* pp. xiii-xiv; *La verdad,* pp. 12-13, 79-80.

8. This is PPH, a collection of Gutiérrez's principal essays following the publication of TL.

9. For an account of Maritain's influence in Latin America, *see* Lima, pp. 70-85, and Caldera. Richard traces the crisis in the pastoral practice of the Latin American church in great detail in his *Death of Christendoms*. Richard uses the expression "New Christendom" in a much broader sense than Gutiérrez to distinguish the church's alliance with political elites after the *old,* that is, pre-independence Christendom of the colonial era.

10. Among these theologians were Yves Congar and M.-D. Chenu. A mistranslation in the English edition of TL has caused many readers to confuse New Christendom with the distinction of planes. The first sentence of Chapt. 5 should read: "The rise of the New Christendom position entails of course a rejection of *the earlier approach* [i.e., Christendom]; it in turn, however, is criticized by the distinction of planes position" (TL 39, emphasis added). The next sentence should begin: "Nevertheless. . . ." Note also the omission of material in PPH 189 (compare the original Spanish version, *La fuerza,* pp. 343-44).

11. As in the previous models, the church has a double mission: 1) sanctification and 2) building up the world, but this time only through moral education of individual Christians.

12. Gutiérrez considered this issue crucial: "In every theology one finds a series of distinctions: spiritual and temporal, sacred and profane. The most important of these distinctions, which constitutes the basis for all the others, is the distinction between the natural (the human) and the supernatural (grace)" (LP 30). Gutiérrez traces the grace debates in TL 43-46; cf. *La verdad,* pp. 175-80.

13. "Salvation—the communion of human beings with God and among them-selves—is something which embraces all human reality, transforms it, and leads it to its fullness in Christ" (TL 85; cf. PPH 31).

14. "Either one loves the neighbor, or one does not; either one is an egoist, or one lives in service of others. This reminds us of St. Augustine's theology of history where the two cities are based on love, the love of God and others and the love of self" (LP 61). "There is no human act which cannot in the last instance be defined in relation to Christ" (TL 153).

15. The issue is central to the church's life and thought in Latin America because of the secularization process under way there. Will industrialization affect Latin America the way it has affected Europe? *See* the interchange at Gutiérrez's doctoral defense between Gutiérrez and Christian Duquoc (*La verdad,* pp. 40-42; cf. pp. 163-64). It is also central to the place of social analysis, relative to faith, in developing political strategy and tactics—and to ethics.

16. *See* Assmann's self-criticism and the remarks of Manzanera, pp. 319-25, 337-39. Gutiérrez has little to say on revolutionary violence—better, counterviolence—first, because official (Catholic) church teaching has been clear for a long time and repeatedly reaffirmed (*see* PP 31) and, second, because he wishes to treat liberation in the broad sense in the light of God's Word (cf. *La verdad,* 109n.19).

17. The various formulations of dependency *theory* have been largely abandoned, even as many theorists maintain the *fact* of the dependency of the Latin American national economies on those of the First World. "It is clear," wrote Gutiérrez in 1988, "that the theory of dependence . . . is now an inadequate tool" (TL xxiv; *see also* TL 199 n. 31 and the bibliographical references there). Cf. Manzanera, 326-28; McGovern, Chapt. 8 and pp. 125-29; Kay; Hunt.

18. *See,* for example, *La verdad,* pp. 220-21; cf. also Early. For a recent conceptu-alization of the first level of liberation, *see La verdad,* pp. 182-88. *See* the fine presentation of issues in Burns and the important study by Castañeda.

19. One must take great care in adapting Gutiérrez's insights, especially at this first level, to other historical contexts, for example, in North America (*see* TL xxxvi). At the same time, Latin American and North American social problems and their

solutions are internal to each other, connected at every level: economic, political, racial, and cultural. As Haight has written (*An Alternative Vision, passim*), liberation theology directly addresses the crucial theological and human problem of our day, namely, the problem of living together.

20. "If indeed our author does not clearly explicitate this," Manzanera comments, "this utopian-historical level already implies a philosophical vision of history in the sense of a reference-to-'being' which explains human existence" (p. 132).

21. Gutiérrez's celebration of the advances of modernity, e.g., of modern science and the Enlightenment, contrasts sharply with Maritain's dour critique (*see* TL 18-19; PPH 49-50, 171-76). As we shall see, however, Gutiérrez's fundamental insights contain seeds undermining some Enlightenment presuppositions.

22. This expression, "el devenir histórico de la humanidad," pervades Gutiérrez's works. *Devenir* is variously translated "future" (TL 17, 92, 147), "process" (19, 75), "development" (75), "destiny" (86 twice). *See also* PPH 27 ("course in history"), 29 ("development"), 31 (twice: "destiny" and "development"); *La verdad*, pp. 148, 177, 187n.71, etc.

23. The Puebla Document (513, 521-23) makes a similar (not identical) distinction between a "broader or global" sense and a "more specific" sense of "political."

24. The concept of the new human being is latent in the writings of Peruvian José Carlos Mariátegui and explicit in Mao Tse-tung, E. Che Guevara, and others. TL organizes the chapters most central to our concerns around the expression which captures the essence of the liberation process: the *creation* (Chapt. 9) of the *new* (Chapt. 11) *human being* (Chapt. 10). The fifteenth anniversary edition of TL translates "el hombre nuevo" as "the new humanity." Although this new person is a social being, "the new human being" is preferable.

25. *See* Mannheim. From a third-world perspective, *see* the rich reflections of Alves, *Tomorrow's Child.* For an updated discussion of the issues, *see* Ricoeur. For a critical appraisal of Gutiérrez's understanding of utopia, *see* Fierro, pp. 274-88.

26. Gutiérrez believes that New Christendom, the theology of revolution, and the theology of development all risk misconstruing faith as an ideology directly applicable to society. To this extent they fail to appreciate the distinctiveness of faith and the autonomy of both society and science. Gutiérrez affirms the autonomy of social science and political action (TL 138). But the autonomy is not absolute. Social science is not dogmatic in the pejorative sense. It advances by hypothesis and is by its nature always open to revision in the light of new data (*see La verdad*, pp. 83-84). Revelation and reason are mutually illuminating.

In early talks and in course notes on Marxism and Christianity, Gutiérrez rejected a rigid epistemological distinction of planes by "Althusserian Christians" who separated faith and "science" (*see* Manzanera, pp. 52-56). "When science dogmatizes and in a certain way ideologizes . . . utopia emerges to break [the] molds. Political action is therefore science on the one hand and utopia on the other" (Gutiérrez, "Marxismo y cristianismo" [mimeogr.], cited in Manzanera, p. 141).

Although Gutiérrez does not attempt to develop an ethic, his insights on the function of utopia have important consequences for the relationship between faith and politics in the practical order—as one can see in his treatment of Christian love and class struggle in both editions of TL (1st ed. pp. 272-79; 15th anniv. ed., pp. 156-61). On the ethical contribution of Gutiérrez, *see* Schubeck, Chapt. 2.

27. "*In the present order* . . . we do not have one history of nature and another history of grace, one of brother- and sisterhood and another of divine filiation; rather the relation between grace and nature, between God's call and the free response of the human being, occurs within the one and only Christofinalized history" (*La verdad*, p. 180; cf. PPH 31 and *La fuerza historica*, pp. 212-13). Míguez Bonino, (p. 71) relates this to Irenaeus's theology of the recapitulation of all things in Christ.

28. The Puebla Document reformulates Gutiérrez's thesis more abstractly with a change of perspective:

Freedom always implies the capacity we all possess in principle to be our own person and to act on our own initiative (GS 17), so that we can go on fashioning community and participation, to be embodied in definitive realities, on three inseparable planes: our relationship to the world as its master, to other persons as brothers or sisters, and to God as God's children. (Puebla 322; cf. 323-29)

29. Teilhard de Chardin "values the dominion over nature that human kind has achieved and speaks of it as the penetration point of evolution, enabling humankind to control" evolution (TL 101). Maritain, for whom the common good is the *summum bonum* of the temporal order, escapes this critique. On optimistic European theologies, *see La verdad,* pp. 46-47.

30. "Creation" here means God's creative *action,* only secondarily its result. Cf. PPH, 31-32 and *On Job,* Chapt. 9.

31. Gutiérrez lays the groundwork here for explaining how the ontological good and the usable and delectable good, which are the gift of nature and the fruit of work, can be incorporated into the work of salvation through the mediation of the moral good, which is above all personal and social. *See* Chapt. 2, note 20, and Chapt. 3, note 21, above.

32. Augustine's *City of God* shaped Christian interpretation of the Old Testament from the fifth century on. In that work, Augustine discusses the Old Testament almost book by book. Yet among the hundreds of pages of commentary, he devotes but a single page to the exodus (Book 16, Chapt. 43; cf. also Book 18, Chapts. 8 and 11).

33. On the use of the exodus story in recent Latin American theology, *see* Croatto; Pixley, *On Exodus;* van Iersel and Weiler. For a different perspective, *see* Yoder.

34. Cf. *La verdad,* p. 198, note. "The sin-grace relation is played out in the deepest part of the human person" (p. 199).

35. "Alienation" recalls Hegel and Marx. Gutiérrez cautions against pushing the parallel too far (*see* TL 226nn.97, 99).

36. But Gutiérrez lacks a systematic Christology. *See* the excellent appraisal of his hermeneutical presuppositions in Manzanera, pp. 383-90.

37. For what follows, see principally TL 91-97; cf. also *The God of Life,* pp. 101-2, 106-7.

38. A frontal attack on spiritualizing is necessary. One could hold that Old Testament promises are indeed realized today in a wholly "spiritual" way. Von Rad himself appears to leave this possibility open (*see Old Testament Theology* 2, Part 3). On the use of the Old Testament and the four traditional meanings of texts, *see* DeLubac, *Exégèse médiévale,* Première Partie II, Seconde Partie II, and Kraeling.

39. "Flesh," which refers to the *whole* human being, is good; it is also weak and mortal. To this Old Testament understanding of "flesh," Paul adds a dynamism away from God and toward death: Sin instrumentalizes the flesh (and law) and leads to death.

40. "Human life unfolds within an option for death or an option for life" (*We Drink,* pp. 69-70). "In the final analysis, to liberate is to give life—life in its totality. It is in this framework that distinctions between the material and the spiritual, the temporal and the religious, the personal and the social, and others of the same kind, must be understood (and not suppressed). The study of Paul shows us that in his eyes the basic opposition is between *death* and *life*" (ibid., p. 3).

41. Cf. TL 106-16, which traces the Bible's revelation of God's presence in the world in ever more universal and *integral* categories; i.e., God's presence touches all persons and the whole person. God is present in Christ, body and soul, and is therefore to be encountered in other corporeal human beings.

42. Manzanera attributes an early formulation of this idea to Yves Congar (*see* Manzanera, p. 103n.28; *see also* Boff and Boff, *Salvation and Liberation,* pp. 58-60).

43. In the present context, Gutiérrez builds on the work of Moltmann (*Theology of Hope*), whom he also regards as insufficiently attentive to human beings' collaboration

in their redemption and who fails to address seriously the particular concrete forms of dehumanization from which God delivers them.

44. Compare Ernst Bloch's understanding of human beings as those who hope and who strive to make their hope real (references at TL 232nn.12-16). Recall Rahner's identification of hope with human transcendence itself, in which God, as the absolute future, comes to us as sheer gift.

45. Liberating action in the present "nourishes" the present-future tension. "It is thus that the attraction of 'what is to come' is the driving force of history." The close connection between present and future action implies that "the action of Yahweh in history and at the end of history are inseparable" (TL 95). God acts now and will act analogously in the future (TL 94-95; PPH 7).

46. "The eschatological promises are being fulfilled throughout history, but this does not mean that they can be identified clearly and completely with one or another social reality; their liberating effect goes far beyond the foreseeable and opens up new and unsuspected possibilities. The complete encounter with the Lord will mark the end of history, but it already occurs in history" (TL 97, trans. emended; cf. TL 104, 155-56; La verdad, 209; cf. PPH 68-69).

47. Shortly before his own death, Rahner wrote, in a celebrated letter on Gutiérrez's behalf: "I am convinced of the orthodoxy of the theological work of Gustavo Gutiérrez. The Theology of Liberation which he represents is entirely orthodox. It is conscious of its limited significance within the totality of Catholic theology" (Letter to Cardinal Juan Landázuri Ricketts, p. 81; cf. TL xxxvi).

48. See DeLubac, A Brief Catechism, pp. 100-9. These last points are valid despite DeLubac's over-sharp distinction of orders. In the 1988 edition of TL, Gutiérrez wrote: "There is no slightest tinge of immanentism in this approach to integral liberation. …any interpretation along those lines is incompatible with my position. . . . The saving, all-embracing love of God is what leads me to speak of history as profoundly one (in saying this I am not forgetting the distinctions also to be found within history)" (TL xxxix).

49. Although the just society is not a necessary condition for God's gift of the kingdom (TL 135), nevertheless, "without liberating historical events, there would be no growth of the kingdom," either (TL 104).

50. Pixley, for example, shows how the various traditions (Yahwist-Elohist, Priestly, etc.) of the Book of Exodus express the relationship between divine and human action in different ways. He draws on Whitehead to achieve a synthesis which can integrate them and satisfy the modern mind (On Exodus, Appendix 8, pp. 76-80; see also Gottwald, pp. 250-60). Cf. the balanced comments of Ellacuría, Mysterium liberationis 1:330-42; cf. also Comisión Teológica Internacional, "Declaración," p. 192. Harvey Cox, whom Gutiérrez cites in this context, was attempting to make the different point that the exodus relativizes all claims to political legitimacy (pp. 22-24; cf. TL 221n.41).

51. Fierro, pp. 326-27. Manzanera is also correct to indicate that Gutiérrez nonetheless pointed the way to a synthesis (p. 292n.27, 181-3, 188).

52. Manzanera summarizes: "In the theological conception proposed by Gutiérrez the fundamental content of the human acceptance of divine self-communication is not faith as intellectual belief, or even charity as love directly for God, but rather altruistic universal love, which in turn implies an attitude of solidarity in praxis of liberation" (p. 110). For a recent summary account of Gutiérrez's position, see La verdad, pp. 51-54.

53. Gutiérrez finds the spirituality of Ignatius of Loyola helpful for integrating gratuitousness and effective action. It "locate[s] efficacy . . . in the space of freely bestowed encounter with the Lord" (We Drink, p. 109). "The experience of gratuitousness . . . envelopes and permeates the effort to achieve historical efficacy" (p. 113). On all these points, see esp. We Drink, Chapt. 7. Compare the profound intuitions of the Puebla Document (274-79) based on Jesus' relationship to the Father and on Israel's collaborative covenant-relationship to Yahweh. For Rahner, human freedom and

dependence on God vary directly, not inversely. Rahner, "Freedom. Theological Aspect," in *Sacramentum Mundi;* idem, *Foundations,* p. 79. Cf. Manzanera, pp. 376-77, 404-6.

54. TL xxxi, my emphasis. God's "gift is accepted *in* the negation of injustice, *in* the protest against trampled human rights, and *in the struggle* for peace and fellowship" (TL 125, my emphasis).

55. Manzanera (pp. 52-56, 79-80, 120, 139-48, 211-24, 328-82) provides an especially thorough analysis of Gutiérrez's critical appropriation of Marxist thought. *See also* Cadorette, *passim.* Gutiérrez also considers Hegel's philosophy vital to contemporary, and future, thinking (see TL 236n.59).

56. What Gutiérrez means is that he rejects philosophical materialism and economic determinism, not to speak of atheism. His stress on freedom and personal responsibility is incompatible with determinism (*see La verdad,* pp. 188, 190).

57. Human beings overcome (*aufheben*) alienation by socially appropriating 1) the means of production and the fruits of labor, 2) the political project, 3) real liberty (*see* TL 138-39, 243n.129; cf. "Liberation Theology and Proclamation," pp. 62-63). The first two appropriations correspond to the first level of liberation, the last to the second (*see* Manzanera, pp. 364-77). Recent studies of Marx, especially the notes of his "master plan," the *Grundrisse,* vindicate this interpretation of Marx's thought.

58. Marx—who recorded his epistemological breakthrough in the *Theses on Feuerbach*—views theory and practice in dialectical tension. Praxis is "the matrix of authentic knowledge and the acid test of the validity of that knowledge" (PPH 59). Recently, Gutiérrez has pointed out that this understanding of theory and practice is not Marx's alone, and it indeed builds on a long and complex development in Western philosophy, as Lobkowicz, among others, has shown (*see La verdad,* 125-130). Gutiérrez once spoke of praxis as "the proving ground of all theory" (TL 21), leaving himself open to the charge that praxis had supplanted Christian faith as ultimate arbiter. He has recently qualified his earlier position (*see* TL xxxiv, 180n.34, 181n.40; *La verdad,* pp. 140-41).

59. Compare, for example, their respective treatments of eschatology. Sigmund's claim that early works of liberation theology neglected scripture crumbles before the evidence in Gutiérrez's case.

60. Fierro has criticized Gutiérrez for this, arguing that his theology is precritical.

61. "As Jean Mouroux wrote, 'if there are in the universe varying levels of analysis (creation, sin, redemption), there are not two different orders of reality, but only one, that of the Covenant which had creation for its first act; and Christ is its Alpha and Omega, its beginning and end; and this order is supernatural'" (cited in DeLubac, *A Brief Catechism,* p. 190).

62. Clodovis Boff has observed how the theological dimension of the liberation process fans out into three subdimensions of its own, namely, the presence of grace in the world, the presence of the (lay) Christian in the world, and the presence of the institutional church (and the hierarchy) in the world (*see* Boff and Boff, *Salvation and Liberation,* pp. 108-16).

63. Clodovis Boff lists several classical metaphors which describe the world in relation to saving grace (Paul: a *schema,* or shape; the New Testament: this age; the fathers of the church: this economy or dispensation; Augustine: the scaffold of the building, or history is pregnant with Christ; Vatican II: the foreshadowing of God's reign, the material of the celestial realm; N. Berdyaev, the *noumenon* of history; Boff suggests the "incarnation" or "installation" of the kingdom in history) *(Salvation and Liberation,* pp. 82-86). DeLubac speaks of a "parable" of God's reign (*A Brief Catechism,* p. 102). Leonardo Boff relates (political) liberation to salvation 1) the way Christ's human and divine natures are related (Chalcedon principle), 2) the way events are related to the grace they mediate sacramentally (in the broad sense), 3) the way love of neighbor and love of God are related, and the way body and soul are related (Boff and Boff, *Salvation and Liberation,* pp. 58-64).

5. NEW BRANCHES FOR AN OLD TREE

1. Of course, non-Christian religions also have much to say to Catholic thought about salvation, but that will have to remain a task for the future. A great deal of fruitful work has recently been done on salvation in Christian and non-Christian traditions *(see* Knitter; Gillis).

2. *See* Ruether's challenge to "the whole Western theological tradition of the hierarchical chain of being and chain of command" *(Sexism and God-talk,* pp. 85-92; quotation from p. 85; cf. Ruether, *To Change the World,* p. 67). This chain of superordination/subordination takes its rise from the original sin of sexism: the dominance of woman by man. Cf. Vaughan, pp. 106-21. We cannot adequately consider what feminist theology says about eschatology or sociality in this section. Ruether develops an eschatology of "conversion to the center, conversion to the earth and to each other, rather than flight into the unrealizable future." Her agnosticism about personal immortality, however, departs from Christian tradition *(Sexism and God-talk,* pp. 252-58). Feminist thought in general converges with much of what we say in the next section about the social character of the human condition.

3. Reality itself has a transcendental character. This does not refer to fixed universal characteristics but to the fact that all reality has a formal character (its "ownness" or "propriety") that is open to the rest of reality and dynamic, that is, open to assuming new forms based on present ones. For the foregoing summary, *see* Zubiri, *Inteligencia sentiente,* esp. pp. 127-32. Ellacuría's principal philosophical work is the posthumously published *Filosofía de la realidad histórica.*

4. "God is not a thing that is beyond things themselves, nor even a type of efficient cause . . . that underlies all of them. God is, as I see it, something more elementary and prior to all theory: . . . God does not *transcend things,* but is transcendent *in things.* And among these, transcendent *in* the human person" (Zubiri, *El hombre y Dios,* p. 308; cf. pp. 174, 202-4, 308-11, 377-79).

5. Ellacuría, *Mysterium liberationis* 1:323-72. For Ellacuría and Zubiri, persons are not subjects, or substances, prior to or underlying their activity. Persons are systems of characteristics. Personal reality is fundamentally self-possession (Zubiri, *Sobre el hombre*).

6. Compare the pan*en*theism espoused by Rahner and others. Johnson conveniently contextualizes this current in *She Who Is,* pp. 230-33. For Zubiri, God and the world are not two different realities, "but neither are they one. . . . [As Zubiri says], 'God transcends the world, but the world is immanent to God' " (González, "La novedad teológica," pp. 255, citing an unpublished text by Zubiri). "Precisely because God does not transcend things, but rather transcends *in* them, precisely for this things are not *simpliciter* not-God, but rather in some way they are a configuration of God *ad extra.* Therefore, God is not the human person, but the human person is in some form God: s/he is God humanly" (Zubiri, *El hombre y Dios,* p. 379).

7. This is not a matter of reducing salvation to human specifications. Rather, as the scholastic dictum states: Whatever is received is received according to the capacity of the receiver. "The 'close accord' and the kind of 'continuity' summed up in the axiom (stated by William of Auxerre and William of Auvergne) 'gratia perficit naturam' or 'gratia proportionatur naturae ut perfectio perfectibili,' or again 'natura praeambula est ad gratiam' by no means preclude, from another aspect, the total transcendence of the supernatural gift, its perfect spontaneity, and its difference in kind from 'nature'" (DeLubac, *Mystery of the Supernatural,* pp. 118-19).

8. Not all of the schools mentioned above have been conscious of the convergence outlined here. A striking example of it is the interest of German neo-Marxist critical theory in American pragmatism and linguistic philosophy. See the interest of Jürgen Habermas in the work of linguistic analysts Ludwig Wittgenstein and John Austin and

in the pragmatist G. H. Mead and philosophers of language like John Austin (Habermas, *Communicative Action*). According to Hans Joas, "misrepresentations concealed even from Marxists the extraordinary proximity between Marx's philosophy of praxis and the fundamental principle of pragmatism" (p. 36).

9. For what follows, see Geertz, "Impact"; idem, "Growth" in his *Interpretation of Cultures*, pp. 33-54 and pp. 55-83, respectively.

10. In the course of human evolution, "man determined, if unwittingly, the culminating stages of his own biological destiny. Quite literally, though quite inadvertently, he created himself" (Geertz, "Impact," p. 48). *See* Landmann, p. 230.

11. The functioning of the nervous system is impossible without culture. Therefore, thought is impossible and affectivity sheer chaos without cultural determinations (Geertz, "Growth," pp. 68-69, 75-81; cf. Landmann, p. 219).

12. "Many animals also live in groups. But, for man, life in the group has an additional, deeper function. An animal that grows up separated from other members of its species . . . will still behave exactly like one that grows up normally. . . . But man becomes a complete man only by growing up in a tradition-bearing group of his own kind" (Landmann, p. 220).

13. For the work of von Uexküll et al., *see* Berger and Luckmann, p. 195, n. 1. The work of these scientists and philosophers has been critically synthesized at greater length by Landmann in *Philosophical Anthropology, passim.*

14. "For Mead the primordial given is . . . the 'social act,' the complex activity of the group" (Joas, p. 112). According to Mead, consciousness of other selves and communication arises from practical cooperation. Consciousness of objects, and then of one's own body, as well as space and time, arise from consciousness of others. Thought emerges in the form of interior conversation among remembered (exterior) voices (ibid., Chapt. 5). Elizabeth Johnson explains clearly and briefly how feminist thought has assumed and extended the idea of the social constitution of the self (pp. 67-69 with bibliographical references, p. 286nn16-22).

15. "The Self must be conceived, not theoretically as subject, but practically, as agent" (Macmurray, *Self as Agent,* p. 38). This is because "the assumption of the primacy of the theoretical in our philosophical tradition . . . institutes a formal dualism which cannot be resolved" (ibid., p. 84).

16. "The personal is constituted by the relation of persons. The reference to the personal Other is constitutive for all personal existence" (ibid., p. 69; cf. pp. 73, 77, 91, 119, 170).

17. Thus his book *Sobre el hombre* begins: "As a living being, the human being finds itself among things, some external, others internal, which maintain him/her in activity that is not only constant, but primary; living beings are constitutive activity" (p. 11). This primary activity is the condition for action in the pragmatists' sense. For Zubiri and unlike classical philosophy, all reality is dynamic. Human beings are "systems" or "structures."

18. Scholars today agree that Marx's works display a fundamental unity of thought. While Marx's thought developed, the basic themes of the sociality of human beings, alienation, and its overcoming by appropriation are central themes from early through late works. "Thus Marx's thought," David McLellan writes, "is best viewed as a continuing meditation on central themes broached in 1844, the high point of which meditation occurred in 1857-8" with the composition of the *Grundrisse,* the immense work which expresses the unity of themes in the *1844 Manuscripts* and later works like *Capital* (McLellan, p. 12; cf. Ollman, pp. xv-xvi; Avineri, pp. 1-7).

19. Marx, "Economics and Philosophical Manuscripts," p. 158. Hereafter: *1844 Mss.*

20. Alienation is first of all a matter of social relations (cf. p. 129).

21. Thus Marx can refer to "religion, the family, the state, law, morality, science, art, etc." as forms of production (*1844 Mss.,* p. 156; cf. Ollman, p. 98). On the centrality of work, *see* Avineri, Chapt. 3.

22. "The *whole of what is called world history* is nothing but the creation of man by human labour, and the emergence of the nature of man" (*1844 Mss.*, p. 166; *see* p. 198). In *The Poverty of Philosophy* Marx wrote that "all history is nothing but the continual transformation of human nature" (cited in Ollman, p. 79). Ollman holds that Marx recognized a "conception of 'human nature in general'," at least in the sense of general characteristics or preconditions of human activity (Ollman, pp. 73-76, 112; quotation from p. 74).

23. "Human beings are animals of distantiation. Their hyperformalization determines them to be sensing, and therefore to be in a certain way in what they sense, but to be so in a distanced way. . . . Distantiation . . . is not separation 'from' things, but distantiation 'in' them" (Zubiri, *Inteligencia sentiente*, p. 70).

24. "Self-identity is impossible without the self already having been constituted by the other in such a way that to *be* requires the overcoming of that predefinition" (Rasmussen, p. 42; cf. pp. 19-25, 41-43; *see also* Unger, p. 204).

25. Assuming the role of another means behaving in anticipation of the reaction of another, not assuming the other's social situation (Joas, p. 118). According to Joas, while Mead is the source of key concepts of the symbolic interactionism school, his starting point is not communication but rather *practical interaction*: "The mechanism of human society is that of bodily selves who assist or hinder each other in their cooperative acts by the manipulation of physical things" (G. H. Mead, cited in Joas, p. 114).

26. In the socialization process, "the child takes on the significant others' roles and attitudes, that is, internalizes them and makes them his own" (Berger and Luckmann, pp. 131-32; *see* Landmann, p. 187). Berger and Luckmann write: "the self is a reflected entity, reflecting the attitudes first taken by significant others toward it; the individual becomes what he is addressed as by his significant others" (Berger and Luckmann, p. 132). The authors are drawing on Cooley, Mead, and Schutz here.

27. The person's identity is always experienced (even if only preconsciously or in memory) as more or less threatened with meaninglessness (*anomie*) and the possibility of dissolution. Marginal or boundary experiences unveil this (*see* Berger and Luckmann, pp. 100-4). I am stressing, in addition, the *material* nature of this threat.

28. Marxists would interpret the dialectic in terms of class struggle. Many feminists consider the male-female dialectic as primordial, the model and root cause of all other forms of oppression. For still others, racial discrimination constitutes the root oppression. The question is fundamental, but we must leave it for another day.

29. "*All* roles represent the institutional order in the aforementioned sense" (Berger and Luckmann, p. 76; cf. p. 79). The authors are developing an expanded notion of Mead's understanding of role, one that can include reference to institutions (p. 197n.22). "Mead situates the formation of the self within social and political praxis" (Joas, p. 134).

30. Not that Marx viewed human beings as outside of nature. The opposite is true. Communism will mean the overcoming of the antagonism between human beings and nature (*1844 Mss.*, p. 155). Under these conditions, nature will be humanized and humanity naturalized (p. 157).

31. *See* Marx, *Preface and Introduction*, where consumption and distribution are construed as aspects of production.

32. Moralist Marciano Vidal suggests we take structural sin as our prime analogue (Vidal, p. 998).

33. Concupiscence in Christian tradition refers most often to humanity's profound tendency to evil or, more broadly, to "man's spontaneous desire insofar as it precedes his free decision *and resists it*" (Rahner, "Theological Concept of 'Concupiscentia' "). For Rahner, "concupiscence" refers not merely to *sensitive* appetite and not merely to an inclination to *evil* but always to (spontaneous) sensitive-*spiritual* appetite. Concupiscence is the inertia or resistance offered by human "nature" (i.e., whatever is given prior to and as a condition for free decision) to the attempt of the person to dispose of

him- or herself in an evil or a *good* free action. It is, therefore, a *bivalent* notion. Rahner also believes that this implies an inherent lack of harmony in the *world* itself: as "concupiscent," the world is never subject to complete ideological or political unification. The world, like the life of the concupiscent individual, is fraught with conflict and struggle (Rahner, "Theological Reflections on the Problem of Secularisation").

34. Metz, like many others, has rightly stressed this "eschatological proviso" (*Theology of the World,* p. 114; cf. Fierro, pp. 281-82).

6. JESUS AND THE REIGN OF GOD

1. It might not have been *the* central theme explaining all others, however (Meier, *A Marginal Jew* 2:237).

2. Norman Perrin reviews the history of life-of-Jesus research from Schleiermacher to around 1960 in his *The Kingdom of God in the Teaching of Jesus.* For more recent trends, *see* Evans, "Life-of-Jesus Research" and idem, *Life of Jesus Research.* For a clear exposition of the various criteria used to establish the earliest materials embedded in available texts, see the masterful assessment by Meier, *A Marginal Jew* 1: Chapt. 6. *See also* the simple, clear exposition of criteria in Bowden, Chapt. 3.

3. Notice the fundamental sin-grace paradigm. There is no neutral ground; one submits to the rule of Satan or to God (Meier, *A Marginal Jew* 2:414-15; cf. Sobrino, *Jesucristo liberador,* pp. 130, 166-70). It is a theme underdeveloped by most commentators.

4. This partly justifies our use of the English word *kingdom* in addition to the increasingly common *reign,* which is generally preferable. The use of *kingdom* and *reign* is problematic for contemporary theology, however: As for *kingdom,* the Hebrew and Greek equivalents are not gender-specific and could as easily mean "queendom." Of course, Jesus transvalues the symbol and invests it with a meaning much more acceptable to contemporary sensibilities than traditional kingships are (*see* Matt 20,25-27). This probably partly accounts for his reluctance to identify with the title Messiah (*see* Bornkamm, Chapt. 8).

5. *See* the classic study of Kümmel, *Promise and Fulfillment: The Eschatological Message of Jesus,* pp. 114-21. John P. Meier criticizes Marcus Borg, John Dominic Crossan and others who minimize the future eschatological elements of Jesus' message (cf. Meier, *A Marginal Jew* 2:9, 269-70, 337-38 and Chapt. 15, *passim*).

6. Dupont, *Les Béatitudes. Le problème littéraire* is the first volume. Volume 2, *Les Béatitudes. La bonne nouvelle* interprets the beatitudes within the framework of Jesus' teaching and ministry. It is the material of the second volume which concerns us principally. Volume 3, *Les Béatitudes. Les évangélistes,* studies the beatitudes within the literary context of the gospels of Matthew and Luke. For a concise summary of Dupont's understanding of the beatitudes, *see* Dupont, "Introduction au Béatitudes"; in English *see* idem, "The Poor and Poverty in the Gospels and in Acts." Dupont has had a profound, if little-noticed, impact on Latin American theology, especially through the work of Gutiérrez.

7. Dupont believes that the fourth beatitude, though part of early tradition, reflects the situation of the early church (2:343). Meier (*A Marginal Jew* 2:322-23) agrees with this reconstruction. For recent discussions, *see* Mealand, Chapt. 2 (with notes 5-9) and pp. 61-63; Schottroff and Stegemann, pp. 19-20, 124n.58.

8. "Second Isaiah" here refers to all of Isaiah 40-66, although chapters 56-66 probably derive from a third Isaian school. Some oracles of the Book of Consolation promise deliverance to the poor and afflicted: Is 61,1-3; 49,13; 57,18; 66,10.13; etc. Others announce satisfaction for the hungry and thirsty: Is 61,6-7; 55,1-3; 65,13; 66,11-12; 23,18 [late text].

9. Hoppe criticizes the well-known thesis of Gelin that "the poor" becomes progressively de-materialized in the later traditions of the Bible (*see also* Lohfink, *Option for*

the Poor, pp. 59-60; Mealand, pp. 101-2, 127-28nn.1-11 and "Appendix B"; Meier, *A Marginal Jew* 2:384n.157).

10. Dupont cites Ps 76,8-10; 68,6-7; 103,6; 140,13; 146,7-10; 9-10 along with Deut 10,17-18 and the Psalms of Solomon and Qumran texts (pp. 67-73).

11. *See* Ezekiel 34 (the good shepherd); Is 14,30; Mi 4,6-7; Zeph 3,15-19; Is 40,9-11. God will intervene like a just king: Dupont cites Jer 21,12; 22,3.12-19; 5,28; Prov 29,14; Amos 2,6-7; 8,4; Is 1,23; 3,14-15; 10,1; Ps 82,2-4. For the ideal king, the messiah, *see* Is 8,23 - 9,3.6; 11,2-9; Psalms of Solomon 17; Ps 72 (Dupont, *Béatitudes,* 2:85-88).

12. For what follows, *see* Berkovits; von Rad, pp. 372f.; Schrenk; Berger, "Justice. I. Scripture"; Walsh, pp. 4-5, 31-32; Miranda, Chapt. 3; Aguirre and Vitoria Cormenzana.

13. *See also* the following texts, which use these concepts to indicate *who God is:* Ex 34,6-7; Num 14,18; Ezr 9,15; Is 5,16; Ps 33,4-5; 85,10; 89,14; 97,1-2; etc.; cf. Is 46,13; 56,1; Hos 2,21-22.

14. *See* Berkovits, pp. 322-26, 331-333. Is 56,6-8 gives a comprehensive definition of *sedeq* (vs. 8). Berkovits distinguishes *sedeq* from *sedaqah* (two terms von Rad and others treat as synonymous).

15. *See* Is 65,17-25; cf. also Is 25,6-9; 29,17-21; 32,15-20; Jer 31,10-17. In this sense, peace equals salvation (Is 52,7; Nah 2,1 [Hebr.]).

16. Cf. Miranda, Chapt. 3, and Walsh, Chapts. 2 and 3. *See also* Pixley, *God's Kingdom,* Chapt. 1. Other gods defended the vulnerable. As Walter Harrelson notes, only Yahweh comes to the aid of an oppressed *people.* Moreover, the subversive elements of Israel's tradition do not disappear, as such elements tend to disappear in other religions. They form part of the "core tradition" of Israel's faith (Harrelson, p. 25).

17. John Riches argues that a rich symbol like "God's reign" retains a core meaning even as different communities invest the symbol with a wide variety of "conventional associations" (Riches, Chapt. 2).

18. Meier remarks: "About 90 percent of Galilean Jews would probably have qualified as 'poor' in some sense of the word" (*A Marginal Jew* 2:1048n2). Peasants typically made up 90 percent of the population of ancient agricultural societies (Horsley, p. xii). Crossan, pp. 43-46, gives a lower, nonnumerical assessment.

19. Oakman calculates that a peasant who withheld grain for seed and paid taxes, tithe, and other social obligations, could be left with one-fifth of the harvest for consumption (p. 72; cf. Crossan, p. 221).

20. Poverty is always an evil in the Bible, and when the Wisdom literature warns that dissolute behavior brings on poverty, this hardly supplants the tradition that the poor are victims. Much less does it intend to portray the poor as lazy. *See* Hoppe, esp. Chapt. 5.

21. Sanders argues that Jesus did not demand repentance of "sinners" (pp. 106-13, 206-8). In any event, he apparently took the initiative with sinners prior to any repentance (Sobrino, *Jesucristo liberador,* pp. 170-75). But we know he also demanded acceptance of his person and message.

22. Merkel (p. 135) considers Jesus' special regard for tax collectors "an outrageous provocation."

23. Jesus did, however, recognize differences and criteria of righteousness and sin: cf. Matt 5,45; 13,49; 25,37.46.

24. The dominant priestly theology stressed strict observance of torah, especially those rituals which distinguished devout Jews from both Gentiles and Jewish Hellenizers (Riches, Chapt. 4; cf. Theissen, Chapt. 8).

25. Crossan (pp. 261-64) argues that Jesus' open informal meals were part of a program of radical egalitarianism. Cf. Theissen, Chapt. 8, *passim,* on inter- and intra-group differentiation.

26. For Jesus' message to the poor, *see* Luke 4,16-22; Luke 6,20-26; Matt 11,2-6 par.; Matt 25,31-46. For his message to sinners, *see* Mark 2,13-17 par.; Matt 21,28-32; Luke

7,29-30; Luke 7,34 par.; Luke 15 *passim;* Matt 9,9-10 par.; Luke 18,9-14; Luke 19,1-10. We could include many more passages from later synoptic traditions. On this double emphasis in early traditions, *see* Schottroff and Stegemann, pp. 18-37.

27. *See* Matt 19,3-9 par.; Matt 5,31-32 (divorce); Matt 5,27-28; Luke 20,47 (secondary?) and many narratives: Mark 15,40-41 par.; Luke 8,1-3; 13,10-17.36-50; John 7,53 - 8,11. On widows, *see* Luke 7,11-17; 18,1-8; 20,47; 21,1-4.

28. Jesus' contemporaries considered children ignorant and insignificant (Jeremias, *New Testament Theology,* p. 227). *Therefore* God's kingdom is especially for them—not because they are innocent or humble, but because God is compassionate to those who are weak and considered unimportant.

29. On Samaritans, *see* Luke 10,29-37 and less sure traditions: Luke 17,11-19; John 4,1-43. On Gentiles, *see* Matt 22,1-10 par. and possibly Matt 20,1-6; Mark 12,1-12; Luke 11,29-32 with the following narrative material: Matt 8,5-13 par.; Mark 5,1-20 par.; 7,24-30 par.; Luke 4,25-30. Virtually all Jesus' contemporaries numbered Gentiles and public sinners among the wicked whom God would destroy.

30. Theissen, Sanders, Lohfink, Schüssler Fiorenza, Riches, Borg, and Crossan all stress this point, with varying nuances.

31. "Twelve tribes of Israel" may simply mean Israel here, with no strictly miraculous gathering of disappeared tribes intended. Some interpret "judge" to mean (or include) rule. For the literature, *see* Beasley-Murray, pp. 273-77, with notes.

32. He may have felt the turmoil over Roman tribute served to distract from Israel's own need to reform: "Render to God what is God's."

33. Criticizing Sanders, Craig Evans has shown that Jesus' temple action protested priestly corruption in the prophetic spirit (Evans, "Jesus' Action in the Temple"). Evans construes the prophetic tradition too narrowly, however. The contexts of the very texts he cites show how it is the abuse of the weak, not just vague corruption, which profanes the cult.

34. Most today hold that the leaders of the Jewish community—the chief priests— were the principal force behind Jesus' execution. But the Romans probably participated more than the gospels suggest (*see* Nolan, Chapt. 18; Borg, p. 178; Theissen, p. 72).

35. For the evidence, *see* Jeremias, *Theology,* pp. 131-41; Kümmel, "Eschatological Expectation," pp. 36-51. The English version of Kümmel's article first appeared in 1971. Cf. also, Beasley-Murray, p. 190 with copious references (381n.161). Jesus gave no date. *See* Meier, *A Marginal Jew* 2:336-48.

36. Riches, pp. 160-67, believes that condemnation-language is incompatible with Jesus' message.

37. The problem of the state of those who die in Christ, the problem of the "intermediate state" between death and Jesus' second coming, was a question for later theology, not for Jesus.

38. Although "fundamentally a corporate concept," God's kingdom equals "life" for the individual (Mark 9,43.46) who will enter the kingdom through resurrection (Beasley-Murray, p. 175).

39. Schweizer, "Psuche," *passim;* quotation, p. 639. Compare Paul VI's teaching in PP 23. "Here, then, the Greek division into body and spirit, into a bodily and earthly life on the one side and a heavenly and spiritual life on the other, is plainly overcome" (Schweizer, "Psuche," p. 644; cf. Jacob, "Psuche"; Wolff, p. 38. "Israelite anthropology is monistic" (Jacob, "Psuche," 631; cf. Wolff, pp. 7-9).

40. While Paul's "new creation" stresses the radical newness of salvation in Christ, it presupposes the same anthropology (see Schweizer, "Pneuma, pneumatikos," 434-36).

41. The second half probably does not go back to Jesus. It is more likely an early interpretation of "Your kingdom come!"

42. "The kingdom of heaven is fundamentally the kingdom of earth" (Beasley-Murray, p. 163). This beatitude (Matt 5,5) and the proclamation of the Jubilee "land reform"

(if historical) surely provoked strong reactions to Jesus. Apocalyptic eschatology does not necessarily entail "the cosmological destruction of the world" or "the temporal end of history" (Collins, p. 64). We need not assume it did for Jesus, either. Nor should we take all apocalyptic heavenly imagery literally. Cf. also Theissen, p. 63; Cullman, pp. 141-46; Viviano, Chapt. 1; Lohfink, *Option for the Poor,* pp. 5-8; Nolan, p. 46; Berkovits, p. 348.

"Treasure [or 'reward'] in heaven" (Matt 5,12 par. Luke 6,23; Matt 6,21 par. Luke 12,33; Mark 10,21 par.) simply refers to treasure kept with God (= "heaven"). It means that God will reward the one who is faithful. It does not mean (at least not necessarily) that one goes to heaven to receive the reward. *See* Miranda, pp. 104-5.

43. Liberal theology enlisted the growth parables (mustard seed, leaven, seed growing slowly) in the service of the ideology of evolutionary progress. But to change the label to "contrast parables," as some propose, would be misleading. The parables portray precisely a divinely inspired process in which the end is implicit in the beginning and results from it. *See* Dahl; Beasley-Murray, pp. 123-27, 194-201.

44. For Paul, Abraham's descendents will "inherit the world" (Rom 4,13; cf. 8,21). "Spiritual bodies" (1 Cor 15,44)—that is, persons transformed by God's spirit—will inhabit the (new?) earth. When 1 Cor 15,50 says that "flesh and blood" will not inherit the kingdom, "flesh and blood" means not *body = soma* but that corruptible "*sarx*" which is the instrument of sin (cf. Gal 5,21). The new creation language of 2 Pet 3,13 and Rev 21,1 (cf. Is 65,17; 66,22) can signify a radical transformation of this world, as in Is 65-66.

45. This suggests that the decisive battle has *already* been won; the "Strong Man" has already been bound (Mark 3,27). *See* Beasley-Murray, pp. 110-11.

46. First-century Palestine knew many popular movements whose discontented members acclaimed the leader messiah-king (Horsley, Chapt. 3; Crossan, pp. 99-123 and Chapts. 9-10).

47. Traditions both early and late reflect these temptations: the demand for signs from God (Mark 8,11-12 par.; John 2,18; 6,30); ostentation (John 7,2-5); the cry for bread (John 6 and discouragement: vs. 66); rejection of the humble way of sacrifice (Mark 8,31-33 par.); the offer of kingship (John 6,14-15); violence against non-Jews (Luke 9,54); Gethsemane (Mark 14,36 par.); violent resistance (Matt 26,51-53 par.; John 18,36); "Let him come down from that cross" (Matt 27,38-43 par.).

48. In what follows, I draw on the well-known article by Ebeling, "Jesus and Faith." Cf. also, Bornkamm, pp. 129-32 and Nolan, Chapt. 4.

49. It is striking that Jesus uses the term faith without reference to God (Ebeling, p. 232). Perrin (*The Teaching of Jesus,* pp. 130-42) over-secularizes the concept, however, in a treatment similar to Ebeling's.

50. Not all we hear Jesus saying about faith in the synoptics derives from him; but this matters little in light of the question we posed above. The gospels, especially the Q source, tell us what the early disciples understood Jesus' teaching about faith to be and how they undertook radically new forms of kingdom-behavior under very trying circumstances. *See* Schottroff and Stegemann, Chapt. 2, *passim;* Mealand, Chapt. 3; Theissen. *See* Ebeling for convincing arguments that the *concept* of faith indicated in the synoptic passages (and outlined here) derives from Jesus.

51. "In the New Testament exegetical literature I have found every possible explanation of the rare occurrence of the theme of 'poverty'. . . . But I have very seldom encountered the notion that among the early Christians, because of a new initiative in common life given them by Jesus and a new way of handling material goods, there might have been something like an abolition of social stratification and the disappearance of real poverty" (Lohfink, *Option for the Poor,* p. 56).

52. Faith therefore must liberate utopian imagination. That genuine hope depends on imagining new truly realistic and possible ways to live together. *See* Lynch; Alves, *Tomorrow's Child;* Lane.

53. "The actual stuff of all historiography is 'abstract', that is, it carves out a part of the real past; it formalizes and provides only images. Thus the historical Jesus, so called, is no less a Jesus-image than the Christ of the believer" (Schillebeeckx, p. 68). Hypothesis and reconstruction is of the nature of this type of research. *See* Sanders, pp. 3, 18-22. According to John P. Meier, the "historical Jesus" which we construct never coincides with the irretrievable real Jesus of Nazareth. Ours are limited and revisable reconstructions (Meier, "The Historical Jesus." Cf. Crossan, pp. 422-26).

54. Scripture confronts our present situation of life and thought with questions and answers, and contemporary life and thought pose questions and answers to Scripture, as well. The hermeneutical circle expands beyond the individual and the text. *See* Tracy, *Blessed Rage,* pp. 45-46. Indeed, we must expand this circle to include praxis as well as reflection and ask which traditions enlighten the path for liberation of the oppressed (Segundo, *Liberation of Theology,* p. 9 and *passim*; cf. Schüssler Fiorenza, "Feminist Biblical Hermeneutics," p. 100).

55. Paradoxically, the fact that our Jesus of Nazareth is a construct "relativizes the sharp contrast supposed to exist between the 'Jesus of history' and the 'Jesus of faith' " (Schillebeeckx, p. 68).

56. From this standpoint, Bultmann fails to render an appropriate interpretation of Jesus' message today. As Dorothee Soelle says, consistent existentialist principles require a political interpretation of human existence (Soelle, Chapt. 4; cf. Metz, *Theology of the World,* pp. 110-11, 128).

57. Perrin argued that Israel inherited two traditions concerning God's royal activity: the Creator-king rules over creation and the Liberator-king rescues Israel in crucial moments of his history (*Jesus and the Language,* pp. 16-32). Beasley-Murray has rightly criticized this view, arguing that God's rule over creation subserves and illustrates God's coming to deliver those in need (pp. 9, 340 and Part 1, *passim*).

7. GOD'S REVOLUTION

1. For this last criterion, see my "Evolución del concepto de justicia con referencia al capitalismo y socialismo." All modern economies, whether capitalist or socialist, will have managers of the means of production. The point is democratic accountability for this decisive power. The critique of the reigning disorder and the search for alternatives is well advanced in Latin America. *See,* for example, Montoya, *La nueva economía popular: una aproximación teórica*; Razeto, *Economía popular de solidaridad;* idem, *Economía de solidaridad y mercado democrático*; *Neoliberales y pobres: El debate continental por la justicia*; González, "Orden mundial y liberación." For a strategy for change, *see* Burbach and Nuñez, *Fire in the Americas;* Castañeda, *Utopia Unarmed.*

In the context of the North, *see* the U.S. Catholic Bishops' pastoral, *Economic Justice for All.* Burns, "The Problem of Socialism in Liberation Theology" (p. 505n.51), offers a rich bibliography of recent works grounded "in cogent economic analysis and argument" for "models of feasible socialism."

2. "The world is sick. Its illness consists less in the unproductive monopolization of resources by a small number of persons than in the lack of fellowship among individuals and peoples" (PP 66).

3. Martin Luther King, Jr., "Love, Law, and Civil Disobedience," p. 52—and frequently. In the second instance, King is quoting William Cullen Bryant.

4. Vatican II had paved the way for this statement. According to the council, the church is sacrament of salvation and of unity (LG 1 and 48; *see* AG 1; GS 38). Its mission is to proclaim and establish the reign of God among all peoples (LG 5; cf. LG 36; GS 45; AG 1). The church "seeks but a solitary goal: to carry forward the work of Christ himself under the lead of the befriending Spirit" (GS 3), "to make God the Father and His Incarnate Son present and in a sense visible" (GS 21). According to GS 42, Christ gave the church "no proper mission in the political, economic, or social

order. . . . But of [its] *religious* mission itself comes a function, a light and an energy which can serve to structure and consolidate the human community according to the divine law" (emphasis added). This suggests that, granted the autonomy of the social order, the church's specifically *religious* mission itself includes, necessarily, a prophetic social dimension. This is not a secondary mission, however, for "the promotion of unity belongs to the innermost nature of the Church, since she is, 'by her relationship with Christ, both a sacramental sign and an instrument of intimate union with God, and of the unity of all [hu]mankind' " (GS 42, citing LG 1). *See* EN 14.

BIBLIOGRAPHY

Aguirre, R., and F. J. Vitoria Cormenzana. "Justicia." In Ignacio Ellacuría and Jon Sobrino, eds. *Mysterium liberationis: Fundamental Concepts of Liberation Theology*. English ed. Maryknoll, NY: Orbis Books, 1993, pp. 539-61.

Alves, Rubem. *A Theology of Human Hope*. St. Meinrad, IN: Abbey Press, 1975.

_____. *Tomorrow's Child: Imagination, Creativity, and the Rebirth of Culture*. New York: Harper and Row, 1972.

Anderson, James F. "The Role of Analogy in Maritain's Thought." In Joseph W. Evans, ed. *Jacques Maritain: The Man and His Achievement*. New York: Sheed & Ward, 1963.

Assmann, Hugo. *Theology for a Nomad Church*. Trans. Paul Burns. Maryknoll, NY: Orbis Books, 1976.

Avineri, Shlomo. *The Social and Political Thought of Karl Marx*. New York: Cambridge University Press, 1968.

Bammel, Ernst, and C. F. D. Moule, eds. *Jesus and the Politics of His Day*. New York: Cambridge University Press, 1984.

Beasley-Murray, G. R. *Jesus and the Kingdom of God*. Grand Rapids, MI: Eerdmans, 1986.

Berger, Klaus. "Justice. I. Scripture." In Karl Rahner, ed. *Encyclopedia of Theology: The Concise 'Sacramentum Mundi.'* New York: Seabury, 1975.

Berger, Peter L., and Thomas Luckmann. *The Social Construction of Reality: A Treatise in the Sociology of Knowledge*. Garden City, NY: Doubleday, 1967.

Berkovits, Eliezer. *Man and God: Studies in Biblical Theology*. Detroit, MI: Wayne State University Press, 1969.

Berryman, Phillip. *Liberation Theology: The Essential Facts about the Revolutionary Movement in Latin America and Beyond*. New York: Pantheon Books, 1987.

_____. *The Religious Roots of Rebellion: Christians in Central American Revolutions*. Maryknoll, NY: Orbis Books, 1985.

Boff, Clodovis. "Society and the Kingdom." In Leonardo Boff and Clodovis Boff, *Salvation and Liberation: In Search of a Balance between Faith and Politics*. Maryknoll, NY: Orbis Books, 1984.

Boff, Leonardo. *Liberating Grace*. Maryknoll, NY: Orbis Books, 1979.

Boff, Leonardo, and Clodovis Boff. *Introducing Liberation Theology*. Trans. Paul Burns. Maryknoll, NY: Orbis Books, 1988.

_____. *Liberation Theology: From Confrontation to Dialogue*. Trans. Robert R. Barr. San Francisco: Harper and Row, 1986.

_____. *Salvation and Liberation: In Search of a Balance between Faith and Politics*. Trans. Robert R. Barr. Maryknoll, NY: Orbis Books, 1984.

Borg, Marcus. *Jesus: A New Vision*. San Francisco: Harper, 1991.

Bornkamm, Günther. *Jesus of Nazareth*. Trans. I. and F. McLuskey with J. M. Robinson. 3rd ed. New York: Harper & Row, 1975.

Bottomore, T. B., and M. Rubel, eds. *Karl Marx: Selected Writings in Sociology and Social Philosophy*. London: Watts and Co., 1956.

Bowden, John. *Jesus: The Unanswered Questions*. Nashville, TN: Abingdon Press, 1989.

Brackley, Dean. *Etica social cristiana: Textos de la doctrina social católica, ensayos bíblicos y comentarios.* San Salvador: UCA Editores, 1995.

_____. "Evolución del concepto de justicia con referencia al capitalismo y socialismo." *Revista Latinoamericana de Teología* 30 (Sept.-Dec. 1993): 263-78.

_____. *Organize! A Manual for Leaders.* Illus. Joey Negrón. New York: Paulist Press, 1990.

_____. *People Power.* Illus. Larry Nolte. New York: Paulist Press, 1989.

Bradley, Denis J. M. "Rahner's Spirit in the World: Aquinas or Hegel?" *The Thomist* 41 (1977): 167-99.

Bromiley, Geoffrey W., ed. *Theological Dictionary of the New Testament.* Grand Rapids, MI: William B. Eerdmans, 1968.

Brown, Raymond. *The Gospel According to John, XIII-XXI.* Anchor Bible 29A. Garden City, NY: Doubleday, 1970.

Brown, Robert McAfee. *Gustavo Gutiérrez: An Introduction to Liberation Theology.* Maryknoll, NY: Orbis Books, 1990.

_____. *Theology in a New Key: Responding to Liberation Themes.* Philadelphia: Westminster Press, 1978.

Buckley, James J. "On Being a Symbol: An Appraisal of Karl Rahner." *Theological Studies* 40 (1979): 453-73.

Bultmann, Rudolf. *Jesus and the Word.* Trans. Louise Pettibone Smith and Erminie Huntress Lantero. New York: Charles Scribner's Sons, 1958.

Burbach, Roger, and Orlando Nuñez. *Fire in the Americas: Forging a Revolutionary Agenda.* New York: Verso Books, 1988.

Burns, Peter J. "The Problem of Socialism in Liberation Theology." *Theological Studies* 53 (1992): 493-516.

Cadorette, Curt. *From the Heart of the People: The Theology of Gustavo Gutiérrez.* Oak Park, IL: Meyer-Stone Books, 1988.

Caldera, Rafael. "Personal Testimony." *New Scholasticism* 46 (Winter 1972): 10-17.

Calvin, John. *Institutes of Christian Religion.* Ed. John T. MacNeill, trans. Ford Lewis Battles. Philadelphia: The Westminster Press, 1960.

Carpenter, James A. *Nature and Grace: Toward an Integral Perspective.* New York: Crossroad, 1988.

Carr, Anne E. *Transforming Grace: Christian Tradition and Women's Experience.* San Francisco: Harper & Row, 1988.

Castañeda, Jorge. *Utopia Unarmed: The Latin American Left After the Cold War.* New York: Knopf, 1993.

Chilton, Bruce. "God in Strength." In his *The Kingdom of God in the Teaching of Jesus.* Issues in Religion and Theology 5. Philadelphia: Fortress Press, 1984.

Chopp, Rebecca. *Praxis of Suffering.* Maryknoll, NY: Orbis Books, 1986.

Christ, Carol P. "The New Feminist Theology: A Review of the Literature." *Religious Studies Review* 3:4 (Oct. 1977): 203-12.

Codina, Victor. "Crónica de Santo Domingo." *Revista Latinoamericana de Teología* 9:27 (Sept.-Dec., 1992): 259-71.

Cohn, Norman. *The Pursuit of the Millennium: Revolutionary Millenarians and Mystical Anarchists of the Middle Ages.* London: Paladin, 1970.

Collins, John J. "Apocalyptic Eschatology as the Transcendence of Death." In Paul D. Hanson, ed. *Visionaries and Their Apocalypses.* Philadelphia: Fortress Press, 1983.

Comisión Teológica Internacional. *Theología de la liberacíon.* B.A.C. Menor 48. Madrid: Biblioteca de Autores Cristianos, 1978.

Congar, Yves. "Apropos: The Peasant of the Garonne." In William J. Nottingham. *Christian Faith and Secular Action: An Introduction to the Life and Thought of Jacques Maritain.* St. Louis, MO: The Bethany Press, 1968.

Cook, Michael L. *Guidelines for Contemporary Catholics: The Historical Jesus.* Chicago: The Thomas More Press, 1986.

Cox, Harvey. *The Secular City: Secularization and Urbanization in Theological Perspective*. Rev. ed. New York: Macmillan, 1966.

Croatto, J. Severino. *Exodus: A Hermeneutics of Freedom*. Trans. Salvator Attanasio. Maryknoll, NY: Orbis Books, 1981.

Crossan, John Dominic. *The Historical Jesus: The Life of a Mediterranean Jewish Peasant*. San Francisco: HarperSanFrancisco, 1991.

Cullman, Oscar. *Christ and Time: The Primitive Christian Conception of Time and History*. Trans. Floyd Filson. Philadelphia: Westminster, 1950.

Dahl, N. A. "The Parables of Growth." *Studia Theologica* 5:2 (1951): 132-66.

Daly, Mary. *Beyond God the Father: Toward a Philosophy of Women's Liberation*. Boston: Beacon Press, 1973.

_____. *Pure Lust: An Elemental Feminist Philosophy*. Boston: Beacon Press, 1984.

DeLubac, Henri. *A Brief Catechism on Nature and Grace*. San Francisco: Ignatius Press, 1984.

_____. *Exégèse médiévale: Le quatre sens de l'écriture*. Paris: Aubier, 1969.

_____. *The Mystery of the Supernatural*. Trans. Rosemary Sheed. New York: Herder and Herder, 1967.

Dodd, C. H. *The Founder of Christianity*. New York: Macmillan, 1970.

Doering, Bernard. *Jacques Maritain and the French Catholic Intellectuals*. Notre Dame, IN: Notre Dame University Press, 1983.

Duffy, Stephen J. *The Graced Horizon: Nature and Grace in Modern Catholic Thought*. Collegeville, MN: Michael Glazier/The Liturgical Press, 1992.

Dulles, Avery. "The Meaning of Faith Considered in Relation to Justice." In John C. Haughey, ed. *The Faith that Does Justice*. New York: Paulist Press, 1977, pp. 10-46.

_____. *Models of the Church*. Garden City, NY: Doubleday/Image Books, 1978.

Dupont, Jacques. *Les Béatitudes*. Vol. 1: *Le problème littéraire: les deux versions du Sermon sur la montaigne et des Béatitudes*. Bruges-Louvain, 1958. Reprint ed. Paris: J. Gabalda, 1969. Vol. 2: *La bonne nouvelle*. Paris: J. Gabalda, 1969. Vol. 3: *Les évangélistes*. Paris: J. Gabalda, 1973.

_____. "Introduction au Béatitudes." *Nouvelle Revue Théologique* 98 (1976): 97-108.

_____. "The Poor and Poverty in the Gospels and in Acts." In Augustin George, et al. *Gospel Poverty: Essays in Biblical Theology*, pp. 25-51. Trans. Michael D. Guinan. Chicago: Franciscan Herald Press, 1977.

Dussel, Enrique. *A History of the Church in Latin America, Colonialism to Liberation [1492-1972]*. Grand Rapids, MI: Eerdmans, 1981.

Eagleson, John, and Philip Scharper, eds. *Puebla and Beyond: Documentation and Commentary*. Trans. John Drury. Maryknoll, NY: Orbis Books, 1979.

Early, Tracy. "Father of Liberation Theology Says Vatican Comments Have Helped Him." NC News Service. July 13, 1988, pp. 6-7.

Ebeling, Gerhard. "Jesus and Faith." In his *Word and Faith*, pp. 201-46. Trans. J. W. Leitch. Philadelphia: Fortress Press, 1963.

Ellacuría, Ignacio. *Filosofía de la realidad histórica*. San Salvador: UCA Editores, 1990.

_____. "Fundamentación biológica de la ética." *Estudios Centroamericanos* 34:368 (June 1979): 219-28.

_____. "The Historicity of Christian Salvation." In Ignacio Ellacuría and Jon Sobrino, eds. *Mysterium Liberationis: Fundamental Concepts of Liberation Theology*. Maryknoll, NY: Orbis Books, 1993, pp. 251-88.

Ellacuría, Ignacio, y Jon Sobrino, eds. *Mysterium liberationis: Conceptos fundamentales de la teología de la liberación*. San Salvador: UCA Editores, 1991.

Ellacuría, Ignacio, and Jon Sobrino, eds. *Mysterium liberationis: Fundamental Concepts of Liberation Theology*. English ed. Maryknoll, NY: Orbis Books, 1993.

Ellis, Marc H., and Otto Maduro, eds. *The Future of Liberation Theology: Essays in Honor of Gustavo Gutiérrez*. Maryknoll, NY: Orbis Books, 1989.

Evans, Craig A. "Jesus' Action in the Temple: Cleansing or Portent of Destruction?" *Catholic Biblical Quarterly* 51 (1989): 237-70.

_____. *Life of Jesus Research: An Annotated Bibliography*. New Testament Tools and Studies 13. Leiden: Brill, 1989.

_____. "Life-of-Jesus Research and the Eclipse of Mythology." *Theological Studies* 54 (1993):3-36.

Evans, Joseph W. *Jacques Maritain: The Man and His Achievement*. New York: Sheed and Ward, 1963.

Fierro, Alfredo. *The Militant Gospel: A Critical Introduction to Political Theologies*. Trans. John Drury. Maryknoll, NY: Orbis Books, 1977.

Fiorenza, Francis Schüssler. "Introduction." In Karl Rahner. *Spirit in the World,* pp. xix-xlv. Trans. W. Dych. New York: Herder and Herder, 1968.

_____. "Political Theology as Foundational Theology." *Proceedings of the Catholic Theological Society of America* 32 (1977).

IV Conferencia General de Episcopado Latino americano. *Nueva èvangelización, promoción humana, cultura cristiana* (Santo Domingo Document). San Salvador: CELAM/Arguidiócesis de San Salvador, n.d.

Fowlie, Wallace. "Maritain the Writer." In Joseph W. Evans, ed. *Jacques Maritain: The Man and His Achievement*. New York: Sheed and Ward, 1963.

Geertz, Clifford. "The Growth of Culture and the Evolution of the Mind." In his *The Interpretation of Cultures,* pp. 55-83. New York: Basic Books, 1973.

_____. "The Impact of the Concept of Culture on the Concept of Man." In his *The Interpretation of Cultures,* pp. 33-54. New York: Basic Books, 1973.

_____. *The Interpretation of Cultures*. New York: Basic Books, 1973.

Gelin, Albert. *The Poor of Yahweh*. Collegeville, MN: The Liturgical Press, 1965.

Gibellini, Rosino. *The Liberation Theology Debate*. Trans. John Bowden. Maryknoll, NY: Orbis Books, 1987.

Gilkey, Langdon. *Reaping the Whirlwind: A Christian Interpretation of History*. New York: A Crossroad Book, The Seabury Press, 1976.

Gillis, Chester. *A Question of Final Belief: John Hick's Pluralistic Theory of Salvation*. New York: St. Martin's Press, 1989.

González, Antonio. "La novedad teológica de la filosofía de Zubiri." *Revista Latinoamericana de Teología* 10:30 (Sept.-Dec. 1993).

_____. "Orden mundial y liberación." *Estudios Centroamericanos* 549 (July 1994): 628-52.

_____. "El problema de la historia en la teología de Gustavo Gutiérrez." *Revista Latinoamericana de Teología* 6:18 (Sept.-Dec., 1989): 335-64.

Goodman, Martin. *The Ruling Class of Judea: The Origins of the Jewish Revolt Against Rome A.D. 66-70*. New York: Cambridge University Press, 1987.

Gorostiaga, Xabier. "¿ Está la respuesta en los países del Sur?" *Envío* 132 (Nov. 1992): 2, 46-55.

Gottwald, Norman K. "The Exodus as Event and Process: A Test Case in the Biblical Grounding of Liberation Theology." In Marc H. Ellis and Otto Maduro, eds. *The Future of Liberation Theology: Essays in Honor of Gustavo Gutiérrez*. Maryknoll, NY: Orbis Books, 1989.

Gross, Heinrich. "Peace." In Johannes B. Bauer, ed. *Sacramentum Verbi: An Encyclopedia of Biblical Theology*. 2 vols. New York: Herder and Herder, 1970, 2:648-51.

Guenther, Titus. "Rahner and Metz: Transcendental Theology as Political Theology." Ph.D. dissertation, University of St. Michael's College, 1988.

Gustafson, James M. *Protestant and Roman Catholic Ethics: Prospects for Rapprochement*. Chicago: University of Chicago Press, 1978.

Gutiérrez, Gustavo. *El Dios de la vida*. Cuadernos de Teología 1. Lima: Departamento de la Teología de la Universidad Católica, 1982.

_____. "Evangelio y praxis de liberación." In Instituto Fe y Secularidad, ed. *Fe cristiana y cambio social en América latina*. Salamanca: Sígueme, 1973.

_____. *La fuerza histórica de los pobres.* Lima: CEP, 1979.

_____. *The God of Life.* Trans. Matthew J. O'Connell. Maryknoll, NY: Orbis Books, 1991.

_____. "Liberation Theology and Proclamation." In Claude Geffré and Gustavo Gutiérrez, eds. *The Mystical and Political Dimension of the Christian Faith. Concilium* 96. New York: Herder and Herder, 1974.

_____. *Líneas pastorales de la iglesia en América latina.* Lima: Centro de Estudios y Publicaciones, 1970.

_____. *On Job: God-Talk and the Suffering of the Innocent.* Trans. Matthew J. O'Connell. Maryknoll, NY: Orbis Books, 1987.

_____. "Option for the Poor." In Ignacio Ellacuría, S.J., and Jon Sobrino, S.J. *Mysterium liberationis: Fundamental Concepts of Liberation Theology.* Maryknoll, NY: Orbis Books, 1993, pp. 235-50.

_____. *The Power of the Poor in History.* Trans. Robert R. Barr. Maryknoll, NY: Orbis Books, 1983.

_____. *Teología de la liberación: Perspectivas.* Salamanca: Ediciones Sigueme, 1977.

_____. "Theology from the Underside of History." In his *The Power of the Poor in History,* Chapt. 7. Trans. Robert R. Barr. Maryknoll, NY: Orbis Books, 1983, pp. 169-221.

_____. *A Theology of Liberation: History, Politics, and Salvation.* Trans. and ed. Sister Caridad Inda and John Eagleson. Rev. ed. Maryknoll, NY: Orbis Books, 1988.

_____. "Toward a Theology of Liberation." In Alfred Hennelly. *Liberation Theology: A Documentary History.* Maryknoll, NY: Orbis Books, 1989, pp. 62-76.

_____. *La verdad los hará libres: Confrontaciones.* Lima: Centro Bartolomé de las Casas/DEP, 1986.

_____. *We Drink from Our Own Wells: The Spiritual Journey of a People.* Trans. Matthew J. O'Connell. Maryknoll, NY: Orbis Books, 1984.

Habermas, Jürgen. *Knowledge and Human Interests.* Trans. Jeremy J. Shapiro. Boston: Beacon Press, 1971.

_____. *The Theory of Communicative Action.* 2 vols. Trans. Thomas McCarthy. Boston: Beacon Press, 1984, 1987.

Haight, Roger D. *An Alternative Vision: An Interpretation of Liberation Theology.* New York: Paulist Press, 1985.

_____. "Grace and Liberation: An Interpretation of History." *The Thomist* 42 (Oct. 1978): 539-81.

Harrelson, Walter. "Life, Faith, and the Emergence of Tradition." In Douglas A. Knight, ed. *Tradition and Theology in the Old Testament.* Philadelphia: Fortress Press, 1977.

Harvanek, Robert F. "The Unity of Metaphysics." *Thought* 28 (1953): 375-412.

Harvey, Van A. *A Handbook of Theological Terms.* New York: Macmillan, 1964.

Hegel, G. W. F. *The Phenomenology of Mind.* Trans. J. B. Baillie. London: George Allen and Unwin, 1949.

Hennelly, Alfred. *Liberation Theology: A Documentary History.* Maryknoll, NY: Orbis Books, 1989.

_____. *Santo Domingo and Beyond.* Maryknoll, NY: Orbis Books, 1993.

_____. *Theology for a Liberating Church: The New Praxis of Freedom.* Washington, DC: Georgetown University Press, 1989.

Hobsbawm, E. J. *The Age of Revolution: Europe 1789-1848.* London: Wiedenfeld and Nicolson, 1962.

Hoppe, Leslie. *Being Poor: A Biblical Study.* Good News Studies 20. Wilmington, DE: Michael Glazier, 1987.

Horsley, Richard A., with John S. Hanson. *Bandits, Prophets, and Messiahs: Popular Movements at the Time of Jesus.* San Francisco: Harper & Row, 1985.

Hunt, Diana. *Economic Theories of Development: An Analysis of Competing Paradigms.* Savage, MD: Barnes & Noble, 1989.

Instituto Fe y Secularidad, ed. *Fe cristiana y cambio social en America latina.* Madrid: Encuentro de El Escorial, 1972; Salamanca: Ediciones Sígueme, 1973.

Jacob, Edmond. "Psuche." In Geoffrey W. Bromiley, ed. *Theological Dictionary of the New Testament* 9:608-31. Grand Rapids, MI: William B. Eerdmans, 1968.

Jeremias, Joachim. *New Testament Theology: The Proclamation of Jesus.* Trans. John Bowden. New York: Charles Scribner's Sons, 1971.

_____. *The Parables of Jesus.* 2d ed. New York: Scribner's, 1972.

Joas, Hans. *G. H. Mead: A Contemporary Reexamination of His Thought.* Trans. Raymond Meyer. Cambridge, MA: The MIT Press, 1985.

John Paul II. *Centesimus annus.* In *Catholic International* 2:2 (June 15-30), 1991.

_____. "Opening Address at the Puebla Conference." In John Eagleson and Philip Scharper, eds. *Puebla and Beyond: Documentation and Commentary.* Trans. John Drury. Maryknoll, NY: Orbis Books, 1979.

_____. *Redemptoris missio.* In *Catholic International* 2:6 (March 16-31), 1991.

_____. *Sollicitudo rei socialis. Origens* 17:38 (Mar. 3, 1988): 641-60

Johnson, Elizabeth A. *She Who Is: The Mystery of God in Feminist Theological Discourse.* New York: Crossroad, 1992.

Kay, Cristóbal. *Latin American Theories of Development and Underdevelopment.* London and New York: Routledge, 1989.

Kee, Alistair. *Marx and the Failure of Liberation Theology.* London/Philadelphia: SCM/Trinity International, 1990.

Kernan, Julie. *Our Friend, Jacques Maritain: A Personal Memoir.* Garden City, NY: Doubleday, 1975.

King, Martin Luther, Jr. "Love, Law, and Civil Disobedience." In James Melvin Washington, ed. *A Testimony of Hope: The Essential Writings of Martin Luther King, Jr.* San Francisco: Harper and Row, 1986.

Knitter, Paul. *A Critical Survey of Christian Attitudes Toward the World Religions.* Maryknoll, NY: Orbis Books, 1985.

Kraeling, Emil H. *The Old Testament Since the Reformation.* London: Lutterworth Press, 1955.

Kuhn, Thomas S. *The Structure of Scientific Revolutions.* 2d ed. Chicago: University of Chicago Press, 1970.

Kümmel, W. G. "Eschatological Expectation in the Proclamation of Jesus." In Bruce Chilton, ed. *The Kingdom of God in the Teaching of Jesus.* Issues in Religion and Theology 5. Philadelphia: Fortress Press, 1984.

_____. *Promise and Fulfillment: The Eschatological Message of Jesus.* 3rd ed. Trans. Dorothea M. Barton. Studies in Biblical Theology 23. London: SCM, 1961.

Küng, Hans. *The Church.* New York: Sheed and Ward, 1968.

Landmann, Michael. *Philosophical Anthropology.* Trans. David J. Parent. Philadelphia: Westminster Press, 1974.

Lane, Belden. "Spirituality and Political Commitment: Notes on a Liberation Theology of Nonviolence." *America,* March 14, 1981, pp. 197-202.

Lehman, Hellmut T., gen. ed. *Luther's Works.* Vol. 45, *The Christian in Society II.* Philadelphia: Muhlenburg Press, 1962.

Lehmann, Karl. "Problemas metodológicos y hermenéuticos de la 'teología de la liberación'." In Comisión Teológica Internacional. *Teología de la liberación.* Madrid: B.A.C., 1978.

Lernoux, Penny. *Cry of the People.* Garden City, NY: Doubleday, 1980.

_____. *People of God: The Struggle for World Catholicism.* New York: Viking Press, 1989.

Lima, Alceu Amoroso. "Testimony: On the Influence of Maritain in Latin America." *New Scholasticism* 46 (Winter 1972): 70-85.

Lobkowicz, Nicolas. *Theory and Practice: History of a Concept from Aristotle to Marx.* Notre Dame, IN: University of Notre Dame Press, 1967.

Lohfink, Norbert. "The Kingdom of God and the Economy in the Bible." *Communio* 13 (Fall 1986).

_____. *Option for the Poor: The Basic Principles of Liberation Theology in the Light of the Bible.* Trans. Linda A. Maloney and Duane Christensen. Berkeley, CA: BIBAL Press, 1987.

Lukás, Georg. *History and Class Consciousness: Studies in Marxist Dialectics.* Trans. Rodney Livingstone. London: Merlin Press, 1971.

Lynch, William. *Images of Hope.* New York: New American Library, 1966.

McBrien, Richard P. *Church: The Continuing Quest.* New York: Newman, 1970.

McCann, Dennis. "Reinhold Niebuhr and Jacques Maritain on Marxism: A Comparison of Two Traditional Models of Practical Theology." *Journal of Religion* 58 (April 1978).

McCool, Gerald A. *From Unity to Pluralism: The Internal Evolution of Thomism.* New York: Fordham University Press, 1989.

_____. "Introduction." In Karl Rahner, *A Rahner Reader,* pp. xxv-xxviii. New York: The Seabury Press, 1975.

_____. "Jacques Maritain: A Neo-Thomist Classic." *Journal of Religion* 58 (Oct. 1978): 380-404.

McGovern, Arthur. *Liberation Theology and Its Critics: Toward an Assessment.* Maryknoll, NY: Orbis Books, 1989.

McLellan, David. "Introduction." In Karl Marx, *The Grundrisse.* Trans. and ed. David McLellan. New York: Harper and Row, 1971.

Macmurray, John. *The Form of the Personal.* 2 vols. Vol. 1: *The Self as Agent.* London: Faber and Faber, 1969. Vol 2: *Persons in Relation.* London: Faber and Faber, 1961. Reprint ed., Atlantic Highlands, NJ: Humanities Press, 1979.

Mannheim, Karl. *Ideology and Utopia: An Introduction to the Sociology of Knowledge.* Trans. Louis Wirth and Edward Shils. New York: Harcourt, Brace and World/A Harvest Book, 1936.

Manzanera, Miguel. *Teología, salvacíon, y liberación en la obra de Gustavo Gutiérrez: Exposición analítica, situación teórico-práctica y valoracíon crítica.* Teología Duesto, No. 13. Bilbao: Publicaciones de la Universidad de Duesto, 1978.

Maritain, Jacques. *Christianity and Democracy.* Trans. Doris C. Anson. New York: Charles Scribner's Sons, 1944.

_____. "Confession of Faith." In his *The Social and Political Philosophy of Jacques Maritain: Selected Readings.* Joseph Evans and Leo R. Ward, eds. New York: Charles Scribner's Sons, 1955; reprinted Notre Dame, IN: University of Notre Dame Press, 1976.

_____. *Distinguish to Unite: Or, The Degrees of Knowledge.* Trans. Gerald B. Phelan et al. London: Geoffrey Bles, 1959.

_____. *Freedom in the Modern World.* Trans. Richard O'Sullivan. New York: Charles Scribner's Sons, 1936.

_____. "The Immanent Dialectic of the First Act of Freedom." In his *Range of Reason.* New York: Charles Scribner's Sons, 1952, pp. 66-85.

_____. "The Immortality of the Soul." In his *The Range of Reason.* New York: Charles Scribner's Sons, 1952, pp. 51-65.

_____. *Integral Humanism: Temporal and Spiritual Problems of a New Christendom.* Trans. Joseph W. Evans. Notre Dame, IN: University of Notre Dame Press, 1973.

_____. *An Introduction to Philosophy.* Trans. E. I. Watkins. New York: Sheed and Ward, 1937.

_____. *Moral Philosophy: An Historical and Critical Survey of the Great Systems.* Trans. Marshall Suther et al. New York: Charles Scribner's Sons, 1964.

_____. "The Natural Mystical Experience and the Void." In his *Ransoming the Time*. Trans. Harry Lorin Binsse. New York: Charles Scribner's Sons, 1941.

_____. *Neuf leçons sur les notions premières de la philosophie morale*. Paris: Téqui, 1951.

_____. *Notebooks*. Trans. Joseph W. Evans. Albany, NY: Magi Books, Inc., 1984. [*Carnet de notes*. Paris: Desclée de Brouwer, 1965.]

_____. *On the Church of Christ: The Person of the Church and Her Personnel*. Trans. Joseph W. Evans. Notre Dame, IN: University of Notre Dame Press, 1973.

_____. *On the Philosophy of History*. Ed. Joseph W. Evans. New York: Charles Scribner's Sons, 1957.

_____. *The Person and the Common Good*. Trans. John J. Fitzgerald. Notre Dame, IN: University of Notre Dame Press, 1966.

_____. *The Range of Reason*. New York: Charles Scribner's Sons, 1952.

_____. "Religion and Culture." In his *The Social and Political Philosophy of Jacques Maritain: Selected Readings*. Joseph Evans and Leo R. Ward, eds. New York: Charles Scribner's Sons, 1955; reprinted Notre Dame, IN: University of Notre Dame Press, 1976.

_____. *Religion and Culture*. Trans. J. F. Scanlan. In Jacques Maritain, Peter Wust, and Christopher Dawson, *Essays in Order*. London: Sheed and Ward, 1931.

_____. *Religion et culture*. 2d ed. Paris: Desclée de Brouwer, 1946.

_____. *Scholasticism and Politics*. Trans. and ed. Mortimer J. Adler. New York: Macmillan, 1940.

_____. *Science and Wisdom*. Trans. Bernard Wall. New York: Charles Scribner's Sons, 1940.

_____. *The Social and Political Philosophy of Jacques Maritain: Selected Readings*. Ed. Joseph Evans and Leo R. Ward. New York: Charles Scribner's Sons, 1955; reprinted Notre Dame, IN: University of Notre Dame Press, 1976.

_____. *The Things That Are Not Caesar's*. Trans. J. F. Scanlan. London: Sheed and Ward, 1932.

Maritain, Jacques, and Raïssa Maritain. *Prayer and Intelligence*. New York: Sheed and Ward, 1928.

Markus, R. A. *Saeculum: History and Society in the Theology of St. Augustine*. Cambridge: Cambridge University Press, 1970.

Marx, Karl. "Economic and Philosophical Manuscripts." In T. B. Bottomore, trans. and ed. *Karl Marx: Early Writings*. New York: McGraw-Hill, 1964.

_____. *The Poverty of Philosophy*. Moscow, n.d.

_____. *Preface and Introduction to "A Contribution to the Critique of Political Economy."* Peking: Foreign Languages Press, 1976.

Marx, Karl, and Frederick Engels. *The German Ideology: Part One*. Ed. C. J. Arthur. New York: International Publishers, 1970.

Mealand, David L. *Poverty and Expectation in the Gospels*. London: SPCK, 1980.

Meier, John P. "The Historical Jesus: Rethinking Some Concepts." *Theological Studies* 51 (1990):3-24.

_____. *A Marginal Jew: Rethinking the Historical Jesus*. 2 vols. Vol. 1: *The Roots of the Problem and the Person*. Vol. 2: *Mentor, Message, and Miracles*. The Anchor Reference Library. New York: Doubleday, 1991, 1994.

Merkel, Helmut. "The Opposition Between Jesus and Judaism." In E. Bammel and C. F. D. Moule, *Jesus and the Politics of His Day*. New York: Cambridge University Press, 1984, pp. 129-44.

Mertens, Herman-Emiel. "Nature and Grace in Twentieth-Century Catholic Theology." *Louvain Studies* 16 (1991): 242-62.

Metz, Johann B. *The Emergent Church: The Future of Christianity in a Postbourgeois World*. Trans. Peter Mann. New York: Crossroad, 1981.

_____. *Faith in History and Society: Toward a Practical Fundamental Theology*. Trans. David Smith. New York: Seabury Press, 1980.

_____. "Foreword." In Karl Rahner. *Spirit in the World.* Trans. W. Dych. New York: Herder and Herder, 1968.

_____. *Theology of the World.* Trans. William Glen-Doepel. New York: Herder and Herder, 1969.

Míguez Bonino, José. *Doing Theology in a Revolutionary Situation.* Philadelphia: Fortress Press, 1975.

Miranda, José Porfirio. *Marx and the Bible: A Critique of the Philosophy of Oppression.* Trans. John Eagleson. Maryknoll, NY: Orbis Books, 1974.

Moltmann, Jürgen. *The Crucified God: The Cross of Christ as the Foundation and Criticism of Christian Theology.* Trans. R. A. Wilson and John Bowden. New York: Harper and Row, 1974.

_____. *Theology of Hope: On the Ground and the Implications of a Christian Eschatology.* Trans. James W. Leitch. New York: Harper and Row, 1967.

Montoya, Aguiles. *La nueva economía popular: una aproximación teórica.* San Salvador: UCA Editores, 1993.

Mora, L. Raul, et al. *Neoliberales y pobres: El debate continental por la justicia.* Santafé de Bogotá: CINEP/CRT/SIC/CRAS, 1993.

Neal, Marie Augusta. *A Theology of Letting Go: The Role of a First-World Church Facing Third-World Peoples.* New York: Paulist Press, 1974.

Nelson, Ralph. "Moral Philosophy Adequately Considered." In *Jacques Maritain: The Man and His Achievement.* Ed. Joseph W. Evans. New York: Sheed and Ward, 1963.

Neuhaus, Gerd. *Transzendentale Erfahrung als Geschichtsverlust? Der Vorwurf der Subjektlösigkeit an Rahners Begriff geschichtlicher Existenz und eine weiterführende Perspecktive transzendentaler Theologie.* Düsseldorf: Patmos, 1982.

Niebuhr, H. Richard. *Christ and Culture.* New York: Harper and Row, 1951; 1975.

Nolan, Albert. *Jesus Before Christianity.* Maryknoll, NY: Orbis Books, 1978.

Nottingham, William J. *Christian Faith and Secular Action: An Introduction to the Life and Thought of Jacques Maritain.* St. Louis, MO: The Bethany Press, 1968.

Novak, Michael. *Does It Liberate?: Questions about Liberation Theology.* New York: Paulist Press, 1986.

Oakman, Douglas. *Jesus and the Economic Questions of His Day.* Studies in the Bible and Early Christianity 8. Lewiston, NY, and Queenston, ONT: Edwin Mellen Press, 1986.

O'Brien, T. C., ed. "Salvation." In *Corpus Dictionary of the Catholic Churches.* Washington, DC: Corpus Publications, 1970.

O'Donovan, Leo J. "A Journey into Time: The Legacy of Karl Rahner's Last Years." *Theological Studies* 46 (1985): 621-46.

_____. "Orthopraxis and Theological Method in Karl Rahner." *CTSA Proceedings* 35 (1980): 47-65.

Oliveros, Roberto. *Liberación y teología: Génesis y crecimianto de una reflexíon, 1966-1976.* Lima: Centro de Estudios y Publicaciones, 1977.

Ollman, Bertell. *Alienation: Marx's Conception of Man in Capitalist Society.* 2d ed. Cambridge: Cambridge University Press, 1976.

Paul VI. *Evangelii nuntiandi* (Evangelization in the Modern World). Washington, DC: U.S.C.C., 1975.

_____. *Populorum progressio* (On the Development of Peoples). Boston: Daughters of St. Paul, 1967.

Peck, M. Scott. *The People of the Lie: The Hope for Healing Human Evil.* London: RIDER, 1988.

Perrin, Norman. *Jesus and the Language of the Kingdom.* Philadelphia: Fortress Press, 1976.

_____. *The Kingdom of God in the Teaching of Jesus.* Philadelphia: Westminster Press, 1963.

_____. *Rediscovering the Teaching of Jesus.* New York: Harper & Row, 1976.

Peruvian Bishops' Commission for Social Action. *Between Honesty and Hope.* Trans. John Drury. Maryknoll, NY: Maryknoll Publications, 1970.

Pixley, George V. *God's Kingdom: A Guide for Biblical Study.* Trans. Donald D. Walsh. Maryknoll, NY: Orbis Books, 1981.

_____. *On Exodus.* Maryknoll, NY: Orbis Books, 1985.

Planas, Ricardo. *Liberation Theology: The Political Expression of Religion.* Kansas City, MO: Sheed and Ward, 1986.

Postel, Sandra. "Carrying Capacity: Earth's Bottom Line." In Lester R. Brown, et al., *State of the World 1994: A Worldwatch Institute Report on Progress Toward a Sustainable Society.* New York and London: W.S. Norton, 1994.

Rahner, Karl. "The Body in the Order of Salvation." Trans. Margaret Kohl. TI 17. (1981): 71-89.

_____. *The Christian Commitment.* Trans. Cecily Hastings. New York: Sheed & Ward, 1963.

_____. "Christian Humanism." Trans. Graham Harrison. TI 9 (1972): 187-204.

_____. "The Christian Understanding of Redemption." Trans. Hugh M. Riley. TI 21 (1988): 239-54.

_____. "The Church and the Parousia of Christ." Trans. K.-H. and Boniface Kruger. TI 6 (1969): 295-312.

_____. "Church and World." In his *Encyclopedia of Theology: The Concise 'Sacramentum Mundi.'* New York: The Seabury Press, 1975, pp. 237-50.

_____. "The Church's Commission to Bring Salvation and the Humanization of the World." Trans. David Bourke. TI 14 (1976):295-313.

_____. "The 'Commandment' of Love in Relation to the Other Commandments." Trans. Karl-H. Kruger. TI 5 (1966): 439-59.

_____. "Concerning the Relationship between Nature and Grace." Trans. Cornelius Ernst. TI 1 (1961): 297-318.

_____. "Experience of Self and Experience of God." Trans. David Bourke. TI 13 (1975): 122-32.

_____. "Experience of the Spirit and Existential Commitment." Trans. David Morland. TI 16 (1983): 24-34.

_____. "The Experiment with Man." Trans. Graham Harrison. TI 9 (1972): 205-24.

_____. *Foundations of Christian Faith: An Introduction to the Idea of Christianity.* Trans. William V. Dych. New York: Seabury Press, 1978.

_____. "Freedom. Theological Aspect." In his *Encyclopedia of Theology: The Concise 'Sacramentum Mundi.'* New York: The Seabury Press, 1975, pp. 544-45.

_____. "The Function of the Church as a Critic of Society." Trans. David Bourke. TI 12 (1974): 229-49.

_____. *Hearers of the Word.* Trans. Michael Richards. New York: Herder and Herder, 1969.

_____. "The Hermeneutics of Eschatological Assertions." Trans. Kevin Smyth. TI 4 (1966): 323-46.

_____. "History of the World and Salvation History." Trans. Karl-H. Kruger. TI 5 (1966):97-114.

_____. "Immanent and Transcendent Consummation of the World." Trans. David Bourke. TI 10 (1973):273-89.

_____. "The Intermediate State." Trans. Margaret Kohl. TI 17 (1981): 114-24.

_____. "Introduction." In James J. Bacik. *Apologetics and the Eclipse of Mystery: Mystagogy according to Karl Rahner.* Notre Dame, IN: University of Notre Dame Press, 1980.

_____. Letter to Cardinal Juan Landázuri Ricketts, Archbishop of Lima, Mar. 16, 1984. In *Algunos aspectos de la teología de la liberación: Instrucción de la Santa Sede y otros documentos.* 2d ed. Colección Documentos y Estudios 9. Madrid: PPC, 1984.

_____. "The Life of the Dead." Trans. Kevin Smyth. TI 4 (1966):347-54.

_____. "Marxist Utopia and the Christian Future of Man." Trans. K.-H. and Boniface Kruger. TI 6 (1969): 59-68.

_____. "Mystical Experience and Mystical Theology." Trans. Margaret Kohl. TI 17 (1981):90-99.

_____. "Natural Science and Reasonable Faith." Trans. Hugh M. Riley. TI 21 (1988): 16-55.

_____. "Nature and Grace." Trans. Kevin Smyth. TI 4 (1966): 165-88.

_____. "One Mediator and Many Mediations." Trans. Edward Quinn. TI 19 (1983):169-84.

_____. "On the Theology of Hope." Trans. David Bourke. TI 10 (1973): 242-59.

_____. "The Order of Redemption Within the Order of Creation." In his *The Christian Commitment*, pp. 38-74. Trans. Cecily Hastings. New York: Sheed & Ward, 1963.

_____. "Profane History and Salvation History." Trans. Hugh M. Riley. TI 21 (1988): 3-15.

_____. *A Rahner Reader.* Ed. Gerald A. McCool. New York: The Seabury Press, 1975.

_____. "Reconciliation and Vicarious Representation." Trans. Hugh M. Riley. TI 21 (1988):239-69.

_____. "Reflections on the Unity of the Love of Neighbor and the Love of God." Trans. K.-H. and Boniface Kruger. TI 6 (1969):231-49.

_____. "Religious Enthusiasm and the Experience of Grace." Trans. David Morland. TI 16 (1983): 35-51.

_____. "Salvation." In his *Encyclopedia of Theology: The Concise 'Sacramentum Mundi.'* New York: The Seabury Press, 1975, pp. 1499-1504 and 1512-30.

_____. "The Significance in Redemptive History of the Individual Member of the Church." In his *The Christian Commitment.* Trans. Cecily Hastings. New York: Sheed & Ward, 1963, pp. 75-113.

_____. "Some Implications of the Scholastic Concept of Uncreated Grace." Trans. Cornelius Ernst. TI 1 (1961):319-46.

_____. *Spirit in the World.* Trans. William Dych. New York: Herder and Herder, 1968.

_____. "The Theological Concept of 'Concupiscentia'." Trans. Cornelius Ernst. TI 1 (1961): 347-82.

_____. *Theological Investigations* (TI). London: Darton, Longman, and Todd, 1961-83; New York: Crossroad, 1988.

_____. "The Theological Problems Entailed in the Idea of the 'New Earth'." Trans. David Bourke. TI 10 (1973): 260-72.

_____. "Theological Reflections on the Problem of Secularisation." Trans. David Bourke. TI 10 (1973):318-48.

_____. "Theology of Freedom." Trans. K.-H. and Boniface Kruger. TI 6 (1969):178-96.

_____. "The Theology of the Symbol." Trans. Kevin Smyth. TI 4 (1966):221-52.

_____. "The Unity of Spirit and Matter in the Christian Understanding of Faith." Trans. K.-H. and Boniface Kruger. TI 6 (1969): 153-77.

_____. "Unity of the Church—Unity of Mankind." Trans. Edward Quinn. TI 20 (1981):154-72.

_____. "Why and How Can We Venerate the Saints?" Trans. David Bourke. TI 8 (1971):3-23.

Rahner, Karl, and Herbert Vorgrimler. *Dictionary of Theology.* 2d ed. New York: Crossroad, 1981.

Rasmussen, David M. "Between Autonomy and Sociality." *Cultural Hermeneutics* 1 (1973).

Razeto, Luis M. *Economía de solidaridad y mercado democrático.* Santiago, Chile: Programa de Economía del Trabajo y Academia de Humanismo Cristiano, 1988.

_____. *Economía popular de solidaridad.* Santiago, Chile: Area Pastoral Social de la Conferencia Episcopal de Chile y Programa de Economía del Trabajo [PRT], 1990.

Richard, Pablo. *Death of Christendoms, Birth of the Church: Historical Analysis and Theological Interpretation of the Church in Latin America.* Trans. Phillip Berryman. Maryknoll, NY: Orbis Books, 1987.

Riches, John. *Jesus and the Transformation of Judaism.* New York: Seabury, 1982.

Ricoeur, Paul. *Lectures on Ideology and Utopia.* Ed. George H. Taylor. New York: Columbia University Press, 1986.

Ruether, Rosemary Radford. *The Radical Kingdom: The Western Experience of Messianic Hope.* New York: Harper and Row, 1970.

_____. *Sexism and God-talk: Toward a Feminist Theology.* Boston: Beacon Press, 1983.

_____. *To Change the World: Christology and Cultural Criticism.* New York: Crossroad, 1981.

Sacred Congregation for the Doctrine of the Faith. *Instruction on Certain Aspects of the "Theology of Liberation."* Vatican City, 1984.

_____. *Instruction on Christian Freedom and Liberation. Origins* 15:44 (April 17, 1986).

Sanders, E. P. *Jesus and Judaism.* Philadelphia: Fortress Press, 1985.

Schillebeeckx, Edward. *Jesus: An Experiment in Christology.* Trans. Hubert Hoskins. New York: Vintage Books, 1979.

Schlosser, J. *Le règne de Dieu dans les dits de Jésus.* Paris: Gabalda, 1980.

Schottroff, Luise, and Wolfgang Stegemann. *Jesus and the Hope of the Poor.* Trans. Matthew J. O'Connell. Maryknoll, NY: Orbis Books, 1986.

Schrenk, Gottlob. "Dikaiosune." In Geoffrey W. Bromiley, ed. *Theological Dictionary of the New Testament.* Grand Rapids, MI: William B. Eerdmans, 1968.

Schubeck, Thomas L. *Liberation Ethics: Sources, Models, and Norms.* Minneapolis, MN: Fortress Press, 1993.

Schüssler Fiorenza, Elisabeth. *In Memory of Her: A Feminist Theological Reconstruction of Christian Origins.* New York: Crossroad, 1983.

_____. "Toward a Feminist Biblical Hermeneutics: Biblical Interpretation and Liberation Theology." In Brian Mahan and L. Dale Richesin, eds. *The Challenge of Liberation Theology: A First World Response.* Maryknoll, NY: Orbis Books, 1971.

Schweizer, Eduard. "Pneuma, pneumatikos." In Geoffrey W. Bromiley, ed. *Theological Dictionary of the New Testament* 6:434-36. Grand Rapids, MI: William B. Eerdmans, 1968.

_____. "Psuche." In Geoffrey W. Bromiley, ed. *Theological Dictionary of the New Testament* 9: 637-56. Grand Rapids, MI: William B. Eerdmans, 1968.

Second General Conference of Latin American Bishops. *The Church in the Present-Day Transformation of Latin America.* Vol 2: *Conclusions.* 2d ed. Washington, DC: U.S.C.C., 1970.

Segundo, Juan Luis. *The Liberation of Theology.* Trans. John Drury. Maryknoll, NY: Orbis Books, 1976.

_____. *Theology and the Church: A Response to Cardinal Ratzinger and a Warning to the Whole Church.* Trans. John W. Diercksmeier. Minneapolis, MN: Winston Press, 1985.

Sigmund, Paul E. *Liberation Theology at the Crossroads: Democracy or Revolution?* New York: Oxford University Press, 1990.

Smith, Brooke Williams. *Jacques Maritain, Antimodern or Ultramodern?: An Historical Analysis of His Critics, His Thought, and His Life.* New York: Elsevier, 1976.

Smith, Christian. *The Emergence of Liberation Theology: Radical Religion and Social Movement Theory.* Chicago: University of Chicago Press, 1991.

Sobrino, Jon. *Christology at the Crossroads: A Latin American Approach.* Trans. John Drury. Maryknoll, NY: Orbis Books, 1978.

_____. *Jesucristo liberador: Lectura histórico-teológica de Jesús de Nazaret.* San Salvador: UCA Editores, 1991; *Jesus the Liberator: A Historical-Theological View.* Trans. Paul Burns and Francis McDonagh. Maryknoll, N.Y.: Orbis Books, 1993.

_____. "Los vientos que soplaron en Santo Domingo y la evangelización de la cultura." *Revista Latinoamericana de Teología* 9:27 (Sept.-Dec. 1992): 273-92.

Soelle, Dorothee. *Political Theology.* Trans. John Shelley. Philadelphia: Fortress Press, 1974.

Synod of Bishops. "A Declaration from the Synod." *Origins* 4 (1974).

_____. Second General Assembly. *Justice in the World.* In Joseph Gremillion, ed. *The Gospel of Peace and Justice.* Maryknoll, NY: Orbis Books, 1976.

Theissen, Gerd. *Sociology of Early Palestinian Christianity.* Trans. John Bowden. Philadelphia: Fortress Press, 1978.

Topel, L. John. *The Way to Peace: Liberation through the Bible.* Maryknoll, NY: Orbis Books, 1979.

Topmoeller, W. G. "Salvation." *New Catholic Encyclopedia.* New York: McGraw-Hill, 1967.

Tracy, David. *The Analogical Imagination: Christian Theology and the Culture of Pluralism.* New York: Crossroad, 1981.

_____. *Blessed Rage for Order: The New Pluralism in Theology.* New York: Winston/Seabury, 1975.

_____. "Response to Fr. Metz." In W. J. Kelly, ed. *Theology and Discovery: Essays in Honor of Karl Rahner, S.J.* Milwaukee, WI: Marquette University Press, 1980.

Trible, Phyllis. *God and the Rhetoric of Sexuality.* Philadelphia: Fortress Press, 1978.

_____. *Texts of Terror: Literary-Feminist Theological Reconstruction of Christian Origins.* New York: Crossroad, 1983.

Unger, Roberto Mangabeira. *Knowledge and Politics.* New York: Free Press, 1975.

United Nations. "Integración social." New York, 1994.

U.S. Catholic Conference. *Economic Justice for All.* Washington, DC: N.C.C.B., 1986.

van Iersel, Bas, and Anton Weiler, eds. *Exodus—A Lasting Paradigm.* English ed. Marcus Lefébre. *Concilium* 189 (1/1987). Edinburgh: T. & T. Clark.

Vaughan, Judith. *Sociality, Ethics, and Social Change: A Critical Appraisal of Reinhold Niebuhr's Ethics in the Light of Rosemary Radford Ruether's Works.* Lanham, MD: University Press of America, 1983.

Vidal, Marciano. "Pecado." In Casiano Floristán and Juan José Tamayo, eds. *Conceptos fundamentales del cristianismo.* Madrid: Trotta, 1993, pp. 983-1001.

Viviano, Benedict. *The Kingdom of God in History.* Good News Studies 27. Wilmington, DE: Michael Glazier, 1988.

von Rad, Gerhard. *Old Testament Theology.* 2 vols. Trans. D. M. G. Stalker. New York: Harper and Row, 1962.

Vorgrimler, Herbert. *Understanding Karl Rahner: An Introduction to His Life and Thought.* New York: Crossroad, 1986.

_____, ed. *Pastoral Constitution on the Church in the World Today.* Vol. 5: *Commentary on the Documents of Vatican II.* New York: Herder and Herder, 1969.

Walsh, J. P. M. *The Mighty from Their Thrones: Power in the Biblical Tradition.* Overtures to Biblical Theology 21. Philadelphia: Fortress Press, 1987.

Williams, George H. *The Radical Reformation.* Philadelphia: Westminster, 1962.

Wolff, Hans Walter. *Anthropology of the Old Testament.* Trans. Margaret Kohl. Philadelphia: Fortress Press, 1974.

Yoder, John Howard. "Exodus and Exile: The Two Faces of Liberation." *Cross Currents* 23 (1973): 297-309.

Zubiri, Xavier. *El hombre y Dios.* 4th ed. Madrid: Alianza, 1994.

_____. *Inteligencia sentiente. Inteligencia y realidad.* Madrid: Alianza, 1984.

_____. *Sobre el hombre.* Madrid: Alianza, 1986.

INDEX